STEAM SHIPS OF EUROPE

STEAM SHIPS
OF EUROPE

ALISTAIR DEAYTON

CONWAY
MARITIME PRESS

Frontispiece: *Blidösund* at Svartloga

First published in Great Britain 1988 by
Conway Maritime Press Limited
24 Bride Lane, Fleet Street
London EC4Y 8DR

ISBN 0 81577 478 4

Designed by Tony Garrett
Typeset by MJL Limited, Hitchin
Printed and bound by Butler & Tanner Ltd, Frome
Colour plates printed by
Bath Press Ltd, Bath

CONTENTS

PREFACE

WHEN I WAS a child, a favourite day out was a sail on the paddle steamer *Jeanie Deans* on her regular Saturday afternoon trip from Gourock to Tighnabruaich. On those lovely summer afternoons of the fifties and early sixties a life-long interest in Clyde steamers was kindled. Then, as the steamers on the Clyde were withdrawn one by one from service, until only *Waverley* remained, that interest spread beyond the Firth of Clyde to European waters. Year by year, in different countries, I explored areas with operating steamers, at first on a random basis, and then by a methodical filling in of the gaps. As I collected books, timetables, and postcards, I realised that no book existed, in English or indeed in any other European language, covering all the surviving steamers of Europe. Thus the idea of this book was born.

The scope of the book is:

a) all operating European passenger steamers

b) a few non-passenger steamers which are preserved and now carry passengers, such as former tugs, inspection steamers and similar vessels

c) all operating European passenger motor vessels originally built as steamers, but later converted to diesel

d) a few cargo ships which were built as passenger steamers but later rebuilt

e) any vessel in the above categories now in static use, for example as a museum or restaurant, currently laid up, or awaiting restoration

In general, those vessels in categories (a) and (b) are listed in Part One of this book, and those in categories (c), (d) and (e) in Part Two.

The gathering of such information, often only obtainable locally, has taken a number of years. While all information is believed to be correct at the time of writing (March 1988), I can offer no guarantee that any vessel listed here will still be operating on a given service, or indeed, be operating at all, in 1988 and beyond.

Information and photographs of any omissions would be welcomed for a possible future edition.

My thanks go to many who have helped and encouraged me on this venture, but especially to:

Geoffrey Hamer, from whose *Trip Out* guides many leads have been obtained for previously unknown veterans

Russell Plummer, Paddle Steamer Preservation Society

Brian Hillsdon, Steamboat Association

Waldemar Danielewicz, Gdansk (information on Polish steamers)

Michael Bor, Prague (information on Czech steamers)

Bernd Langensiepen, Hamburg, and Selim San, Izmir (information on Turkish steamers)

Heinz Trost (Germany and Berlin)

Claus Rothe (East Germany)

Antonio Scrimali (Italy), and his *Latest News from the Mediterranean* newsletter

Olaf Engwig, Arne Holm and Per Alsaker (Norway)

Professor Jim Parratt (lake Balaton)

Max Kuhn, Interlaken (Dutch tugs)

A number of operators who have also given useful information

All photographs are my own unless otherwise indicated.

THE SURVIVORS

AT THE TURN OF THE CENTURY, steamships and steamboats dominated the coasts and lakes, the rivers and canals, the harbours and estuaries of every country in Europe. Busy excursion steamers took full loads of passengers from the great port cities to holiday resorts in the summer months, and on excursions to scenic areas from these resorts. Harbour ferries crossed busy rivers with workers, longer distance ferries brought commuters into port cities; glistening white paddle steamers steamed majestically along the lakes of Alpine Europe; screw steamers, glistening just as white, cruised the archipelagos of Sweden and Finland; and on the great European rivers, the Rhine, the Elbe, and the Danube, fleets of paddle steamers sailed beneath castle-topped crags. Here and there was a unique steamer, of an unusual design, often in a remote tourist area. The coasts of Norway saw many small communities linked to the main towns by passenger and cargo steamers, sailing from the remote islands at around 5am and returning in the afternoon after their passengers had spent a day at the market selling their produce or shopping in the town.

As the century has worn on, these steamers have all but disappeared, replaced first by motor vessels, then by 'roro' car ferries and by express boats, by hydrofoils and by catamarans. As these words are written the last major commercial fleet of steamers, at Istanbul on the Bosporus, has been drastically cut; withdrawal of the coal-fired ferries was completed by the end of 1986, and withdrawal of many of the oil-fired examples in 1987.

Not only have the steamers disappeared, but their trade has often gone too, with roads built to remote communities, islands, particularly in Scandinavia, linked to the mainland by bridge or tunnel, and the holiday resorts of northern Europe emptied by the rush to the sun and by currency movements that made Spain, Greece, and Italy much more economical for the family holiday than Switzerland, Germany and Austria.

Yet, of those thousands of early twentieth century steamers, and of those that followed them until the final decline of steam in the fifties and early sixties, around 120 survive in steam, preserved by groups of enthusiasts, or kept on by owners mindful of their historical heritage. Some have been restored to original condition, others altered over the years; alterations which have usually meant greater comfort for passengers at the expense of historical authenticity. A few have been restored from much altered ships to beautiful original condition. It is those remaining 120 steamers, plus a further 20 or so undergoing restoration at present, that form the core of this book, and the content of Part One.

To these are added a handful preserved as museums, and a few more used as restaurants, sometimes so much altered as to be unrecognisable, sometimes in near original condition.

Many steamers, especially the smaller screw vessels, had their steam engines replaced by motors, occasionally gasoline in the early days, then diesel, with the odd diesel-electric conversion. A few paddlers were also altered, but this was a much more complex operation, so that where a screw vessel might have been dieselised (an ugly but inevitable word) a paddle steamer would generally have been scrapped. These former steamers are often little documented outside their local area; while some owners are proud of an antique ship, others conceal age. Most former steamers were converted in the thirties, or in the fifties and sixties, although a few went over to petrol or diesel before 1914. Sadly, one or two have been converted in the past few years. Of these ex-steamers, some have been restored to a traditional steamer profile with tall funnel and traditionally designed superstructure, while others, notably whole groups of ex-steamers on the Thames and at Berlin, have had their funnels removed so as to pass readily under low bridges, have had additional modern saloons added in an incongruous marriage with old-fashioned hull lines, and are unrecognisable as veterans. All these converted steamers are listed in Part Two of this book.

Passenger accommodation varies tremendously, from basic harbour ferries with standing room only and a few wooden benches to the Belle Epoque dining saloons of the Swiss paddlers. Catering also varies from the trestle table with bottles of soft drinks which serves for a buffet on *Diessen,* through basic bars and cafeterias as on *Waverley* to the wood-panelled dining saloons of the Swedish steamers, which even have a special dish, 'steamer steak'. There are surprises too, such as the half-saloon on *Patria,* with plush leather settees, and the seemingly bare lower deck saloons on *Gisela,* with walls hung with historic steamer photographs.

Public awareness of a steamer's historic value also varies; while on some steamers, such as those at Prague, even postcards are unobtainable, on others not only cards, but also stickers, books, and even models are sold. Obviously this is more prevalent on the enthusiast-preserved steamers such as *Kingswear Castle* and *Bohuslän* than on such steamers as the Istanbul ferries, yet even in areas where public interest in steam is strong, awareness of particular steamers varies. Lake Lucerne is much more enthusiast-oriented than lake Geneva, some Stockholm steamers cater more to public interest than others, and *Suomi* more so than some of the Saimaa steamers.

Engines, of course, vary, although this is not the place for a technical description of the steam engine and how it works. Paddle steamers use, in the main, diagonal engines, mainly compound two-cylinder, though a few sport triple expansion, three cylinder engines. Most, like *Waverley,* are open, visible through a railed-off space on the main deck, and have an almost hypnotic attraction with their valves and cranks, rods and eccentrics moving in perfect time. This attraction accounts for the expression 'going down to see the engines', an excuse for visiting the bar, traditionally situated below decks on the Clyde steamers; one of the nineteenth century pioneers of the temperance movement was converted to it after narrowly escaping death by falling into the engine of a Clyde steamer while drunk. Some paddle steamers, notably those on the Elbe at Dresden, plus *Gisela* and *Hjejlen,* have oscillating engines where the cylinders themselves move to and fro. In general, the oscillating engine is not so clearly visible from the main deck, but is most impressive when viewed from the floor of the engine room.

Screw steamers have upright engines, not normally open to public view (except on the Turkish steamers) although on a number of preserved Scandinavian steamers it is possible for enthusiasts to climb down a steep ladder into the engine room. Here one may be given a technical description, scarcely audible above the noise of the machinery (if indeed it is in a language one can understand) to which one just nods, looks on in wonder, and, if one has come prepared, leaves a postcard of one's own favourite steamer to be propped on a ledge and admired. Details of diesel engines are not given in this book, for reasons of space and because they are generally of less interest to the steam enthusiast.

Of remaining steamers, many were converted to oil, but a few remain coal-fired, and an odd one or two wood-, or even peat-fired.

Paddle steamers, in the main, thrived on the British coast, the Swiss and Italian lakes, and the great rivers Rhine, Danube, and Elbe. Stern-wheelers were not popular in Europe, and indeed I have come across records of only two stern-wheel passenger steamers: *Elsa* (1892), on the Fulda at Kassel, which operated as late as 1971, albeit with a diesel engine from 1960, and *Indalen* (1887) on the remote Indal river in Sweden, scrapped many years ago. This of course, excludes the many Mississippi-type fake paddlers that have been built in recent years, most of which have an unpowered paddle, split in two, and moving in the wake of twin screws. Stern-wheel paddle tugs were more common, mainly on the rivers and canals east of the Elbe, on the Havel and Spree at Berlin and on the rivers Oder and Vistula and connecting canals, while an odd one or two sailed on the Weser and Rhine. None, sadly, have been preserved though the hull of possibly the last example has served as a workshop for many years at Decin on the Czech section of the Elbe. A few side-wheel paddle tugs have been preserved and made into excellent museums, including *Oscar Huber* at Duisburg, *Ruthof* at Regensburg, and *Württemberg* at Magdeburg.

Screw propulsion was preferred for small launches and ferries out Europe, and for larger steamers in northern Germany and Scandinavia, and also in Turkey. In Norway, the screw steamer was obviously more suited to stormy coastal waters than paddlers, while in Sweden and Finland narrow canals made paddlers, with their bulky sponsons, difficult to use. A special type of violin-shaped fiddle-paddler was designed for Göta canal use, and one has recently been found at the bottom of lake Vättern, perhaps eventually to be raised.

Fares and tickets vary. Fares range from the 10p or less on the Bosporus ferries, which can take you on an hour or more's sail on the commuter steamers, and 75p for a half-day trip on the Elbe paddlers at Dresden, to £170 for a trip from Vienna to Budapest on *Schönbrunn* with a night in a hotel at Budapest, and bus back. Most day excursions are around £10, with Sweden notably cheaper, probably because the steamers that run as part of the local transport network are subsidised, and Finland notably more expensive. In many areas, for example in Switzerland, season tickets are available, often including rail and bus travel. Stockholm's Waxholm company issues the Båtluffarkort, little known but probably the finest value anywhere with a week's unlimited sailing for £10, and Commodore tickets for a whole season's sailings are offered on *Waverley, Kingswear Castle* and *Balmoral*.

Tickets themselves vary, from basic paper machine-issued tickets to elaborate souvenirs. In Istanbul metal tokens, known as *jetons*, are used. These are used to operate a turnstile at the pier of embarkation, except on car ferries, where paper tickets are issued and collected on disembarkation. Swiss steamers retain the Edmondson card ticket, one of Britain's little-recognised legacies to the transport systems of the world, and now on the verge of extinction because of computerisation in many countries. Tickets can be purchased in some places on the boat, in other places at a shore ticket office, sometimes in advance from tourist information offices; in other places, for example at Prague, tourist information offices have never heard of the steamers.

So, all in all, Europe's surviving steamers represent a picture of fascinating variety. But don't just read about them, sail on them! Support the preservation societies, enjoy a sail, with the pleasure of fresh air, historic surroundings, often majestic, changing scenery, and the sight and smell of the steam engine. Sail on the converted vessels, visit the museums, eat in the static restaurants as well. Pressure the owners of unrecognisable historic ships to consider restoration; advise those few who mistakenly label motor vessels as steam of their error. Don't be afraid of venturing behind the Iron Curtain; once the visa red tape has been completed, there is generally freedom for the tourist. Any steamer I have been on has been full of locals enjoying themselves, and snapping away with their Zeniths and Prakticas. Obviously you must avoid photographing anything that may remotely be construed as military, and take plenty of film, as the only film available on the Dresden paddlers, ORWO, is difficult to get processed in the UK.

For those involved in preservation there should be a number of future targets: the restoration of the *Medway Queen,* surely not impossible with the large population in the greater London area, and the return to Britain (if not already scrapped) of three examples of British shipbuilding, the former Thames paddle steamer *Smialy,* the former steam yacht *Libertatea* (surely London or Glasgow could support a hotel conversion of this to the same quality as Stockholm's *Mälardrottningen*) and one of the Clyde-built Bosporus ferries, *Sarayburnu* or *Halas.*

NOTES ON ENTRIES

1) As will be imagined, data has come from a large number of sources; where these have conflicted, a choice has had to be made. I apologise for any errors.

2) Practically all vessels, unless otherwise mentioned, operate in summer only. Summer seasons vary; generally from early June to mid-September, although a lot of Swedish and Finnish operators sail from the last week in June to the middle of August.

3) The mention of any vessel in this book is no guarantee that it will still be in operation on any particular route, or indeed in operation at all, in future years.

4) Engine details are given for steamers, but not motorships. Note that quoted horse-power figures vary depending on whether they are indicated horsepower, shaft horsepower, or nett horsepower, so care should be taken in comparing these figures.

5) UK, Eire, and Norway dimensions are in feet; for the remainder of Europe the metric system is used. For paddle vessels, the two breadth measurements given refer to the hull breadth and overall breadth across the paddle boxes respectively.

6) Similar types of vessel are known by different names in different countries. Here the term 'motor vessel' has been standardised, although it is unwieldy, exept when a vessel is known to be small, with a single deck, and then the term 'launch' has been used; likewise a privately owned steamer is normally termed a 'yacht'.

7) Where a vessel is believed to continue in operation, but no positive news has been forthcoming for some time, the phrase 'No recent information' is used.

8) The vessels of each country are listed in geographical order, generally with coastal waters preceding inland waters. Where there are several vessels at one place, they are generally listed in chronological order of building, with vessels under the same ownership grouped together, and those on scheduled service taking precedence over those operating charters only, and over static vessels.

9) Asterisks by ships' names indicate that photographs of them appear in the colour sections.

PART ONE

OPERATING STEAM SHIPS

SCOTLAND

FIRTH OF CLYDE

WAVERLEY*

Preserved paddle steamer
Operator: Waverley Excursions Ltd, Glasgow
Owner: Waverley Steam Navigation Co Ltd
(both controlled by the Paddle Steamer Preservation Society)
Built: 1947, A & J Inglis Ltd, Pointhouse, Glasgow; 693gt; 235.5ft ×
30.2/57.3ft; 1350 pass
Machinery: triple expansion, Rankin & Blackmore, Greenock; new
boiler 1982; 2100hp; 15kn
Route: excursions from many places on coast of Britain

It is perhaps fitting that the list of steamers in this book should start with *Waverley*, Widely known as the last sea-going paddle steamer in the world, she has the most extensive and ambitious sailing programme of all Europe's preserved steamers, having visited over the past decade many piers and harbours that had not seen a paddle steamer for half a century or more.

Built for the London and North Eastern Railway to replace *Waverley* of 1899, which had been lost at Dunkirk in 1940, her early years were spend on the route from Craigendoran (near Helensburgh) up Loch Long to Lochgoilhead and Arrochar. Becoming part of the British Railways fleet on nationalisation of the railways in 1948, she adopted their colour scheme of buff funnel with black top. She became part of the Caledonian Steam Packet Co fleet, still under British Railways control, in 1951, and in 1965, British Rail's corporate image brought a dark blue hull and lions on the funnels. She was converted from coal to oil firing in 1957.

A more varied programme of sailings was undertaken in the fifties, and she sailed from Craigendoran in conjunction with her elder sister *Jeanie Deans* until the latter's withdrawal in 1964, and subsequently with the ex-LMSR paddler *Caledonia* until 1969. Her hull reverted to black in 1969, when the CSP became part of the Scottish Transport Group, and the Clyde fleet were no longer under railway control. Her last season before preservation was 1973 and in that summer she sported new funnel colours.

In August 1974 she was sold to the Paddle Steamer Preservation Society for the symbolic sum of £1, and, rather to the surprise of Caledonian McBrayne, who had expected her to be statically preserved, returned to service in May 1975 after a thorough overhaul, with much work by volunteer PSPS members. A new image brought back the LNER's red, white and black funnels, while imaginative itineraries and enthusiastic marketing brought a return to steam over the entire summer. In 1977, a week's visit to Liverpool brought her first sailings outside the Firth of Clyde, and by the mid-eighties a pattern had emerged with the season starting on the Clyde in late April, sailings from Oban and Fort William in early May, the Bristol Channel from late May to mid or late June, on the Clyde in July and August, and on the South Coast of England and the Thames in September. Visits were paid to the Humber, Tyne and Forth in 1981 and 1982, Dublin in 1985 and 1986, and Waterford and Cork in 1986; sailings from Portree and Kyle of Lochalsh were planned for spring 1988. Sailings have included special school cruises, introducing many to the joys of a steamer excursion.

Waverley, 1980

Waverley has had problems over the years, and these, unfortunately, generate more press publicity than her success does. In 1977 she stranded on the Gantocks rocks off Dunoon, 1981 saw the fitting of a new boiler, 1985 a much-criticised trip from Garlieston to the Isle of Man in stormy weather, (although as Garlieston harbour dried out at low tide she had no alternative), and 1987 a premature end to sailings in mid-August because of boiler problems.

As on most paddlers, the engine room is open to view, the movement of the three pistons and cranks exercising an almost hypnotic effect on passengers. A souvenir shop is manned by PSPS volunteers and there are two bars and a self-service cafeteria.

Her 40th anniversary voyage was on 16 June 1987, an evening trip from Greenock to Loch Long, turning off the now-closed pier at Arrochar. A birthday cake was cut by Capt John Cameron, who had been master of the previous *Waverley*.

In late 1987 it was announced that the boiler would be repaired, and that *Waverley* would be in operation for the Glasgow Garden Festival year of 1988. The problems were apparently complex, but had, in the main, been due to lubricating oil finding its way into the cooling system. A new boiler could possibly be needed by 1989.

FIRTH OF CLYDE, CALEDONIAN CANAL

VIC 32

Screw steamer; ex Royal Navy VIC steamer (puffer type), in service
Operator: Nick & Rachel Walker, Lochgilphead
Built: 1943, R Dunston & Co, Thorne, Yorks; 96gt; 62ft × 18ft;
12 pass
Machinery: compound, Crabtree, Great Yarmouth; 130hp; 6kn;
coal-fired
Route: 6/7 day cruises on Caledonian Canal from Banavie (early and
late season), and on Firth of Clyde from Ardrishaig (high season)

Built as one of a series of 63 VICs (Victualling Inshore Craft) to provide wartime coastal cargo transport for the Admiralty, *VIC 32* was purchased for preservation in 1970, and by her present owners in 1975. She has been expertly converted, and her hatch covers have been raised a little to provide space for cabin accommodation. Passengers are encouraged to fire the boiler and help in the running of the steamer. In 1987 she won the British Coal Steam Heritage Award.

The VICs were based on the Clyde puffers, whose design had evolved to enable them to pass through the Crinan Canal locks, and to take the beach to load and unload cargo on the smaller Hebridean Islands.

GLASGOW, WEST HIGHLANDS

VITAL SPARK

ex *Auld Reekie* 1988, ex *VIC 27* 1969
Screw steamer, ex VIC naval water tanker
Owner: Bathgate Bros (Marine) Ltd, Edinburgh
Built: Isaac Pimblott & Sons, Northwich, Cheshire; 96gt; 66.9ft ×
18.5ft;
12 pass
Machinery: compound, Crabtree, Great Yarmouth; 130hp; coal-fired
Only occasional passenger trips

Built as a sister to *VIC 32*, *VIC 27* was used as a fresh water tanker for the Admiralty until about 1962. Converted in 1969 to provide more basic accommodation than her sister, she was mainly used for groups of young people. Previously owned by Sir James Miller, she was purchased by her present

owners in about 1976, and has been used as a bunkering ship for a fleet of charter yachts. Some charters were continued, although by 1986 these had almost ceased. Based at Oban, and wintering at Crinan until 1985, she spent the 1986 summer in Loch Carron, and in 1987 commenced a fifteen month charter to Argyll & Bute District Council, who took her to Campbeltown for a major overhaul before planned exhibition at the Glasgow Garden Festival in 1988. She has recently been renamed *Vital Spark* after the ficticious puffer of Neil Munro's *Para Handy Tales*.

Other preserved VICs are *VIC 56* at Chatham, *VIC 96* at Maryport, *Victual* (ex *VIC 77*) in Holland, and the dieselised *Spartan*, ex *VIC 18*, preserved at the Scottish Maritime Museum at Irvine.

VIC 32 laid up for the winter, Inverness, 1981

Sir Walter Scott off Trossachs pier, 1978

Lady Rowena, Loch Awe, 1987

CHARLOTTE DUNDAS II

¾ scale replica of pioneer stern-wheel (recessed wheel) tug of 1803
Owner: Falkirk District Council
Built: 1988, Cockenzie Slip & Boatyard Co, Cockenzie/Falkirk District
Council; original was 56' × 18'
Machinery: horizontal single cylinder; 10hp

William Symington's *Charlotte Dundas* was the first practical application in Europe of steam propulsion. Unfortunately protests by farmers over excessive wash stopped her sailing, and she was scrapped in 1861 after many years laid up.

The replica will be of three-quarters scale, in view of the low bridges on the Forth and Clyde Canal, and it is planned she will pull passenger barges and come into operation in 1989.

LOCH KATRINE

SIR WALTER SCOTT

Screw steamer
Operator: Strathclyde Water Dept
Built: 1900, Wm Denny & Bros, Dumbarton; 115gt; 110.5ft × 19.1ft;
416 pass
Machinery: triple expansion, M Paul & Co, Dumbarton; 140hp; smokeless coal-fired; new boiler 1956
Route: Trossachs Pier–Stronachlachar; 1 hour cruises from Trossachs
pier

Scotland's oldest steamer has sailed on Loch Katrine since her building. She is little changed with the exception of the replacement of large saloon windows on the lower deck by portholes in 1956, and red and white awnings rather than the old white canvas ones. As Loch Katrine provides a water supply for Glasgow, smokeless fuel has been used since 1967 to prevent pollution. Originally owned by the Loch Katrine Steamboat Co, she was later taken over by Glasgow Corporation Water Dept, which became part of the Lower Clyde Water Board, now Strathclyde Water Dept. A sail on her is rewarding, not only for the pleasure of sailing on a veteran, but also for the magnificent scenery, especially as there is no public road access around the Loch.

LOCH AWE

LADY ROWENA

ex *Water Lily* 1986
Steam launch, ex motor launch 1986
Operator: Dalriada Steam Packet Co, Glasgow
Built: 1927, C R Breaker, Windermere; 36ft; 30 pass
Machinery: compound, E Langley (Sissons design) 1986; peat-fired
Route: cruises from Loch Awe pier

Lady Rowena was rebuilt by owner Harry Watson from a motor launch of classic Windermere design, and fitted by him with a new engine and boiler before entering service on Loch Awe in 1986. Sailings connect with trains at the recently re-opened Loch Awe station. She is a smart-looking launch with a white funnel, and well worth sailing on.

LOCH LOMOND

MAID OF THE LOCH

Paddle steamer, laid up at Balloch
Owner: Alloa Brewery
Built: 1953, A & J Inglis Ltd, Pointhouse, Glasgow; 555gt; 191ft ×
28.1/55ft; 1000 pass
Machinery: compound diagonal, Rankin & Blackmore; 1060hp; 13kn

Built for British Railways to replace the paddlers *Princess May* (1898) and *Prince Edward* (1905), *Maid of the Loch* was ill-conceived and far too large for the traffic offering on the loch. Rapid increase in car ownership had meant a major decrease in excursion steamer traffic, and, in a European context, no other paddle steamers had been built since the war except *Waverley* and a group of Hungarian-built paddlers for Russian rivers. In hindsight a couple of *Countess*-sized motor vessels would have been far more sensible. As a result *Maid of the Loch* faced withdrawal on economic grounds from 1961 onwards. She did in fact last until 1981, by which time she was under the aegis of Caledonian MacBrayne.

She was purchased by her present owners in 1982, and plans have been announced from time to time for her return to service, initially under steam, and latterly with diesel-hydraulic propulsion, keeping the old machinery intact; and also for use as a restaurant. All have so far come to nothing. Berthed at Balloch pier and used as a landing stage for *Countess Fiona*, she is lapsing into very poor condition.

As far as design goes, she is similar to the Clyde steamer *Marchioness of Lorne*, and deserves preservation as one of only a handful of extant British excursion paddlers. Members of the PSPS have carried out some work on her in recent years, but this has been mainly a holding operation against total deterioration.

In late 1987 talks were taking place between Ind Coope and the PSPS about a secure future for the ship.

Sir Walter Scott, Trossachs pier, 1987

ENGLAND

IT IS SURPRISING how many veterans there are in England. Highlights are *Kingswear Castle,* preserved river paddler; *Gondola,* expertly restored lake steamer; *Alaska,* privately owned but for many years on upper and middle Thames passenger service; and *Connaught,* finest of the many London-based veterans. Hopes for the future lie in eventual restoration of *Medway Queen* to service, of *Wingfield Castle* as a museum, and the eventual opening of *Queen Mary* as a restaurant.

One surprising fact is the survival of so many pre-1914 ex-steamers on the Thames, particularly the Salters fleet. Possibly the fact that they lost their funnels when dieselised, and thus do not look so appealing, has contributed to a general lack of interest among enthusiasts in such Thames veterans.

RIVER MEDWAY

KINGSWEAR CASTLE

Preserved paddle steamer
Owner: Paddle Steam Navigation Co
Operator: Kingswear Castle Excursions, Chatham
(both controlled by the Paddle Steamer Preservation Society)
Built: 1924, Philip & Son, Dartmouth; 94gt; 108ft × 17.5ft/28ft;
235 pass
Machinery: compound diagonal, Cox & Co, Falmouth, 1904, formerly
in *Kingswear Castle* (1904); 130hp; coal-fired; 8kn
Route: excursions from Strood and Chatham; also short trips
from Southend

The culmination of many years' preservation work on *Kingswear Castle* by PSPS members came in 1985, when she resumed commercial service. She has been well restored to original condition and, as southern England's only operating paddle steamer, deserves full enthusiast support.

She was built for the River Dart Steamboat Co to replace her predecessor of the same name, whose engines she inherited. Her

Kingswear Castle, Whitstable, 1987

normal route was from Dartmouth to Totnes, and she lasted here until 1965, by which time she was the last surviving steamer in the fleet.

Purchased in 1967 by the PSPS, she was laid up awaiting restoration on the river Medina on the Isle of Wight until 1971, before moving to Rochester. Complete restoration took many years, and she did not steam again until late 1983, and ran in 1984 as a yacht for 12 passengers only until starting full passenger service in 1985. She is much in demand for special sailings, and makes occasional trips to Whitstable through the Swale, and on the Thames at Gravesend and from Tower Pier. Restrictions on her passenger certificate prohibit her from carrying passengers across the Thames Estuary. Sailings are probably not as well patronised as they should be, and there must be a possibility of a move to a more lucrative location at some time in the future. *Kingswear Castle* won the British Coal Steam Heritage Award in 1986.

RIVER MEDWAY

MEDWAY QUEEN

Paddle steamer, undergoing restoration
Operator: Medway Queen Preservation Society
Built: 1924, Ailsa Shipbuilding Co Ltd, Troon; 316gt; 179.9ft × 24.2ft/49.5ft; formerly 828 pass
Machinery: compound diagonal; 1000hp; 13kn

Built for the New Medway Steam Packet Co, *Medway Queen* spent her years in service sailing from Strood and Chatham to Southend and other Thames Estuary piers. She was withdrawn in 1963, and was moved to the river Medina, Isle of Wight

in 1965. Used for a while as a restaurant, she later became derelict, and eventually returned to the Medway in 1984 on a pontoon. She has lain on a mud berth at Chatham since then and the enthusiasts in her preservation society have been fighting a battle with the mud that floods in at every high tide. This appears to be slowly being won, and, if a dry dock or slipway can be found for her, preservation will progress much faster.

Medway Queen has a notable war record, having rescued more troops (around 7000) from Dunkirk, and made more trips there, than any other vessel smaller than a destroyer. This alone makes her worthy of preservation, but she also represents the typical British coastal excursion paddle steamer of a type little changed from the 1880s to the 1930s.

Note: Medway Queen was refloated in November 1987, and towed to a new berth at Damhead Creek, on the Hoo peninsula, where restoration will continue.

RIVER MEDWAY

JOHN H AMOS

ex *Hero* 1970s ex *John H Amos* 1975
Paddle tug/tender, undergoing restoration at Chatham
Owner: Medway Maritime Museum, Chatham
Built: 1931, Bow, McLachlan & Co, Paisley; 202t; 110ft × 22.6ft; formerly 134 pass
Machinery: two compound diagonal, one for each paddle; 500hp

John H Amos was used on the river Tees until 1967. Following abortive attempts at preservation at Stockton, she was moved to the Medway in 1975. Now berthed in the Medway outside Chatham Historic Dockyard, she is undergoing restoration by a small group of enthusiasts. It is uncertain if she ever operated public passenger sailings, but she was used as a workboat for dredger crews in post-war years, and also as an inspection steamer by the Tees Conservancy Commissioners.

SOUTHAMPTON

*SHIELDHALL**

Twin screw sludge steamer, undergoing restoration at Southampton
Owner: Southern Water Authority/Southampton Museum/
SS *Shieldhall* Project
Built: 1955, Lobnitz & Co, Renfrew; 1753gt; 268ft × 43ft; 80 pass
(when on Clyde)
Machinery: two triple expansion; 1600hp

Operated by Glasgow Corporation on the river Clyde for many years, *Shieldhall* carried invited parties, mainly senior citizens but also occasional enthusiast groups, on her sailings from Shieldhall Sewage Works to the sludge dumping grounds off Garroch Head. The passenger-carrying tradition dated back to the years following World War I when convalescent soldiers were carried on *Shieldhall*'s predecessors. This practice is continued on her successor *Garroch Head* and for 12 passengers only on the Forth's *Gardyloo*.

Sold to the Southern Water Authority in 1977, thoroughly overhauled then and in use at Southampton from 1980, she was withdrawn in 1985. There are plans for her restoration to steam, and for future passenger sailings.

Medway Queen in service

Shieldhall at Dalmuir sewage works, river Clyde

Carola, after repainting, 1987 (Plysolene Ltd)

Left: Carola, deck view (Plysolene Ltd)

BUCKLER'S HARD

CAROLA

Preserved steam yacht
Operator: Mark Varvill, Lymington
Built: 1898, Scott & Sons, Bowling; 40gt; 70.7ft × 13.3ft; 12 pass
Machinery: compound, Ross & Duncan, Govan; 80hp; coal-fired
Route: charters from Buckler's Hard, Beaulieu River

One of only a handful of traditional steam yachts left in the world, *Carola* was constructed for her builders for use as a private yacht and also as a tug. Her hull was based on the design of steam drifters then being built by Scott's. During World War II she was used as a fire-fighting steamer on the Clyde. A new boiler was fitted in 1952, but she was then laid up in the river Leven at Dumbarton, becoming very derelict. She was sold to an English owner in 1970, and steamed to Buckler's Hard. Her present owner bought her in 1981, and has completed restoration. She is now used for charters from Buckler's Hard for up to 12 passengers, as she has no full passenger certificate. Photographs of her show that restoration has been carried out to a very high standard. She has two gaff-rigged masts, a tall buff funnel, and black hull. Her main saloon is fitted with plush velvet upholstery, and there is also a six-berth cabin, although at present she is only used for day charters. There is a small fore deck saloon, with an open bridge between this and the funnel.

BIRKENHEAD	MARYPORT

BEN MY CHREE

Twin screw steam turbine cross-channel car ferry, laid up at Birkenhead
Owner: Penespy Ltd
Built: 1966, Cammell Laird, Birkenhead; 2762gt; 325ft × 50ft; 1400 pass, 90 cars
Machinery: 2 steam turbines; 9500hp; 21kn; steam turbine powered bow thruster (500hp) fitted 1978

SCHARHÖRN

Twin screw inspection steamer, undergoing restoration
Owner: A & W Treloar, for sale 1987
Built: 1908, Janssen and Schmilsky, Hamburg; 125ft
Machinery: two triple expansion; coal-fired

Built for the Isle of Man Steam Packet Co and their services from Liverpool and other ports to the Isle of Man, *Ben My Chree* was fitted with an unusual car loading system based on a spiral roadway down to the car deck. Heavily used for summer tourist traffic to the island and for the TT motor cycle races, she became an anachronism with her uneconomic steam engines. When withdrawn at the end of the 1984 season, she was the last turbine cross-channel steamer in northern Europe. She was sold to an American for proposed use in Georgia, USA, but chartered back by the Steam Packet Co for a few weeks in 1985 to provide extra capacity on the Heysham to Douglas route during the TT period. She has remained at Birkenhead, and has reportedly been sold again in 1987, either to be used as a floating restaurant in Manchester or for a Llandudno to Douglas service.

Built as a yacht for the Hamburg harbour commissioners, and used as such until 1914, *Scharhörn* was laid up from 1918 to 1925, then used until 1971 as an inspection and survey steamer at Cuxhaven. She was used in 1944-5 in the evacuation of the eastern territories (see *Albatros*). She was bought in 1973 by a Scottish owner who planned to operate her on passenger cruises on the west coast of Scotland, but instead was laid up at Buckie for six years. She was then sold to her present owners, taken to the Tyne, and moved to Maryport in about 1985, where restoration has proceeded slowly. *Scharhörn* is presently up for sale, and apparently not too much work would be needed to put her into steam again. She is often erroneously referred to as the Kaiser's private yacht. In 1987 she was inspected by Norwegian enthusiasts with a view to purchase. She is similar to, but with less passenger accommodation than, *Alexandra* (Flensburg), which came from the same builders.

Scharhörn, Maryport, 1987

Ben My Chree, Douglas, Isle of Man, 1980

CONISTON WATER

GONDOLA

Preserved screw steamer
Operator: National Trust
Built: 1859, Jones, Quiggin & Co, Liverpool; major rebuild to original
design 1978-80, Vickers, Barrow; 42gt; 84ft × 14.2ft; 86 pass
Machinery: V-shaped oscillating, Locomotion Enterprises, Gateshead,
1980 (copy of original engine); 16hp; coal-fired; 10kn
Route: Coniston Water; Coniston–Park-a-Moor

One of those unusual steamers that have somehow survived, possibly because of their rarity, *Gondola* ran on Coniston Water for the Furness Railway. Their successors, the LMSR, ran her, mainly as a spare steamer, up to the outbreak of World War II. The engine was removed in 1944 to power a sawmill, and she was used as a houseboat for a while, then semi-sunk to stop her from rotting away completely. She had degenerated to little more than a shell when the National Trust purchased her in 1977, and the steamer of today can be seen as more a replica on that shell than a genuine veteran. On the other hand, she has been expertly restored, with her passenger cabin boasting opulent plush red settees; with gleaming gold-plated serpent figurehead, she sails silently along the lake several times daily. It is well worth a special trip to sail on her.

LAKE WINDERMERE

OSPREY

Preserved steam launch, ex motor launch, ex private steam launch
Operator: Windermere Steamboat Museum
Built: 1902, Shepherds, Bowness on Windermere; 8gt; 45.5ft × 8ft.;
12 pass
Machinery: compound, Sissons
Route: short trips from Windermere Steamboat Museum

Windermere's Steamboat Museum has probably the finest collection of steam launches anywhere. Those exhibited were almost all built and used as private steamers, but *Osprey*, used for a number of years as a motor passenger launch on the lake, has been restored to steam and offers trips from the museum. *Osprey* is a small launch with varnished wood hull and small saloon aft. A unique feature is the 'Windermere kettle' which uses water from the boiler to heat a kettle and thus make a cup of tea for passengers.

NORWICH, RIVER WENSUM

OLIVE

Steam launch
Operator: G & O Sutton, Norwich
Built: 1985, Steam & Electric Launch Co, Wroxham; 21ft; 12 pass
Machinery: compound, A Ritchie & S Turner
Route: excursions from Norwich

Reported in operation here 1986, *Olive* is one of a number of similar wooden steam launches built in recent years to traditional designs.

Opposite top: Gondola, Lake Coniston

Opposite: Osprey, Windermere Steamboat Museum

BRENTFORD, RIVER THAMES

RESOLUTE

Double ended screw steamer, awaiting restoration
Owner: Thames Steam & Navigation, Chiswick
Built: 1903, Edwards & Co Ltd, Millwall; 71gt; 73ft × 17.3ft; formerly
316 pass
Machinery: compound, Plenty & Co, Newbury, 120hp; new
boiler 1983

Resolute was a Yarmouth to Gorleston ferry, later used on excursions from Yarmouth. She was acquired for preservation by the Veteran Steamship Society in 1968, but it would appear that the project ran out of money after a few years. The steamer is believed still to be undergoing restoration, berthed on the Thames at Brentford. While *Yarmouth* is flush-decked, *Resolute* has a small upper deck.

RICHMOND, RIVER THAMES

*DUCHESS DOREEN**

ex *Duchess of York* 1900
Motor vessel, ex steamer, undergoing restoration
Owner: A Collier, Richmond
Built: 1894; H Tooley, Hampton Wick; 64.3ft; 12 pass

This vessel operated on the Thames from 1894 to 1900, and then was sold to Worcester, but returned to the Thames in 1973 for 'nostalgia' dinner cruise business for 12 passengers only at Maidenhead. She sank in 1981, and has been out of service since then. She was sold to her present owners at auction in late 1983, for a planned restoration to steam. No recent information.

EGHAM, RIVER THAMES

ECLIPSE

Steam launch, ex motor launch 1982, ex steam launch
Operator: Nichole's Boatyard, Egham
Built: 1901, E Cawston & Co, Reading; 52ft; 12 pass
Machinery: compound, J Ashton, Sheffield, 1980s
Route: executive charters from Egham

Eclipse is an excellently restored steam launch, offering luxury dinner cruises (£90 per person!). She was operated by her builder at Reading 1901-1930, then at Kingston, London, Richmond, Hampton Court, and latterly at Kingston by Parr's, who presently operate the similar *Em*. At some stage she was fitted with a petrol engine and later a diesel. A steam engine has been refitted, and she claims to be the only Edwardian steam launch with a mains microwave oven in the galley. A very attractive and little known steamer.

HURLEY, RIVER THAMES

ALASKA

Preserved steam launch, ex passenger steamer
Owner: unknown (privately owned)
Built: 1883, Horsham & Son, Bourne End; rebuilt P Freebody & Co,
Hurley, 1977-87; 60ft; formerly 70 pass
Machinery: twin simple expansion, Seekings; 10hp

Alaska was Salter Bros' first steamer when they opened their Oxford to Kingston service in 1888, having operated from Walton on Thames the previous year. Replaced by more

Eclipse, Egham, 1987

modern steamers, she was used latterly on charters, and withdrawn during World War II. A 1920 brochure lists her charter rate as £8.40 Thursdays and Saturdays, £7.35 other weekdays. She may have been used in the London area in the forties, but her history since then is uncertain, and she was reportedly in use as a pontoon when restoration started in about 1976. An outstanding job has been done, and she has a gilt figurehead of a bird in flight, white hull, white funnel and small cabin aft. She is one of the finest restoration jobs anywhere in Europe.

HURLEY, RIVER THAMES

WINDSOR BELLE

Preserved screw steamer, ex motor vessel 1986, ex steamer c1949
Operator: Windsor Belle Ltd, Hurley
Built: A Jacobs, Windsor, 1901; rebuilt P Freebody & Co, Hurley, 1986; 23gt; 70ft; 40 pass
Machinery: compound, 1895; coal-fired
Route: charters from Hurley

Windsor Belle was operated by her builders on cruises from Windsor up to 1977; restoration started in 1983 and she has been very well restored, catering for the luxury 'nostalgia' charter market (afternoon cruises £25 per head). She has a varnished wood hull, but her appearance in wet weather is rather spoiled by awnings with perspex windows. She has a small saloon amidships.

MANCHESTER, HEATON PARK

WILLIAM SHARP II

Paddle steamer
Operator: Manchester City Council
Built: 1986, G Lancaster Jones, Port Dinorwic; 30ft; 16 pass
Machinery: D C Burnage, Bedford; 3hp; wood-fired
Route: Heaton Park Lake, Manchester

William Sharp II is a new steam paddle launch, which ran trials in the Menai Straits in 1986 before going to Manchester. A quasi-sister named *Minerva* was completed in 1987 for a private owner in Colwyn Bay, while a further clipper-bowed paddle launch *Jersey Lily* from the same builder was built in 1984 for a private owner for use on the Thames, but was later sold in the north of England.

ELLESMERE (SHROPSHIRE)

MERLIN

Steam launch
Operator: The Boathouse Restaurant, Ellesmere, Shropshire
Built: 1985, G Lancaster Jones, Port Dinorwic; 12 pass
Route: short sailings on the Mere, Ellesmere

Merlin is a small traditional-styled steam launch operating on a small lake south of Chester.

ELLESMERE PORT

ALEXANDRA

Steam inspection launch, planned for restoration
Owner: Boat Museum, Ellesmere Port
Built: 1882 near Hull

*A*lexandra is a former Leeds and Liverpool Canal inspection steamer, used until 1967. She is now at the Boat Museum and here eventual restoration to steam with her original engine is planned. It is possible that she will offer passenger trips when restored.

IRISH REPUBLIC

No operating steamers; *see Part Two.*

Top: Clipper bow and figurehead on *Alaska*, 1987

Windsor Belle, Freebody's yard, Hurley, 1987

NORWAY

Børøysund, Oslo, 1985

As BEFITS A NATION with a long coastline and many islands, Norway has a number of preserved coastal steamers. However, the title of best-known and finest of Norway's steamers must go to an inland steamer, the 130-year-old paddler *Skibladner* on lake Mjøsa. The pattern in Norway generally seems to be for small local groups to preserve steamers, sometimes taking many years in restoration. Rather surprisingly, quite a number of older steamers were sold and converted to coasters in the sixties.

In addition to the vessels mentioned, the Norwegian Maritime Museum at Oslo has on display a three-deck-high section, including the staircase, a de-luxe cabin and the dining saloon of the passenger steamer *Sandnes* (1914), which operated on the Bergen to Stavanger night route and was scrapped in 1973.

Dimensions are given in feet, as most Norwegian maritime histories have used this measurement.

OSLO, OSLOFJORD

BØRØYSUND

ex *Hyma* 1969, ex *Børøysund* 1960, ex *Skjærgar* 1925, ex *Odin* 1923
Preserved screw steamer
Operator: Norsk Veteranskibsklub, Oslo
Built: 1908, Trondhjems Mek Verksted, 1908; rebuilt 1925 Bergen Mek Verksted, and 1935, Tromsø Mek Verksted; 181gt; 108ft × 18.3ft; 100 pass
Machinery: triple expansion; 256hp; coal-fired; 9kn
Route: charters and occasional public sailings from Oslo

A typical medium sized Norwegian coastal steamer, familiar to many visitors to Oslo, where her regular berth is near the Town Hall, *Børøysund* was built as a combined tug and passenger steamer for local services on the Trondheimsfjord. She was sold to Bergen owners in 1923, and again in 1925 to Vesteraalens Dampskibsselkap. Rebuilt in 1925, and also in 1935, she served the Vesteraalen and Lofoten islands until her withdrawal in 1960. Used in the sixties as a stationary training steamer for engineers at Melbu, she was purchased by the Norwegian Veteran Ship Club in 1969, sailed to Oslo, and restored. In 1982 she steamed all the way north to the Vesteraalen Islands for the centenary of her former owners. She is Norway's last coal-fired steamer.

She is difficult for an enthusiast to sail on, as her few public sailings seem only to be advertised locally, and unlike most enthusiast groups operating steamers, her owners do not publish a sailing programme at the beginning of the season. The same club also owns the steam tug *Styrbjørn* (1910), restored and based at Oslo, and the coastal cargo steamer *Hestmanden* (1911, 775gt), undergoing restoration at Trondheim, notable for being the first cargo steamer back in operation on the Norwegian coast after World War II.

TRONDHEIM

HANSTEEN

ex *Ivar Elias* 1978, ex *Haarek* 1950, ex *Hansteen* 1899
Preserved screw steamer, undergoing restoration at Trondheim
Owner: Restaureringskomiteen for *Hansteen*, Oslo
Built: 1866, Nyland Mek Verksted, Oslo, as oceanographic research
ship, wrought iron hull; rebuilt 1899 and 1916, both by Bakklandet
Mek Verksted, Trondheim; 114gt; 101.6ft × 16.4ft
Machinery: compound, 1915; 125hp

Norway's first survey steamer, later used for many years as a passenger steamer, *Hansteen* is the subject of a long-term preservation project. One of the few survivors of the sail and steam era, she was built with a schooner rig, and her wrought iron plates were made by Bloomfield of Tipton, Staffs. In the forefront of scientific research in the latter half of the last century, she carried out meteorological, magnetic, and oceanographic research. She was sold in 1898 for use on the Trondheimsfjord as a local steamer, but only lasted one season during fierce competition on the service. Purchased the following year by the Helgeland Dampskibsselskab, and rebuilt with raised forecastle and midships section, she was used as reserve steamer from 1905 onwards; her strong hull saved her from scrapping, and in 1916 she was rebuilt with an upper deck the full length of the ship. She operated from Sandnessjoen to Træna until 1952, and was then used as a hostel for seasonal workers in the fishing industry until 1962, and then as a hostel at Oslo for the Norwegian Inland Mission. In 1957 a shed structure was built over her.

Restoration of *Hansteen* has continued well, and in December

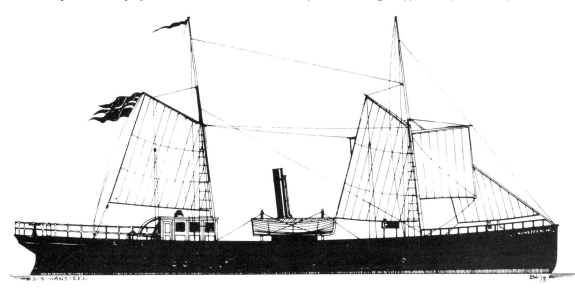

Hansteen's original appearance (Bard Kollveit)

1987 she was towed to Trondheim, surviving a 12-knot tow and a force nine gale en route. Here her engine and boiler will be restored, with new pipework installed, and also the interior woodwork will be renovated. Remarkably, much of this is the original woodwork from 1866. Plans for her restoration had started when an enthusiast explored inside her hull in 1975, while she was still in use as an accommodation ship, and found, to his surprise, all the original fittings intact. So good was the condition of the hull that only 24 of 128 plates had to be replaced. It is hoped to return her to steam in summer 1988 and to 1860s condition. She must be the only survivor in steam anywhere in the world from the steam and sail era of the mid nineteenth century.

Hansteen before restoration, Oslo, 1985

PELLE

ex *Pippi* 1884
Steam launch, undergoing restoration at Oslo
Owner: Stiftelsen Norsk Fartøyvern, Oslo (Norwegian Foundation for Preservation and Restoration of Ships)
Built: 1882, Motala Verkstad, Motala, Sweden; 15gt; 45ft × 12ft; formerly 63 pass
Macninery: single cylinder; 18hp

This vessel was built as a private launch, but used as a local ferry from Arendal to two nearby islands from 1884 right up until 1963. She was purchased as Norsk Veteranskipsklub's first steamer in 1964, but work on their other steamers prevented restoration, and she was sold in 1972 for conversion to a tug. In 1985 she was taken over by her present owners, a group of four enthusiasts who had got together to preserve the steam tug and former whaler *Forlandet* (1921). Having made an excellent job of restoring her, they have now started restoration of *Pelle* on land at Oslo. The engine is still extant, but a new boiler is needed, as the old one was scrapped in 1972. It is planned to start work in 1988 to rebuild her to original condition and name her *Pippi* again.

REIGUN

ex *Oscarsborg I* 1954, ex *Styrsö I* 1910
Cargo motor vessel, ex-steamer, planned for restoration to screw passenger steamer
Owner: Fred Olsen Line (or associates)
Built: 1904, Södra Varvet, Stockholm; 98ft × 22ft

Built for local services from Göteborg to Styrsö, this vessel was sold in 1910 for commuter service from Oslo to Nesodden and the Oslofjord. She was rebuilt in 1918 for winter service there and converted to a diesel coaster in 1954, in which role she was used at least until 1981. There are plans by her present owners, associated with the well-known shipping

Pelle at Christiania, now Oslo, 1905 (Arne Holm, Norsk Fartoyvern)

Opposite: Kysten I, Tønsberg, 1981

company Fred Olsen, who owned her from 1920, to restore her as a passenger ship. When she was seen in spring 1985, no conversion work had been done.

KYSTEN I

ex *Askaas* 1970, ex *Kysten* 1964
Preserved screw steamer. in service
Operator: AS Jubilemskipet, Tønsberg
Built: 1909, Trondhjems Mek Verksted; lengthened 1950; 383gt; 140ft × 21ft; 150 pass
Machinery: triple expansion; 383hp; 9kn
Route: excursions in Tønsberg archipelago (west side of Oslofjord)

A more imposing steamer than *Børøysund, Kysten I* has been preserved at Tønsberg since 1970, and is Europe's finest preserved coastal cargo-passenger steamer. She was built for Namsos Dampskibsselskab, and operated from Trondheim to the Namsos area until 1964, along a very exposed part of the Norwegian coast. The service left Trondheim at 8am on a Saturday, and reached Namsos after 45 stops at 1am on a Monday. During the war she was requisitioned by the Germans for use as a ferry in northern Norway, and in 1950 was converted to oil-firing and lengthened by 14 feet in order to make space for the fuel tanks without sacrificing cargo space. From 1964 to 1968 she was used as a training ship, and then for a short period as a hostel, until purchased by her present owners in 1970, the 1100th anniversary of the founding of the town of Tønsberg. Her normal trips operate daily in summer if there are more than 20 passengers, and sail a very scenic route amongst small rocky islands, but in certain years she has made a trip around the coast as far as Mandal, taking 3½ days each way. She is very well restored and accommodation includes a dining saloon on the lower deck and a small post office. Passengers are welcomed in the engine room. Highly recommended.

Stord I undergoing restoration, Bergen, 1986

Below: Detail view of *Suldal,* Suldalsvatn, 1986

BERGEN

STORD I

ex *O T Moe* 1980, ex *Stord* 1969
Preserved screw steamer, ex motor vessel 1987, ex steamer 1949,
undergoing restoration
Owner: Veteranskipslaget Fjordabåten, Bergen
Built: 1913, Laxevaag Maskin & Jernskibsbyggeri; rebuilt 1931; rebuilt
1987, Mjellem & Karlssen, Bergen to 1931 condition; 469gt;
155.2ft × 33.8ft
Machinery: triple expansion, Yarwood, Northwich, 1942; 500hp (formerly in Royal Navy oil lighter *C609 (F)*)

One of preservation's most tragic stories, *Stord I* had been completely restored over a number of years when she made her second maiden voyage on 9 May 1987. Eleven days later she suffered a serious fire en route from Bergen to Stord, when the boiler blew back, igniting oil on the engine-room floor, which set fire to the whole steamer. Following a survey which indicated that the engine and hull were sound, it was decided that she would be restored again. This will be undertaken at the Eide yard at Høylandsbygd, but she is not expected to sail again until 1989.

She is western Norway's only preserved fjord steamer, and was built for the overnight service of the Hardanger Sunnhordlandske company from Bergen to the Hardangerfjord and Stavanger. She was rebuilt and lengthened in 1931, converted to diesel in 1949, and used as reserve ship by the company from 1959 until 1969. She then lay at Oslo for 11 years as a rehabilitation centre for alcoholics until purchased for preservation in 1980.

She was moved back to Bergen in 1982 and restoration was undertaken in the shipyard of Mjellem & Karlssen from 1983 until 1987. The Royal Navy oil lighter *C609 (F)* was purchased, and her engines and boiler used to re-convert *Stord I* to steam. The HSD logo of her former owners was placed on a new tall funnel in place of the over-large motorship one. Funds for the restoration came from many firms in the area. It had been planned to operate her on excursions and charters from Bergen to the nearby fjords, surely one of the most scenic routes of Europe's preserved steamers.

C609 (F) was used until 1980 by the Royal Navy, and was one of a number of steamships purchased by the Treloar family, and berthed on the Tyne for a while. Later *Scharhörn* and others were taken to Maryport.

Note: Stord's owners claim engines were built by Cammell Laird, but British records show they came from Yarwoods. Possibly *C609F* had been fitted with a new Cammell Laird boiler at some stage.

ÅLESUND

THOROLF

Screw steamer, undergoing restoration
Owner: Foreningen til Dampskipet *Thorolf*'s
Built: 1911, Skaaluren, Rosendal, Hardanger; 27gt; 60ft × 14.5ft
Machinery: compound, Brunholmens Mek Verksted, Ålesund,
1912; 75hp

Thorolf is a small wooden-hulled steamer, originally used by the firm of O A Devold for supplying their products to firms along the Norwegian coast. She was used latterly as the private yacht of her owners, and acquired for restoration

after being laid up in the sixties. She is reported to be in good condition, but no details are available as to whether any passenger sailings are offered.

SULDALSVATN

SULDAL

Preserved screw steamer, ex motor vessel 1985, ex steamer 1953
Operator: Foreningen Suldalsdampen, Sudalsosen
Built: 1885, Stavanger Stoberi & Dock; rebuilt 1955, 1985; 39gt;
63.9ft × 14.2ft; 135 pass
Machinery: compound, Stavanger Maskinistskole, 1985; 150hp
Route: Suldalsvatn, charters and special sailings

A relatively unknown restoration project, *Suldal* was restored to original condition for her centenary in 1985. She operates on the scenic Suldalsvatn, inland from Stavanger, and was built for use as part of a tourist itinerary from Stavanger to Bergen, involving steamers and stage-coaches, via the most scenic part of the fjord country. She was dieselised and rebuilt in 1953, having operated from 1939 as reserve vessel to the car ferry *Suldalsporten*. In 1978 a road was built along the lakeside, and *Suldalsporten* withdrawn and scuttled at a deep part of the lake. At this time interest was kindled in *Suldal* and restoration started. This has been done very effectively, but when she was seen in Autumn 1986 there was no indication anywhere, either on the steamer, at the pier where she was berthed, or at any nearby village, of possible sailings or even of her historic importance.

SETESDAL

BJØREN

Screw steamer, undergoing restoration
Owner: Foreningen Setesdalsbanen, Grovarne
Built: 1860s

Bjøren was a lake steamer on the Byglandsfjord, and was reported scuttled in the 1950s. She was raised in the 1980s, moved to the preserved Setesdal railway near Kristiansand, and restoration was planned; her hull, machinery, and boiler were reported intact. Her superstructure is to be rebuilt when funds permit.

TINNSJØ

*AMMONIA**

Twin screw steam train ferry
Operator: Norsk Transport AS-Rjukanbanen
Built: 1929, Moss Værft & Dock; 929gt; 230.6ft × 35.1ft; 150 pass, 15
freight wagons
Machinery: two triple expansion; 450hp; 11kn
Route: reserve steamer on train ferry service on Tinnsjø, from Mæl to
Tinnoset (38km)

Ammonia was built for a service on the Tinnsjø, which connects a short section of railway from Rjukan to Mæl at the north end of the lake with the Norwegian State Railways at Tinnoset. The train ferry is used for loads of fertiliser from Norsk Hydro's plant at Rjukan, served by a large hydro-electric power station. This plant was used by the Germans during World War II to produce heavy water for their planned atomic bomb, and in 1944 the ferry *Hydro* was sunk by the resistance while carrying a train load of heavy water in tank wagons. *Ammonia* was disguised as *Hydro* in the 1964 film *Heroes of Telemark*

about this exploit. Passenger traffic was carried on the ferries until 1985. Since the introduction of the diesel ferry *Storegut* in 1956, *Ammonia* has been used as reserve steamer, and normally sees about two weeks of service each year. In addition to her passenger accommodation, she has two director's saloons, reported to be unchanged since her construction.

Ammonia, lake Tinn, 1986

Opposite: Deck view, *Skibladner*, 1985

LAKE MJØSA

SKIBLADNER *

Paddle steamer
Operator: Oplandske AS, Eidsvoll, lake Mjøsa
Built: 1856; Motala Verkstad, Motala; 264gt; 165ft × 16.6ft; 230 pass
Machinery: (new engines 1888) triple expansion, Akers Mek Verksted, Oslo; 606hp; 14kn
Route: lake Mjøsa; Eidsvoll–Hamar–Gjovik–Lillehamar

Skibladner, the magnificent 'White Swan of Mjøsa', is the oldest steamer in Europe to have seen constant use as a passenger steamer. (Rumania's *Tudor Vladimirescu* is two years older but was a tug until comparatively recently). She sails daily in summer on an arduous twelve-hour roster the length of the lake from Eidsvoll to Lillehamar and back again, indeed the first few miles from Eidsvoll are along the river Vorma, apparently wide but with a meandering channel. She first plied this route on 2 August 1856, but then only sailed in one direction each day.

The paddler was built with two funnels, but when she was rebuilt in 1888 a new engine was fitted, and her present appearance is little changed since then. She has an aft half-saloon, containing a dining saloon, whose specialities are fresh salmon from the lake followed by strawberries and cream, and a small obser-

vation lounge, situated aft of the dining saloon. A short fore saloon has a shop and souvenir stall. Her wheel is on a raised platform behind a structure one would imagine to be the wheelhouse, actually the captain's cabin and post office, and is in a position abaft the paddle wheels.

She was converted to oil-firing as early as 1921, and a new boiler was fitted in 1983. She is laid up through the icy winter, and twice, in 1937 and 1967, the weight of ice was so great that she sank, but both times was raised and returned to service. Recovery after the later sinking focussed attention on the steamer, and helped to set the operation on a sure footing, with the Opplandske Company being re-formed as a preservation venture then. It is supported by 'Skibladner's Venner' (Friends of *Skibladner*), who promote the steamer, and a new mast fitted in 1985 was donated by them.

A small cannon sits on the bows and can be fired for a fee; this can be done when *Skibladner* passes a particular house on the lake shore, for example for a birthday or other celebration. Parties even come out to meet her on the small preserved car ferry *Helgøya*, and have the cannon fired.

Skibladner is a true veteran, very well maintained, and following an interesting route on a lake bounded by rolling hills in the south and mountains in the north.

1

1. *Waverley* paddlebox

2

2. *Waverley*

3

3. *Duchess Doreen* at Maidenhead, 1972

4. *Shieldhall* at Southampton, 1986

5. *Skibladner* approaching Lillehamer, 1981

6. *Ammonia* berthed at Mael, lake Tinn, 1986

4

7. *Storskär* in the evening sun, 1985

8. *Blidösund* on an evening cruise from Stockholm

9. *Bohuslän* funnel

10. *Boxholm II* at Malexander

11. *Ejdern* on lake Malar, 1985

8

9

10

11

13. *Figaro* funnel

12. *Suomi* leaving Jyväskylä, 1981

14. *Karjalankoski* at Imatra, 1982

15. *Skjelskor* at Roskilde, 1985

16. *Kaiser Wilhelm* at Lauenberg, 1986

17. Small upright compound engine, Elbe Shipping Museum

18. *Alexandra* laid up at Flensburg, 1983

SWEDEN

SWEDEN IS PROBABLY the richest country in Europe for steamers and ex steamers, not only in numbers, but also in the high standard of preservation and the variety of ships. A feature of Sweden is the large number of lakes and archipelagos, and the Swedes have long used the myriads of islands for holiday homes. There has thus grown up a considerable summer commuter traffic in the Stockholm area. The steamers are of a size that has made them easier to preserve than the larger British paddle steamers; some have been laid up for years rather than being sold for scrap, and eventually restored. Even when vessels are near-derelict, the cold winter climate seems to preserve their basic fabric remarkedly well.

With so many to choose from, it is difficult to single out one particular favourite, but *Bohuslän* must be the finest coastal excursion steamer anywhere, and a sail on her brings back memories of Oban's *King George V*. *Trafik's* restoration has a wealth of remarkable detail, while *Boxholm II* gives the passenger the almost unique experience of sailing on a wood-fired steamer. At Stockholm *Blidösund* and *Mariefred* have a special 'preserved' feel, while on Södertalje's friendly *Ejdern*, enthusiasts may even be invited to take the wheel.

Stockholm, of all the cities of Europe, must vie with Istanbul for being the most rewarding for the steamer enthusiast. From the centre of the city, services operate both eastwards to the archipelago (Skärgården) on the Baltic (Saltsjön), and westwards to lake Mälar. Some seven operating steamers are based in the city, six in regular service. Highlight of the steamer year is Skärgårdsbåtens Dag (Archipelago Steamer Day), the first Wednes-

day in June, when all the steamers, with a number of motorships as well, sail from Stockholm to Waxholm. Tickets for this, the official start to the summer season, are usually sold out weeks in advance.

Swedish steamers are mainly of similar design, with an open foredeck, free space for cargo forward on the 'tween deck (on the same level on the Stockholm steamers, whereas on smaller Swedish steamers the foredeck is raised a few feet above this), a passageway to starboard and the galley, toilets, and other facilities to port on this deck, and a restaurant on the upper deck, with outside seating accomodation facing outwards. These seats are very close to the side of the steamer, and there is not really enough space to walk around on this deck without constant obstruction from the knees of seated passengers. The bridge is normally at the forward end of this deck, except on *Norrskär* and ex-steamer *Gustafsberg VII*, on which it is above the upper deck; thus, on these two, passengers can sit facing forward. Steering in some vessels is by a lever rather than a wheel. There is even a speciality dish in the steamer restaurants, 'steamer steak', with great competition for the best cuisine in each year.

The Stockholm archipelago is completely different from the archipelago of the west coast, with many wooded islands with small holiday cabins on their shores. The exposed outer skerries have a beauty all of their own, with rugged bare rocks. A timetable book, *Skärgårdsboken* is published annually for all the steamer and boat services in the Stockholm area; this also carries an historical article or two on steamers, and the 1987 issue ran to 180 pages. Every steamer has its own berth at Stockholm,

Bohüslan on lake Vänern, 1985

and a plan of these is included in the *Skärgårdsboken*, as are data for all vessels. An excellent map is published by SL, the regional transport authority, showing all public transport routes in the greater Stockholm area, including all steamer routes. The steamers themselves are publicised by a folder *Stockholms Vita Ångbåtar* (Stockholm's White Steamers) with brief details of each steamer, its history and routes. If this is stamped by the purser's office of at least six of the eight steamers (including Södertalje's *Ejdern*), a certificate is awarded and a free ticket for a journey on the steamer of your choice (also valid for the following year).

In addition to the vessels listed here, Sweden offers a number of areas of general interest to the steam enthusiast. Lake Siljan is the home of a surprising number of former warp-tugs; that is, tugs fitted with a winch, which was used to warp rafts of timber along channels at the edge of the lake, using a cable. The winch was fitted in a characteristic housing amidships, and the tugs also had normal screw propulsion. This system was in use up to the 1960s with steam right to the end. Survivors in steam are *Tomten* (1862); *Siljan* (1868); *Norsbro* (1873); *Insjön I* (1873); *Elfdalen* (1888); and *Flottisten* (1890). *Orsa* (1888) and *Göran* (1881) are similar, but with diesels fitted in the late sixties. These are all used as private steam yachts, with an annual regatta on the lake. *Norsbro* and *Siljan* still have the wire and warping machinery intact.

Nearby lake Runn has the similar steamers *Domnarfvet* (1863),

Engelbrekt (1903), and *Bäsingen* (1905), also the former passenger launch *Sveden*, built in 1943 with a steel hull to replace an earlier *Sveden* (1904), which had a wooden hull, and fitted with her predecessor's engine.

Another important inland waterway offers a further unique piece of steamship history. In early years what were known as 'fiddle-steamers' were used on the Göta canal; that is, paddle steamers shaped like a fiddle in order to minimise the breadth and thus pass through the canal locks. One of these, *Eric Nordevall*, built in 1836, and sunk on lake Vättern in 1856, has recently been found on the lake bed, and there are plans to raise her and restore her.

One or two words of Swedish may help: *rederi*, shipping company; *-ö* and *-holm* at the end of a word, island; *skärgård*, archipelago; *skär*, skerry or small island; *ång*, steam; *fartyg*, ship; *båt*, boat; *sjö*, lake.

It should be noted that certain parts of the Göteborg and Stockholm archipelagos are restricted areas with no access by non-Swedish citizens. This, however, applies to landing on the islands, and probably not merely to sailing the waters around them. The areas are well marked, and are not covered by the main steamer routes.

Bohüslan, Marstrand, 1981

GÖTEBORG

BOHUSLÄN*

Preserved screw steamer
Operator: Sällskapet Ångbåten, Göteborg
Built: 1914, Eriksbergs Mek Verkstad, Göteborg; 327gt; 42.42m ×
7.26m; 300 pass
Machinery: triple expansion; 600hp; 12kn
Route: Göteborg–Marstrand; evening excursions from Göteborg; many
special trips and charters

*B*ohuslän, one of the first European steamers to be preserved by an enthusiast group, has been operated by Sällskapet Ångbåten since 1966. She was built in 1914 as flagship of the fleet of steamers operated by Marstrands Nya Ångfartygs AB (New Marstrand Steamship Co) from Göteborg north along the Bohuslän coast as far as Lysekil and Smögen. Her design was a development of the largest Stockholm steamers *Norrtelje* and *Express*, but in fact the result looked every inch a coastal steamer. In 1951 she was converted to oil firing, and escaped the fate of the rest of the fleet, which had diesels fitted. From 1953 to 1961, she ran on an all-year service on the Öresund from Copenhagen to Malmö, returning to her old route for the summers of 1957 and 1958, and from 1961 to 1963 on a service from Strömstad to Sandefjord across the mouth of the Oslofjord.

She was sold for scrap in February 1965, and only after that event was Sällskapet Ångbåten (Steamboat Society) founded. She was purchased from the scrapyard in January 1966. Her sailings started that summer, and have continued ever since. The operations have been imaginative, she has on occasion visited Oslo and Copenhagen, and an innovation in 1987 was regular trips right through to Smögen, returning the next day.

She has a dining saloon on the upper deck, with waiter service, and, as on most Swedish steamers with restaurants, seats are booked for the various sittings immediately on boarding the steamer. There is a cafeteria aft on the main deck, an area which was open deck until the fifties, and a smoking saloon aft on the upper deck. Passengers have access to the bridge deck, aft of bridge and on the bridge wings. She is manned entirely by volunteers.

The west coast of Sweden is extremely scenic and *Bohuslän* weaves her way past small islets often with smooth rounded rocks and little vegetation, through narrow canals cut through the rock, and past small fishing villages. The coast is rather exposed, so sailings occasionally have to be cancelled or curtailed because of the heavy swell. She also sails once a year up the Göta river to Trollhättan on Falls Day, when the hydro-electric power station is turned off, and the waterfall flows full blast.

She is a personal favourite of mine, and well worth a trip to Sweden just to sail on her alone.

Färjan 4 before preservation, 1966 (Lennart Nilsson)

GÖTEBORG

FÄRJAN 4

Preserved screw steam ferry
Operator: Sällskapet Ångbåten, Göteborg
Built: 1920, Motala Verkstad, Motala; 48gt; 20.5m × 5.35m;
195 pass
Machinery: compound; 86hp; coal-fired
Route: Göteborg harbour; Lilla Bommen (Göteborg's Maritime
Centre)–Fiskhamnen (summer weekends); charters and excursions at
Göteborg

*F*ärjan 4 is a typical double-ended Swedish harbour ferry, operated in Göteborg harbour until 1954, then kept as reserve ferry until 1970, by which time she was the last steam ferry in Göteborg. Acquired for preservation in 1972, she has been used from time to time since then on trips to Nya Älvsborg fortress, and as relief for other ferries when they were on overhaul. After number of years out of service, she started operating from Göteborg Maritime Centre, home of a large number of preserved vessels of all types, in late summer 1986.

GÖTEBORG

MARIEHOLM

Restaurant ship, steamer
Owner: Restaurant SS *Marieholm*, Göteborg
Built: 1934, Odense Staalskibsværft
1186gt; 70m × 11m; formerly 148 pass
Machinery: triple expansion; 950hp; 12kn

*B*uilt for Swedish America Line, who operated both a Stockholm-Turku route and a weekly circular service in the southern Baltic from Stockholm to Memel, Königsberg, Gdynia, Zopot, and returning to Stockholm via Karlskrona, *Marieholm* was placed on this latter route on entering service in 1934, with an emphasis on the emigrant traffic from the Baltic States to connect with the company's transatlantic liners. Taken over by the Swedish navy in 1940 and used as the Commander-in-chief's staff ship until 1976, she then had one season in 1977 operating from Strömstad to Sandefjord. She was later laid up at Malmö and then Helsinki for a number of different owners

Norrskär, Sandhamn, 1982

while a number of plans failed, eventually arriving at Göteborg in December 1984. After considerable refitting at the Falkensberg yard to repair damage caused by vandals while she was at Malmö, she opened as a restaurant and conference centre in Göteborg in summer 1986. Her owners have a true sense of history, and intend to keep her as a historic ship. She has regained her Swedish American funnel with three gold crowns. There is a possibility that she might return to operation, with short cruises for conference delegates.

STOCKHOLM

STORSKÄR*

ex *Strängnäs Express* 1939
Screw steamer
Operator: Waxholms Ångfartygs AB
Built: 1908, Lindholmen, Göteborg; 235gt; 38.9m × 7m; 418 pass
Machinery: triple expansion; 560hp; 13kn; new boiler 1976
Route: Stockholm–Ramsöberg (mid-day);–Ljusterö (evening);–Husarö (weekends)

Built for service on lake Mälar from Stockholm to the town of Strängnäs, *Storskär* was sold to the Waxholm company, Stockholm's largest steamer operator, in 1939. She ran in the northern part of the archipelago, and was converted to oil-firing in 1953. One of only three steamers retained when the company failed in 1964 and a new local government controlled company was founded, she was the fastest steamer in the area, and the only one with a triple expansion engine. Sailings cover many small jetties, including, for example, 17 calls on her evening trip

to Ljusterö, and as the Waxholm company's routes are part of the public transport network, some cargo is carried, and fares, being subsidised, are also very cheap compared to prices generally in Sweden. The 19 Waxholm boats are the only means of transport to many of the islands in the archipelago. Although not enthusiasts, her owners are sensitive to enthusiast pressure, and 1987 saw the extension of her season into September.

STOCKHOLM

NORRSKÄR

ex *Sandhamns Express* 1949
Screw steamer
Operator: Waxholms Ångfartygs AB
Built: 1920; Eriksbergs Mek Verkstad, Göteborg; 236gt; 34.8m × 6.9; 385 pass
Machinery: compound; 320hp; 11kn; new boiler 1970
Route: Stockholm–Sandhamn (day);–Ramsö (evening)

Norrskär was built with an icebreaker bow for all-year-round service to Sandhamn, a yachting centre and pilot station and the most popular destination in the archipelago. Her original owners gave up the service after the 1947 season, and sold her to the Waxholm company. Used on various routes in the archipelago, she was brought back to her original route in the summer season after the company's flagship steamer *Waxholm* was destroyed by fire in 1978. Following enthusiast suggestions, her homeward journey time from Waxholm has been brought forward, and she can now also operate an evening cruise to Ramsö. Each winter for the past few years she has been gradually restored and completely renovated.

STOCKHOLM

DJURGÅRDEN 3

ex *Nybron* I 1901, ex *Stadsgården* I 1898
Preserved steam ferry
Operator: Ångslups AB, controlled by Stiftelsen Skärgårdsbåten
Built: 1893; Brodins Varvet, Gävle; 20.9m × 5.4m; 199 pass
Machinery: compound; 55hp; 7kn; coal-fired; new boiler 1984
Route: charters; occasional public sailings, mainly for special events

*D*jurgården 3 was returned to steam in 1985 after many years restoration by Stiftelsen Skärgårdsbåten, the local equivalent of the PSPS. Originally withdrawn in 1969, she is now fully restored and in excellent condition. *Djurgården 3* is often used as special ferry for events in the harbour area and also used on Djurgården route alongside modern ferries on Sweden's national day; she is also in occasional winter use.

STOCKHOLM

MÄLAREN 3

ex *Sexan* 1913
Steam ferry, awaiting restoration
Owner: Ångslups AB, controlled by Stiftelsen Skärgårdsbåten
Built: 1903, Södra Varvet, Stockholm; 15.5m × 4.5m
Machinery: compound; 34hp

*M*älaren 3 is a smaller steam ferry of the classic type, out of service since 1950. She was saved for restoration in 1983, and planned for eventual restoration. She is the last lake Mälar steam ferry in existence and moved to Stiftelsen Skärgårdsbåten's base at Beckholmen in September 1987.

Mälaren 3 before restoration, Klara Mälarstrand

Tärnan as *Brynhilda* before preservation, 1985

Björkfjärden, Klara Mälarstrand, 1981

STOCKHOLM

TÄRNAN

ex *Amaranth* 1985, ex *Tarnan* 1951
Screw steamer, ex motor vessel, ex steamer, undergoing restoration
Owner: Ångslups AB, controlled by Stiftelsen Skärgårdsbåten
Built: 1901, Södra Varvet, Stockholm; 20m × 4.9m; 155 pass

Stiftelsen Skärgårdsbåten are now restoring *Tärnan* to steam at their base at Beckholmen, as the last example of the classic ångslup, or steam launch. These were often used for connecting services from the larger steamers for the smaller islands. Many have survived as diesel boats, generally rebuilt, but *Tärnan* will be the only one in steam. She had a diesel engine fitted in 1951, ran at Norrköping for a while, and later bore the alias *Brynhilda* for a part in a TV series before purchase by the society in 1985. The steam engine from similar launch *Frithiof*, almost destroyed by fire in 1977, is being placed in *Tärnan*, while a second-hand tug boiler may be fitted. *Frithiof* is also at the Beckholmen base, although it is unlikely that she will eventually be restored.

STOCKHOLM

BJÖRKFJÄRDEN

ex *Saltsjön* 1970
Preserved steamer, in service
Operator: Ångfartygs AB Stromma Kanal
Owner: Ångfartygs AB Saltsjön-Mälaren
Built: 1925, Eriksbergs Mek Verkstad, Göteborg; 249gt; 37.5m × 7m;
454 pass
Machinery: compound; 383hp; 11kn
Route: Stockholm–Waxholm and Waxholm castle; occasional special
excursions to Utö or Huvudskär; jazz evening cruises

Last of the classic Stockholm steamers to be built, *Björkfjärden* was operated for many years on the Utö service for the Waxholm company. She has a cafeteria in the foresaloon on her lower deck, and the restaurant is in twenties style. She was damaged by fire in 1951, and brought back in service in 1954. In operation from Stockholm to Utö under separate ownership 1966-7, she was converted to oil-firing then. She was purchased by Stromma Canal Co and used in service on lake

Mälar from Stockholm to the island of Björkö, then laid up after the 1974 season. She was taken over by her present owners, a small group of enthusiasts including her captain and engineer, in 1977, in order to allow engine and boiler repairs to proceed. Transferred to the Waxholm route in 1984, she has an ice-strengthened hull, and therefore is used for pre-Christmas cruises with a traditional smörgåsbord meal. In 1987 two-hour trips operated thrice daily from 30 November to 23 December, with two special weekend trips to Utö. *Björkfjärden* is a well restored steamer, enjoyable to sail on, with a slightly more modern feel than the others, and is described as 'Stockholm's floating twenties museum'.

STOCKHOLM

BLIDÖSUND*

Preserved screw steamer
Operator: Roslagens Skeppslag, Stockholm
Built: 1911, Eriksbergs Mek Verkstad, Göteborg; 167gt; 35.29m ×
6.85m; 374 pass
Machinery'; compound; 320hp; 12kn; coal-fired; new boiler 1982
Route: services in Stockholm and to Stockholm archipelago

Distinguished by a tall buff black-topped funnel, *Blidösund* is the last coal-fired steamer in the Stockholm archipelago. She was built for a service from the small communities on the Blidö Sound, in the north of the archipelago, into Stockholm, and maintained this until 1960, by which time easier access by motor car and by express motor vessels had made the trade uneconomic. Laid up for a number of years, she returned to steam in 1969, saved by a small group of enthusiasts. She now has an innovative and varied sailing programme, with a weekend sailing to her old haunts (outward on Friday evening to the Blidösund with return to Stockholm by express boat) and a full day Sunday trip from the Blidösund, with connection from Stockholm, to the island of Svartlöga in the outer archipelago, and back all the way to Stockholm. Evening cruises have always been a strong feature of her programme, with an emphasis on jazz, and a recent innovation has been a lunch-time sailing around Södermalm from the eastern side of Stockholm around to the lake Mälar side and back. Frequently used for charters, she is well-maintained, and one of the most enthusiast-oriented of the Stockholm steamers. Like *Björkfjärden*, she sails on lunch cruises in the month preceding Christmas.

STOCKHOLM

HEBE (steam)

Private steam launch
Owner: unknown, Waxholm
Built: 1889, Wilhelmsberg, Göteborg; 15.6m × 3.6m
Machinery: compound, Härnösand, 1909; 85hp

Hebe was built for passenger traffic and timber towing on the remote lake Landösjön, north of Östersund. Passenger service ceased in the 1930s but timber towing continued until 1967. The steamer was on Storsjön from 1971 to 1985, then sold to a Waxholm owner for use as a private yacht.

STOCKHOLM, LAKE MÄLAR

MARIEFRED

Preserved screw steamer
Operator: Gripsholms-Mariefreds Ångfartygs AB (owned by Stiftelsen Skärgårdsbåten)
Built: 1903, Södra Varvet, Stockholm; 178gt; 31.0m × 6.1m; 335 pass
Machinery: compound; 298hp, 11kn; new boiler 1983; coal-fired
Route: Stockholm–Mariefred

Possibly Stockholm's most notable steamer, *Mariefred* is distinguished by a tall black funnel, and remarkable for being on the same route since building, the route even being painted on the bridge front below the steamer name. She is one of only two remaining coal-fired steamers on lake Mälar. Mariefred is an old-world village adjoining the royal castle of Gripsholm, and the pier is connected to the village by a steam narrow-guage railway, which even operates a boat train for *Mariefred*. Her owning company was taken over by the enthusiast group Stiftelsen Skärgårdsbåten in 1966 and the service has been maintained since then. Her restaurant was badly damaged by fire in 1980 but quickly repaired. Stiftelsen Skärgårdsbåten members get a voucher for one return trip at half price. She is a fascinating steamer to sail on, with an excellent restaurant.

Mariefred at Mariefred pier, 1981

Blidösund on an evening cruise, Stockholm, 1981

Drottningholm, Klara Mälarstrand, 1985

STOCKHOLM, LAKE MÄLAR

DROTTNINGHOLM

ex *Nya Strömma Kanal* 1969, ex *Valkyrian* 1968
Screw steamer
Operator: Ångfartygs AB Strömma Kanal
Built: 1909, Motala Verkstad, Motala; 128gt; 22.7m × 5.3m; 203 pass
Machinery: compound; 85hp; 8kn
Route: Stockholm Klara Mälarstrand–Drottningholm Palace

This Stockholm steamer began life as an ångslup, but after a couple of rebuildings now has an enclosed upper deck and appears like a smaller edition of the traditional design. She and *Prins Karl Philip* between them give an hourly service from Klara Mälarstrand, the quay near Central Station from which the lake Mälar steamers sail, to Drottningholm Palace, a very popular tourist destination. Built for SÅA (Stockholms Ångslups AB) as a larger edition of the usual ångslup, she was sold to the Waxholm company in 1918 and used by them until 1964, when she was sold back to SÅA. Originally with an open upper deck, she had a shelter added in 1911, and a saloon in the forties. She was purchased by the Strömma Kanal Co in 1968 when SÅA gave up archipelago services. Operated to Sandhamn via the Strömma canal for one season, she was then placed on her present service in 1969. The basic upper deck saloon was rebuilt as a restaurant, and she was converted to oil-firing the following winter. Gutted by fire in May 1980, the steamer was however completely rebuilt and returned to service in 1982. Her passengers are almost entirely tourists, whereas the other steamers attract mainly local people and enthusiasts.

SÖDERTALJE, LAKE MÄLAR

EJDERN*

Preserved screw steamer
Operator: Museiföreningen Ångfartyg *Ejdern*, Södertalje
Built: 1880, Göteborgs Mek Verkstad, Göteborg; 38gt; 22.4m × 4.3m; 110 pass
Machinery: compound; 65hp; 9kn; coal-fired
Routes: Södertalje–Björkö; special excursions from Södertalje

A charming veteran, *Ejdern* is enthusiast operated, with a very friendly crew. She is steamer of a previous generation to the other Stockholm steamers. Built for service in Göteborg's northern archipelago, she was used 1898-1906 on lake Roxen at Söderköping, and from 1906 at Södertalje on a service south from there, along the Skanssund. Withdrawn in 1957, she was used as a floating café 1959-60, then became almost derelict. The steamer was saved by an enthusiast group, who fitted a diesel engine in 1965, then a second-hand steam engine and boiler from the tug *Wikingen* in 1966, and finally in 1974 her original engine, which had been put in a museum when it was thought the steamer would be scrapped. In 1975 she visited Göteborg for dry-docking at the yard where she was built. She operates a variety of day and evening cruises both north from Södertalje into lake Mälar, and south into the archipelago, and it should be noted that these leave from different quays in Södertalje, north and south of the large lock in the middle of the town. A regular Saturday trip to Björkö has been operated since 1986. A trip on *Ejdern* should not be missed.

VÄSTERÅS LAKE MÄLAR

BORE

Steam icebreaker, undergoing restoration; eventual passenger sailings
Owner: Swecox Internation AB, Västerås
Built: 1894, Kockums, Malmo; 374gt; 39.8m × 8.9m; 100 pass
Machinery: compound, with unusual valve system; 605hp; 12kn

*B*ore was used as the Malmö Harbour icebreaker until 1984, though latterly she saw only occasional service. Last in full service in 1968, she steamed in 1981 for film use. She was purchased by Swecox/ASEA and is undergoing full restoration at Västerås. She is planned for use by her owners, who are boiler-makers, on guest trips representing the company. *Bore* is an unusual steamer, smaller than other preserved icebreakers such as *Stettin*. One hopes that her owners will operate some public cruises on her.

KARLSTAD, LAKE VÄNERN

POLSTJÄRNAN AF VÄNERN

ex *Polstjärnan* 1985
Preserved screw steamer, ex inspection steamer
Operator: Ångbåts AB Polstjärnan, Karlstad
Built: 1929, Lindholmen, Göteborg; 115gt; 30.1m × 5.8m; 100 pass
Machinery: compound, Motala Verkstad, Motala; 190hp; 10kn
Route: excursions from Karlstad

*B*uilt as an inspection steamer for the lights and buoys on lake Vänern, *Polstjärnan*, third of the name on these duties, operated until 1983. She was lengthened and rebuilt in 1960 at Karlstad, and converted to oil-firing in 1966. Sold after her withdrawal to a Stockholm owner, she was taken to the capital, but no work was done on her, and in 1984 she was brought back to Karlstad by local enthusiasts. They have totally restored her, and operate short passenger excursions. She had previously had a certificate for 40 passengers while an inspection steamer, but now carries 100 on short cruises in the north of lake Vänern.

HJO, LAKE VÄTTERN

TRAFIK

Preserved screw steamer
Operator: SS *Trafik* Ekonomisk Förening
Built: 1892, Bergsund, Stockholm; 129gt; 29.7m × 6.3m; 225 pass
Machinery: compound; 240hp; coal-fired; 11kn
Route: varied trips from Hjo, lake Vättern

*O*ne of Sweden's finest preserved steamers, *Trafik* has been restored with great attention to the smallest detail. She ran until 1958 on a cross-lake service from Hjo to Hästholmen, with narrow guage rail connections at either side. A restaurant from then until 1972, she had lapsed into very poor condition by the time restoration work was started in that year. She returned to service in 1978, and has operated since then, about once or twice a week, mainly from Hjo, with occasional ventures along the Göta canal. She is of an older type than most of the Swedish steamers, and a trip on her is highly recommended.

Ejdern at a jetty on lake Mälar, 1985

Preserved steamer *Trafik* at Hjo, 1982

Below: Thor, Kronoberg pier, Växjö, 1982

Motala Express at the mole at Vadstena, 1982

ASKERSUND, LAKE VÄTTERN

MOTALA EXPRESS

Screw steamer
Operator: Rederi AB Kind, Askersund
Built: 1895, Jönköpings Mek Verkstad; 186gt; 35.7m × 6.6m; 250 pass
Machinery: triple expansion; 360hp; coal-fired; 12kn
Route: excursions from Askersund; weekly trip in high season to
Vadstena

Known as the 'Prisoner of Vättern' because she is too long to get through the Göta canal locks, *Motala Express* operated from Jönköping to Motala for many years, and was saved in 1962 by her present owner Bertil Bergman. He converted her back to coal-firing in 1980 reportedly after buying a large supply of coal from Swedish Railways who at that time got rid of a strategic reserve of steam locomotives. She is similar to, but larger than, *Trafik*, and has the atmosphere of a pleasant survivor rather than a restored steamer. She was placed up for sale at the end of the 1987 season and an enthusiast society, Askersunds Ångbåtsförening, was founded to save her; at the time of writing a local campaign had been started to raise the money to purchase her for continued operation.

VÄXJÖ, HELGASJÖN

THOR

Preserved steam launch
Operator: Smålands Museum, Växjö
Built: 1887, Bergsund, Stockholm; 12gt; 15.4m × 3.4m; 60 pass
Machinery: single cylinder; 35hp; coal and wood-fired; new boiler 1970
Route: excursions from Kronoberg castle, near Växjö

Thor is a unique preserved steam launch with boiler and engine on deck. Sailings are at weekends in July and early August. She has a small after saloon, but the fore part of the steamer has open sides, with a fixed canopy, and blinds that can be drawn down in case of rain. The funnel can be lifted off for passing under low bridges. The single cylinder is fascinating to watch and remarkably smooth. *Thor* was built for the Räppe-Asa Kanal company, for passenger/cargo service on the Helgasjön, and operated until 1957, when she was acquired by the museum, by which time the cargo service had ceased and purely tourist trips were being offered. A new boiler was fitted in 1970, and the steamer was completely restored on land between 1967 and 1971. While most cruises are on Helgasjön, once or twice a season there is a long cruise through the Räppe-Asa canal to Asa with return by bus, with a second group doing the trip in a reverse direction. *Thor* is highly recommended and an unusual vessel.

Boxholm II, Malexander, lake Sommen, 1985

TRANÅS, LAKE SOMMEN

BOXHOLM II*

Preserved screw steamer
Operator: R Hektor & S-O Sjöberg, Boxholm
Built: 1904, Ljungrens Mek Verkstad, Kristianstad; 37gt;
20.3m × 4.5m; 116 pass
Machinery: compound, 1904; 85hp, wood-fired
Route: lake Sommen from Tranås

Europe's last wood-fired passenger steamer, *Boxholm II* was acquired by her present owners, the captain and engineer, in 1982, and since then a support group known as Ångbåtens Vänner has been formed. Sailings have been increased and the steamer has been better publicised. For many years her main sailing has been a Friday market day trip from the small communities around the lake to Tranås, with produce being carried inwards to the town, and the return trip in the evening being operated as an excursion from Tranås to Malexander and back. She was built as a combined passenger steamer and tug, being used for timber towing until 1966. Her aft deck was rebuilt in 1922 with seating, and she can present two completely different appearances, as boards with windows can quickly be put in place in wet or stormy weather to protect the passengers in this aft section. Her engine is open to view, and it is fascinating to watch the boiler, the original from 1904, being fed with planks of wood. There is a short stretch on the river Svartån before the lake is reached, and the unusually-shaped lake is surrounded by low wooded hills. She is an unusual steamer, on a scenic trip.

ÖSTERSUND, STORSJÖN

THOMÉE

Preserved screw steamer
Operator: Östersunds Kommun
Built: 1875, Motala Mek Verkstad, Motala; 106gt; 27.0m × 4.8; 190
pass
Machinery: compound, Bergsund, Stockholm, 1919, installed 1933;
150hp; 8kn; coal-fired boiler built 1916, installed 1937
Route: excursions from Östersund

Thomée is an interesting steamer, of typical older Swedish type with a sunken 'tween deck (or raised foredeck and aft deck), and a small cabin on the upper deck. Named after Anders Thomée, pioneer in opening up this remote area, *Thomée* originally ran on the Revsundsjö as a single-deck steam launch, but was moved to Storsjön in 1880, when the upper deck was added. She was rebuilt in about 1930 with an icebreaker bow, and fitted with an engine formerly in the Storsjön steamer *Framat*, and a boiler from the tug *Viking* at Sundsvall. Used as an icebreaker on the lake for many years, she has operated on tourist service since 1957. She was taken over by a local authority for preservation in 1972 and a major restoration took place in 1975. *Thomée* normally operates daily on the lake in summer with two-hour cruises, and some longer cruises landing on Andersön or Verkön islands. She is well restored, and, like *Östersund*, must be one of the most northerly operating steamers in the world.

ÖSTERSUND, STORSJÖN

ÖSTERSUND

ex Las Vegas 1973, ex Östersund 1960
Screw steamer
Operator: Föreningen *Östersunds* Vänner
Built: 1874, Oskarshamn; 25.2m × 4.5m
Machinery: compound; 1903, Härnösand Mek Verkstad; 120hp
Route: excursions on Storsjön from Östersund

This veteran returned to steam in September 1986 after 23 years out of service. She was built for service at Östersund, being constructed from sections and not entering service until 1875. She operated on the lake until 1959, having been modernised in 1902, when a new engine was fitted; a large upper deck saloon was fitted in 1960. She was used on sightseeing trips and later as a floating night-club at Östersund, then sold for scrapping in 1971. Saved from the scrapyard, she was laid up on the slipway and used as a houseboat. Restoration continued over a period of years, and included the replacement of almost all the wood on board. She now has an aft saloon, and a small saloon aft on the upper deck. This alteration from her original condition will make her more comfortable for passengers without altering the classic appearance too much. She is based at the north of the lake, at Arvesund. No information is available at the time of writing about future passenger services.

LAHOLM

SOFIERO

Steam launch
Owner: S-O Svenson, Laholm, north of Helsingborg
Built: 1888; 9m × 3m; 12 pass
Machinery: 35hp; 6kn

Sofiero is a small ångslup formerly in service on the Kind canal and now owned by the owner of the Sofiero Brewery. Passenger trips are planned in 1988, centenary of both boat and brewery.

LAKE REVSUNDSSJÖN

ALMA

Steam launch
Owner: unknown, Gällö, Revsundssjön, south of Östersund
Built: 1873, Lindberg, Stockholm; 17.4m × 4.0m
Machinery: compound; 15hp

Alma was built for passenger/cargo service on lake Revsundssjön, then used as a timber towing tug 1883-1957. She was used as a summer cabin until 1966, then sold to a Stockholm owner who converted her to a steam yacht. She was sold to a Göteborg owner in 1971. *Alma* returned home in 1985, and restoration and probable passenger trips on the lake are planned.

Thomée, Östersund, 1981

FINLAND

WITH ITS MANY LAKES, Finland has always been a stronghold of steam. A considerable number of steamers are still in service, almost all of a similar type. In addition, many steam tugs are still around in private ownership. Most of these tugs are wood-fired, as they were traditionally used for towing large loads of timber, and thus the wood was easily available. A third type of steamer found in Finland is the 'tar steamer', an engines-aft cargo steamer, built to fit the dimensions of the old Saimaa canal in the same way that the Clyde puffers were built to fit the Crinan Canal. The name arose because the hulls were normally coated with tar.

The typical Finnish passenger steamer differs from the Swedish steamer, although it is of similar size. Passenger accommodation is on both main and upper decks, with fore and aft deck-houses on each deck. Normally there is a small restaurant on the main deck, and a bar on the upper deck, but the remainder of the space is taken up with small cabins. Traditionally, these were used at the beginning and end of long all-day voyages, rather than en route. These cabins are not really relevant for present-day needs, and on some steamers the after deckhouse on the upper deck has been removed, to make a sun deck, while on others, further saloon space has been made in place of former cabins.

Finland's largest lake system, lake Saimaa, more than 250 miles from end to end, offers steamers scattered through the main towns on the lake. Prior to 1981, almost all were owned by Saimaan Laivamaktat (Saimaa Laketours), and used on services radiating like the spokes of a wheel from Savonlinna, but the company went bankrupt at the end of the 1981 season. The steamer fleet was auctioned in March 1982, and all the steamers except one sold for further service, the exception being sold as a museum. Almost all were bought by the local authorities around the lake, so most are probably safe for the future, although one enthusiast there in 1987 reported only about 20 passengers on some sailings. While the older format was sailings lasting all day between the towns, at present this has generally been superseded by short cruises of an hour or two from various locations or return trips on the same day.

A brochure was published by Kuopio Tourist Office in about 1980 with a brief history of the steamers, entitled 'Come, stay and feel at home on board the steam barge'. This quotes a 1918 account of a steamer journey and gives some idea of the golden days of the lake steamers:

'Anyone who has been to Kuopio in summertime knows that the numerous steamboats resting at the quays of the town, all leaving for their own remote points of water route at noon and coming back to town from these farthest-off corners every morning, are crammed with passengers. These travellers are farmers, cottagers, poor lodgers, beggars coming from innumerable landing-places and their surroundings. Beggars always travel free of charge. It is the passenger fees that yield good annual returns to these boats. The cargo hardly brings them any return.

'At least half of the passengers are trip-makers, who have gone to town just for amusement and enjoying themselves. A quarter of them can be included among those who have taken with them

Ukko-Pekka, as *Hamina*, Helsinki, 1982

a kilo of butter, a can of buttermilk or a score of eggs only to conceal their enthusiasm for travelling. The rest of them are then going to do business at the market.'

The booklet also has an anecdotes section with such gems, distorted by translation, as

'Passenger: Why doesn't this boat leave now?

Captain: The machinist went fetching some buttermilk and he may have stayed cuddling with the womenfolk again.

Passenger: I wonder if this boat is driven with the energy of buttermilk.

Captain: So is it. This is a sort of buttermilk rocket. Men are charged with buttermilk and then the boat keeps going. Sir, do you understand that kind of circulation?'

Other vessels of interest on lake Saimaa include 27 steam tugs preserved as private yachts (including one ex British war-built TID tug, *Tommi*, ex *TID 35*), and a further two preserved on land; among the tugs in steam is *Olli* (1920) which has been rebuilt to resemble a small passenger steamer. There are also two small steam launches, two former wood-bundling steamers, and the inspection steamer and buoy tender *Saimaa* (1893), which is expected to join the museum steamers at Savonlinna when retired.

One further tar steamer converted to a steam yacht and a number of other tugs and similar vessels which have been converted to diesel propulsion are in existence also.

Almost all these steamers are wood-fired, and many of the owners are in the Suomen Höyrypursiseura (Finnish Steam Yacht Club) which has regular rallies on the lakes.

In addition to the vessels mentioned, there are number of other former passenger ships which are either fitted with a diesel engine and used as private yachts, or have been laid up for many years, and for which no information is available.

The Finnish National Maritime Museum at Hylkisaari island at Helsinki has on display a passenger cabin from the steamer *Ariadne*, which operated for the Finland Steamship Company from 1914 to 1969. It also is in the process of restoring the steam icebreaker *Tarmo*, built in 1907 by Armstrong Whitworth, of Newcastle.

Finnish is one of the most difficult languages in the world to understand, but a few basic Finnish words are: *laiva*, ship; *järvi*, lake; *höyry*, steam; *matkailiji*, tourist. It should be noted by anyone studying Finnish steamer books that word endings differ according to the use of the word, so references to steamers can be misleading; for example, *Paasiveden* refers to the steamer *Paasivesi*.

TURKU

UKKO-PEKKA

ex *Hamina* 1986, ex *Turku* 1981
Operator: Naantali Höyrylaiva Oy, Naantali
Built: 1938, Wartsila, Helsinki; 231gt; 35.0m × 7.3m; 199 pass
Machinery: triple expansion; 400hp; 10kn
Route: Turku–Naantali (3 hours)

This vessel is a former lighthouse tender and inspection steamer, retired in 1979. She was then sold to Hamina owners and used for passenger trips, including a short season out of Helsinki in 1982. Alterations were limited to extending the upper deck aft to provide more deck space. She started operating on her present route in 1986, and now has an all-black funnel with a flag on the upper part. She was the first inspection steamer to be built after Finland's independence from Russia.

Tarjanne leaving Ruovesi, 1981

TAMPERE, LAKE NÄSIJÄRVI

TARJANNE

Screw steamer
Operator: Runoilijan Tie Oy (Poets Way Ltd), Tampere
Built: 1908, Lehtoniemi & Taipale, Joroinen; 133gt; 29.5m × 6.2m;
133 pass, 27 berths
Machinery: triple expansion; 300hp; 10kn
Route: Tampere–Virrat

The last operating steamer in the Tampere area, *Tarjanne* sails three days a week in each direction. The journey, through wooded lake scenery with isolated holiday cabins by the lakeside, takes 7¾ hours in each direction. The route is known at the Poet's Way after the Finnish national poet J L Runeberg, who lived for a while at Ruovesi at the mid-point of the route. *Tarjanne* is a typical Finnish lake steamer, with the fore saloon on the main deck extending to the sides of the steamer. She has been on this service all her life, and like all Finnish passenger steamers, is oil-fired, having been converted in 1954.

Preserved steam tug *Aure* at Tampere, 1981

TAMPERE, LAKE NÄSIJÄRVI

POHJOLA

Screw steamer, laid up, possibly undergoing restoration
Owner: Runoilijan Tie Oy (Poets Way Ltd), Tampere
Built: 1950, Oy Sommers af Hällström & Waldens, Tampere; 147gt;
29.5m × 5.7m
Machinery: triple expansion; 185hp; 10kn

Pohjola is a similar steamer to *Tarjanne*, in service on lake Näsijärvi since she was built. She was withdrawn after engine failure in 1976. It is believed that there are plans to restore her to service.

TAMPERE, LAKE NÄSIJÄRVI

AURE

Preserved steam tug, in passenger service
Operator: Aure Höyrylaiva Oy, Tampere
Built: 1926, A Ahlström, Varkaus; 45gt; 20.0m × 4.5m; 62 pass
Machinery: compound; 136hp; wood-fired; 7.5kn
Route: excursions from Tampere on lake Näsijärvi

A typical Finnish steam tug, *Aure* was formerly used for towing large rafts of timber from the forests to the sawmills. She has been preserved since 1980 and offers regular passenger trips. She was converted for passenger use by fitting an awning aft. The similar tug *Näsijärvi II* (1929) is also preserved, and owned by Tampere town council.

JYVÄSKYLÄ, LAKE PÄIJÄNNE

SUOMI*

Screw steamer
Operator: H Hilden, Jyväskylä
Built: 1906, Lehtoniemi & Taipale, Joroinen; 239gt; 31.7 × 6.4m;
199 pass
Machinery: compound; 200hp; 10.8kn
Route: Jyväskylä–Lahti; Jyväskylä–Heinola–Lahti; evening cruises

One of the most attractive, and largest, of the Finnish lake steamers, *Suomi* has been well restored, and is operated by owner-captain Hannu Hilden. She is more suited to the day trip traffic than some of the Saimaa steamers, and the upper deck saloon is fitted with what appear to be second-hand aircraft seats. Her lower deck saloons have always been totally enclosed, unlike the Saimaa steamers which have walkways around the saloons. She operates a very full schedule, and is partnered by *Suometar* (1959), formerly Kiel ferry *Düsternbrook*, on an identical but opposite schedule. The full trip from Jyväskylä to Lahti takes 11½ hours through magnificent lake scenery, and calls at a number of isolated points on the lake shore, from which a surprising amount of traffic is generated. Highly recommended both for the scenery and for the atmosphere on board.

Suomi leaving Jyväskylä, evening, 1981

LAHTI, LAKE PÄIJÄNNE

LAHTIS

ex *Lahti*, ex *Lahtis* 1904
ex tar steamer, ex paddle steamer
Owner: R Höylä
Built: 1865, Crichton & Co, Lahti; 33.7m × 4.9m

Built as a paddle steamer, *Lahti* was used on lake Paijanne until about 1903, when she was converted to a screw steamer She was used as a tar steamer during the 1920s, and later as a barge. Bought for preservation by her present owner, a motor mechanic, in 1974, she had a steam engine fitted in 1975. She was seen in 1981 with both screw and paddle wheels, although the lack of sponsons on the paddle wheels would indicate that restoration work was in hand. No recent information is available.

LAKE PÄIJÄNNE

KAIMA

Privately owned steam yacht, ex passenger steamer
Owner: O Ruutu, Helsinki
Built: 1898, Paul Wahl, Varkaus; 47gt; 21.2m × 4.6m
Machinery: compound; 87hp; wood-fired; 7kn

Kaima operated on a local service out of Jyväskylä until 1950, and was then based at Heinola until 1958. She is an attractive small steamer with a half-saloon.

LAKE PÄIJÄNNE

TOIMI

Privately owned steam yacht, ex passenger steamer
Owner: E Puranen, Mikkeli
Built: 1898, Stenberg, Helsinki; 26gt; 15.5m × 3.3m
Machinery: compound; 57hp; wood-fired; 7kn

A small former passenger launch, *Toimi* was in service until 1937 at Jyväskylä, then on lake Keitele from Suolahti to Viitasari until 1968. She returned to Päijänne 1973, and is now a privately owned steam launch.

LAPEENRANTA, LAKE SAIMAA

SUVI SAIMAA

ex *Kallavesi* 1981, ex *Kuopio* 1976, ex *Heinävesi II* 1967
Screw steamer
Operator: Karelia Lines Oy, Lapeenranta
Built: 1907, Paul Wahl, Varkaus; 149gt; 26.7m × 6.6m; 116 pass;
20 berths
Machinery: compound; 150hp
Route: Lapeenranta–Puumula; Lapeenranta–Saimaa canal cruise (non-landing)

Refurbished in 1983, *Suvi Saimaa* is a typical lake Saimaa steamer, still retaining a few cabins which can be reserved before or after her cruise. She stops en route to Puumula at the Suur Saimaa holiday centre, and the entire journey to Puumula takes about five hours in each direction. This part of

Suvi Saimaa at Suur Saimaa pier, 1982

the lake system is more open than further north. From illustrations she seems to be very well restored, and is little changed since building. She was built for service from Kuopio to Savonlinna via the Heinävesi route. When her owners were taken over by Saimaan Laivamaktat in 1967, she was renamed *Kuopio* and later *Kallavesi*, and remained on her original route until 1981.

IMATRA, LAKE SAIMAA

KARJALANKOSKI*

ex *Apollo*, ex *Karjalankoski*
Screw steamer
Operator: Imatran Höyrylaiva (Imatra Steamship)
Built: 1905, Lehtoniemi & Taipale, Joroinen; 107gt; 24.2m × 6.5m; 125 pass
Machinery: compound; 134hp; 11kn
Route: 2-hour cruises from Imatra; weekly full day cruise

One of the steamers with an open upper deck aft, *Karjalankoski* has been operating at Imatra since 1982. She had previously operated excursions from Kuopio for a few years, and had been built for a route north-east from there to Karjalankoski and Akonpohja. She was used for a short period in the late sixties on the Savonlinna-Joensuu route, when she was named *Apollo*. She is well restored. Her operating company is 30 percent owned by the town of Imatra, and the rest by private enterprise.

Karjalankoski arriving at Suur Saimaa, 1982

PUUMULA, LAKE SAIMAA

WENNO

ex *Vetehinen*
Preserved tar steamer (cargo steamer); used for passenger trips
Operator: Puumula Kunta (municipality)
Built: 1907, Savonlinna; 167gt; 30.7m × 6.7m
Machinery: compound; 96hp; wood-fired
Route: excursions from Puumula

O ne of two preserved tar steamers which operate passenger sailings, *Wenno* operated some 20 such trips in
the 1987 season. Owned by a Puumula sawmill until
1910, she later had a succession of owners before finally coming under the ownership of Enso-Gutzeit Oy, who changed her
name because all their ships have five-letter names. She regularly carried birch firewood to St Petersburg (now Leningrad),
Stockholm, and Kotka, but also occasionally to Lübeck and even
to England. She came back to Saimaa filled with wheat, rye, sugar
and oil. Out of service by the seventies, *Wenno* was presented
by Enso-Gutzeit to Puumula town for preservation. Restoration
has been undertaken by a local enthusiast society.

SAVONLINNA, LAKE SAIMAA

FIGARO*

ex *Saaristo* 1974, ex *Norkulla* 1938, ex *Nagu* 1919
Screw steamer
Operator: Kyrönsalmen Höyrywenhe Oy, Savonlinna
Built: 1911, Lehtoniemi & Taipale, Joroinen; 25.2m × 4.9m; 78 pass
Machinery: compound; 1917; 120hp; 9kn
Route: 90-minute lake excursions from Savonlinna

A steamer with an interesting history, *Figaro* is notable for
having been, until 1974, Finland's last lake or coastal
steamer in regular all-year service, as distinct from tourist
trips. She originally sailed in the Turku archipelago, then from
1919 to 1938 at Helsinki, having been lengthened and re-engined
in 1917. From 1938 she sailed from the Sääminki islands to
Savonlinna, inwards early in the morning with milk and market

Preserved steam tug Wenno *(Puumula Tourist Office)*

produce, and back in the afternoon. Replaced on this service by
the modern motor vessel *Sääminki* in 1975, she was purchased
for the excursion trade at Savonlinna, and she was the only Savonlinna steamer not to be sucked into the Saimaan Laivamaktat
fleet. She continues to sail at two-hourly intervals throughout
the day, and is a fascinating steamer to sail on. Her upper deck
aft is open, and aft on the lower deck are two hanging basket
chairs for those who want a touch of luxury.

SAVONLINNA, LAKE SAIMAA

HEINÄVESI

ex *Heinävesi I* 1976, ex *Heinävesi* 1907
Screw steamer
Operator: Oy Savonlinnan Laivat, Savonlinna
Built: 1906, Paul Wahl, Varkaus; 145gt; 26.9m × 6.7m; 126 pass
32 berths
Machinery: compound; 150hp; 8kn
Route: Savonlinna–Punkuharju

H einävesi is a traditional Saimaa steamer, in service from
building on the scenic route from Savonlinna to Kuopio
via Heinävesi, in conjunction with *Heinävesi II*, now *Suvi
Saimaa*, after her first season. She was taken over by Saimaan
Laivamaktat in 1967. The number was dropped in 1976. At the
auction of Saimaan Laivamaktat vessels in 1982, *Heinävesi* was
bought by a group of business interests and local communities.
She now sails the 2¼ hour route to Punkuharju, with an afternoon cruise from there.

Opposite top: Figaro *at Savonlinna*
Opposite bottom: Heinavesi *at Savonlinna quay, 1981*

Preserved tar steamer *Mikko* at Savonlinna

Preserved tar steamer *Mikko* at Savonlinna

SAVONLINNA, LAKE SAIMAA

MIKKO

ex *Ensi*
Preserved tar steamer; occasional passenger trips
Owner; Savonlinnan Kaupunki (Town of Savonlinna)
Built: 1914, Savonlinna Workshop; 212gt; 30.9m × 7.1m
Machinery: compound; 75hp; wood-fired; 6kn

Mikko is a tar steamer normally moored at a museum berth near *Salama*, but offering occasional passenger excursions. She is one of two remaining such vessels in steam, of around 150 between the wars. *Mikko* is Finland's equivalent of the Clyde puffer.

JOENSUU, LAKE SAIMAA

PUNKUHARJU

ex *Kerttu* 1960, ex *Osuuskunta I* 1949
Screw steamer
Owner: Hotelli Joensuun Karleia Oy
Built: 1905, Emil Kliveri, Savonlinna; 74gt; 22.5m × 4.9m; 74 pass
Machinery: compound; 92hp; 9kn
Route: local excursions at Joensuu

Punkuharju is the smallest of the Saimaa steamers, and so tender that a man stands at the bottom of the stairway to the upper deck to stop too many passengers going up. She remained in service until about 1983 on excursions from Savonlinna, having continued on this for a year or two after her change of ownership following the auction. She was built for a route which is no longer operated, from Savonlinna south to Vuori-miemi, and in the sixties and early seventies she worked on *Heinävesi's* present route, from Savonlinna to Punkuharju. She has an open upper deck aft, and no cabin accommodation. Purchased by her present owner in 1987 and moved to Joensuu, she was also used for theatre cruises from Jakokoski canal museum; this canal connects the main Saimaa lake system at Joensuu with lake Peilinen to the north. The same owner also operates the former Norwegian 'sea-bus' *Bruvik* from Joensuu.

Punkuharju at Savonlinna, 1981

Leppävirta, Savonlinna, 1981

VARKAUS, LAKE SAIMAA

PAUL WAHL

ex *Paasivesi* 1982, ex *Joensuu* 1976, ex *Mikkeli* 1970, ex *Vehmersalmi* 1959, ex *Maaninka* 1939
Screw steamer
Operator: Taipaleen Laivaosakeyhtio, Varkaus
Built: 1919, Paul Wahl, Varkaus; 125gt; 297.0 × 6.0m; 107 pass; 34 berths (possibly cabin space now converted to saloon accommodation)
Machinery: compound; 150hp; 11kn
Route: Sunday excursions from Varkaus; also charter sailings; use as restaurant for rest of week

Renamed after the most famous shipyard in the Finnish lakeland, *Paul Wahl* has been restored since her purchase by Varkaus town council in 1982. Previously she had been on the Imatra-Lapeenranta route, and prior to that on the Savonlinna-Joensuu service. From 1959 until 1970 she had been owned by a Mikkeli company, on routes from there, and it would seem that the stranding of *Mikkeli II*, now *Hopeasalmi*, in that year dealt a fatal blow to the company, as Saimaan Laivamaktat took her over and changed her name the same year. She was originally built for a service north from Kuopio to Maaninki. *Paul Wahl* is of the usual Saimaa type with fore and aft deckhouses on the upper deck.

KUOPIO, LAKE SAIMAA

LEPPÄVIRTA

ex *Leppävirta II* 1976
Screw steamer
Operator: Roll-Laivat, Kuopio
Owner: Leppävirta town council
Built: 1904, Paul Wahl, Varkaus; 161gt; 26.9m × 2.1m; 52 berths (127 day pass)
Machinery: compound; 129hp; 9kn
Route: six-day cruises from Kuopio, also sold as three-day cruises from Savonlinna

The only one of the lake Saimaa steamers on regular cruises of several days duration, *Leppävirta* is, however, of similar design to the others, and one of only two reciprocating-engined steamers in Europe offering cruises of several days length (the other being *VIC 32*). Her sailing takes her from Kuopio by the tortuous Heinävesi route to Savonlinna, and on to Punkuharju, returning to Kuopio via Varkaus, a more direct route that can be used by quite large coasters. She operated similar cruises from 1953 to 1977, being rebuilt in 1955 with more berths, and became part of the Saimaan Laivamaktat fleet. Following the stranding and sale of *Imatra* in 1977, she was in service on the southern triangle, connecting Savonlinna, Mikkeli and Lappeenranta. As with the other steamers, her appearance has been virtually unchanged all her life. Built for the Kuopio-Savonlinna service via Leppävirta and Varkaus, she operated this for many years, being taken over by Saimaan Laivamaktat in 1967. Her cruises are patronised mainly by Finns and Germans, but a British group from *Waterways World* made a special cruise in 1987.

Lokki leaving Kuopio, 1982

Puijo at Kuipio, 1981

KUOPIO, LAKE SAIMAA

PUIJO

ex *Imatra* 1978, ex *Sinikolmio* 1970, ex *Punkuharju* 1960, ex *Orivesi* II
1951, ex *Liperi* 1912
Screw steamer
Operator: Roll-Laivat, Kuopio
Built: 1907, Paul Wahl, Varkaus; 148gt; 27.6m × 6.5m; 90 pass;
56 berths
Machinery: compound; 135hp; 10kn
Route: Kuopio–Varkaus (5hr 40min)

Purchased by Roll Lines in 1977 after running aground en route from Savonlinna to Mikkeli while under Saimaan Laivamaktat ownership, *Puijo* was renovated then, with extra cabins built below decks. Her cruise, as well as being offered five days a week as a day excursion from Kuopio, is also offered, including bed and breakfast, from Varkaus. She was built for the Joensuu-Savonlinna service and a change of ownership and name in 1912 kept her on the same service, while the name changes of the post-war years were all part of a confusing swopping of names, possibly to identify steamers with specific routes. From the late fifties until 1977 she ran three-day cruises on the southern triangle, for a year or two under her present ownership she sailed on the Kuopio-Savonlinna service, and in other years she has purely been available for charter; the present service however, has remained more stable. She also offers angling cruises of several days on the lake at the beginning and end of the season, although these are normally charters rather than publicly advertised sailings.

KUOPIO, LAKE SAIMAA

LOKKI

Screw steamer
Operator: Roll-Laivat, Kuopio
Built: 1913, A Ahlström, Varkaus; 99gt; 24.4m × 6.1m; 150 pass;
30 berths (probably not in use)
Machinery: compound; 129hp; 9.5kn
Route: excursions from Kuopio, thrice daily

Lokki is a slightly smaller steamer than most of her type, with an open upper deck aft. She was used at Iisalmi, north of Kuopio, in 1981, before returning there in 1982 to fill the gap left when *Karjalankoski* moved to Imatra. Built for local service from Kuopio, she was used there until 1971, and then until 1978 as a private yacht by founder of Roll Lines, Rolf Stellberg. She is an attractive, well kept steamer.

Kuopio has a new steam museum at the harbour, opened in 1985, with old steamer engines on display.

KUOPIO, LAKE SAIMAA

RIISTÄVESI

Privately owned passenger steamer
Owner: O Ebeling & R Lunden, Helsinki
Built: 1927, Lehtoniemi & Taipale, Joroinen; 99gt; 24.5m × 5.9m
Machinery: compound

Riistävesi is a traditional passenger steamer, to the usual Finnish design though built a few years later than the other steamers. She was used until the 1950s on route eastwards from Kuopio, and 1968-72 north from Kuopio to Iisalmi. Since then she has been used as a private steam yacht, with the after deckhouse on the top deck removed, but a canopy retained and extending the full length of the deck.

LAKE KEITELE

KEITELE I

ex *Äänekoski I*, ex *Keitele*
Privately owned passenger steamer
Owner: J Korpivaara, Vantaa
Built: 1877 Paul Wahl, Varkaus; 21.0m × 3.7m
Machinery: compound; 95hp; wood-fired

Keitele I is of traditional design, but has no upper deck. She is used on lake Keitele, north of Jyväskylä. She is a former tug, but saw some passenger service in post-war years, and is now used purely as a private steam yacht.

KAJAANI, LAKE OULUJÄRVI

KOUTA

ex *Vuokatti II*
Owner: M Kuorikoski & A Sointamo, Kajaani
Built: 1921, A Ahlström, Varkaus; 22.5m × 5.3m
Machinery: compound; 121hp

Kouta is a small passenger steamer, also used as a tug at some time in her history, and is based at Kajaani on lake Oulujärvi, to the north of Finland.

DENMARK

RATHER SURPRISINGLY, in view of its many islands, Denmark has only two remaining steamers. The major reason for this is probably that car ferry services have been well established since before World War II, serving the islands by the shortest crossing; thus the local steamers of other countries had already been made redundant in Denmark by the thirties.

As far as is known there are no veteran passenger vessels in the Faroes or in Iceland. However, four steam whalers may possibly remain in survice in Iceland, operating from an onshore whaling station at Hvalurfjordur. They are *Hvalur 6*, ex *Southern Sailor* 1961 (1946/434gt; Smiths Dock); *Hvalur 7*, ex *Southern*

Hjejlen at Silkeborg, 1981

Wilcox (1946/427gt, Smiths Dock); *Hvalur 8* ex *Gos XII* 1962 (1948/481gt, Kandness, Tønsberg); and *Hvalur 9* ex *Tyr* 1977, ex *Hvalur 9* 1973, ex *Tiger* 1966 (1952/611gt, Langesund). With increasing interest in steam preservation, and the steady rundown of whaling, it would not be surprising if one or more of these were eventually preserved.

SILKEBORG, SILKEBORG LAKES

HJEJLEN

Paddle steamer
Operator: AS *Hjejlen*, Silkeborg
Built: 1861, Baumgarten & Burmeister, Copenhagen; 39gt; 26.9m × 3.8m; 175 pass
Machinery: two cylinder oscillating; 25hp; coal-fired; 8kn; new boiler 1900 and 1947
Route: Silkeborg lkes: Silkeborg–Himmelbjerget–Laven

A unique steamer, like *Gondola* on Lake Coniston, *Hjejlen* is Europe's oldest paddler in anything like original condition; *Skibladner*, although older, was rebuilt in 1888. *Hjejlen* was steamed from Copenhagen under her own steam, and has sailed on the Silkeborg lakes from Silkeborg town to Denmark's highest hill, Himmelbjerget, ever since. The journey runs along a river and several connecting lakes. Laven, beyond Himmelbjerget, is a jetty at the edge of a field, with a railway station at the other side of the field. *Hjejlen* is a charming little paddler, and has one of of only two easily visible oscillating engines still in service. She usually sails twice daily in summer from Silkeborg. Competition prior to the grant of an exclusive concession for the lakes to her owners in 1922 came from hand-powered paddlers carrying a couple of passengers, and a home-made motor paddle boat.

ROSKILDE, ROSKILDE FJORD

SKJELSKØR *

Preserved screw steamer
Operator: Dansk Veteranskibsklub
Built: 1915, J Ring-Andersens Skibsværft, Svendborg; 49gt; 18.3m × 4.86m; 100 pass
Machinery: compound, Steen & Kaufmann, Elmshorn, Germany, 1914; 75hp; coal-fired; 7kn
Route: short excursions on Roskilde Fjord from Roskilde, summer weekends only

Denmark's only operating preserved screw steamer is of rather a dumpy appearance, with a tall funnel. She was built for service from Skælskør to the small islands of Agersø and Omø, off the coast of Sjælland, and sailed there until replaced by a car ferry in 1961. Then sold to shipbreakers, she was rescued by the newly formed Danish Veteran Ship Club. Returned to steam in 1964, she has been based at Roskilde since 1968 after a short period at Bandholm on Lolland. She usually makes two afternoon trips on Roskilde Fjord each Saturday and Sunday from June to August. She is an enjoyable steamer to sail on, and enthusiasts are welcomed into the engine room. She had a major overhaul in 1981. The club also own the preserved steam tug *Bjorn* (1908), used at Randers until 1981.

Bow view of *Skjelskør*

19

19. *La Suisse* arriving at Evian,
1983

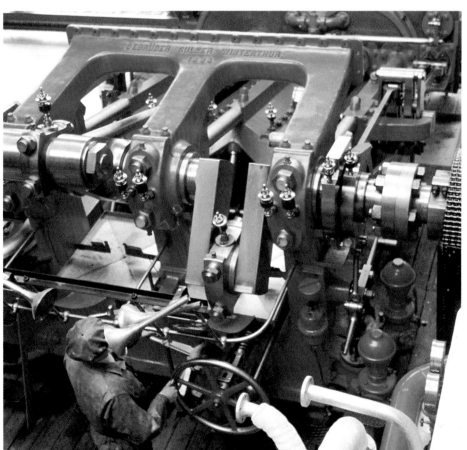

20. Compound diagonal engine,
Swiss Transport Museum, Lucerne

21/22

21. *Uri* at Alpnachstad, 1987

22. *Gallia* leaving Trieb, 1984

23. *Concordia*, lake Como, 1983

24

24. *Savoie* approaching Lausanne-Ouchy, 1987

25

25. *Gisela* leaving Gmunden, 1987

26. *Yalova* approaching the
Bosporus Bridge, 1986

26

27. *Schönbrunn*'s funnel being lowered

28. Triple expansion Hawthorn Leslie engine, Istanbul, 1986

29. *Ataköy*, Istanbul

32

33

32. *Pirna* on the Elbe near Stadt Wehlen

33. *Leipzig* in Saxon Switzerland

30. *Burgaz* leaving Haydarpasa, 1984

31. *Stadt Wehlen* on the Elbe

34. *Tudor Vladimirescu* on the Danube. *Author's collection; photograph G Douglas*

35. *Labe* and *Devín* at the Slapy terminus

WEST GERMANY

WEST GERMANY HAS an interesting and varied collection of veteran passenger steamers, embracing both river paddlers and coastal steamers, including probably Europe's most powerful preserved steamer, the steam icebreaker *Stettin*.

West Berlin is an area of particular interest. Its waters contain two large lakes, the Tegelersee and the Wannsee, connected by a canalised stretch of the river Havel, passing through Spandau lock. Around 40 passenger vessels ply in the city, many modern, but with a few veterans, and also some modern ones built on old hulls. The main operator is Stern & Kreis-Schiffahrt, who are publicly owned. The lakes are pleasant areas to sail on, a green lung for the crowded city. As can be imagined, there is a lot of competition, and at Tegel, where the route from the U-bahn station to the lake is pedestrianised, long rows of large boards advertise the various sailings, in addition to similar ones at the piers, and the various crew members touting for business with loud hailers. Some of the sailings pass along the border, protected by East German patrol boats, and with the infamous wall visible set back from the water's edge on the DDR side.

Several vessels not included below are also well worth a visit.

The paddle tug *Oscar Huber* (1922) is preserved as a museum at Duisburg-Ruhrort. She is a typical Rhine paddle tug, with two funnels fore and aft of the paddles. She operated until 1966, and has been open as a museum since 1974. A nearby building houses the Museum der Deutsches Binnenschiffahrt (German Inland Shipping Museum).

The preserved paddle tug *Ruthof* (1923) is moored as a museum ship in Regensburg; she worked on the Danube for Bayerische Lloyd until sunk in Hungary in 1944 by a mine, and was later raised by the Hungarians and sailed as *Erseksanad* until the mid-seventies, then purchased for preservation and returned to Regensburg in 1979.

The Westphalian Industrial Museum at Munster is restoring the steam tug *Fortuna* (1909) and the small inspection steamer *Nixe* (1939), and there is a possibility that they may be used for passenger trips when restored.

HAMBURG, RIVER ELBE

TIGER

Preserved screw steamer, tug
Owner: Museumshafen Oevelgönne e V, Hamburg
Built: 1910, Schiffswerft & Maschinenfabrik AG, Hamburg; 38gt; 16.0m × 4.8m
Machinery: compound; 240hp; coal-fired
Route: charters in Hamburg area

*T*iger is typical of many coal-fired steam harbour tugs. She was in operation as a tug until 1966, then laid up until 1978, when she was purchased for preservation. The vessel is normally based at Oevelgönne museum harbour.

Tiger, Hamburg Oevelgönne museum harbour, 1986

HAMBURG, RIVER ELBE

CLAUS D

ex *Moorfleth* 1956, ex *Schulau* 1933
Preserved screw steamer, tug
Owner. Museumshafen Oevelgönne e V, Hamburg
Built: 1913, Schiffswerft & Maschinenfabrik AG, Hamburg;
17.5m × 5.5m
Machinery: compound; 220hp
Route: charters in Hamburg area

*C*laus D is a typical harbour tug, converted to oil-firing in 1956. She was in operation until the early eighties, then purchased for preservation in 1984. Now with diesel generators, she does not offer *Tiger*'s 'steam' atmosphere.

HAMBURG, RIVER ELBE

OTTO LAUFFER

ex *Hafenpolizei VI*
Preserved steam launch
Owner: Museum für Hamburgische Geshichte, Hamburg
Built: 1928, H C Stülcken, Hamburg; 17m × 3.9m
Machinery: compound; 147hp; coal-fired
Route: charters in Hamburg area

A former harbour police steam launch, *Otto Lauffer* was in operation until 1968, preserved in 1969 and had a major overhaul 1978-84.

Otto Lauffer at Hamburg (Heinz Trost)

FLENSBURG, BALTIC SEA

ALEXANDRA*

Preserved screw steamer, expected to be in service 1988
Operator: Fördeverein Salondampfer *Alexandra* e V
Built: 1908, Janssen & Schmilsky, Hamburg; 140gt; 33.6m × 7.2m;
400 pass
Machinery: compound; 420hp; coal-fired; 12kn
Route: excursions from Flensburg

*G*ermany's last coastal excursion steamer, *Alexandra* last operated in 1975. A preservation group was set up in the late seventies to save her, but it was not until late 1986, after her former owners, Förde Reederei, donated her to the society, that any work was able to be done on her. She was slipped in December 1986, and is expected to be fully restored and back in service in 1988. She has operated out of Flensburg all her life, and is of a type once common on the coastline of Germany. *Alexandra* is not too different in design from the standard Swedish screw steamer, but with only a small saloon aft on the upper deck, and a small open deck aft. The steamer was used in World War I for target towing, and as a diving tender in World War II. She was used at Kiel yachting olympics as an official steamer both in 1936 and in 1972, when she was painted in a strange psychedelic colour scheme. Her services were very intensive (in 1914, for example, there were 50 daily departures by the fleet of steamers from Flensburg) and her regular run was to Sonderburg (then German, now Danish) and Gravenstein. It is to be hoped that, after a long period out of service, she can return to steam as a unique German steamer.

Alexandra laid up at Flensburg, winter, 1983

KIEL

ANNA

ex *Ute* 1987, ex *Anna* 1936
Screw steamer, ex motorship 1989 (planned), ex steamer 1936,
undergoing restoration
Owner: Lebendiges Kiel Verien, Kiel
Built: 1906, Howaldt, Ellerbek; 38gt; 17.0m × 4.7m; formerly 186 pass

Anna is a small former Kiel ferry; she operated at Rügen 1922-1930 and was rebuilt and converted to a motorship in 1936. Withdrawn in 1970, she was then used as a clubhouse. She was purchased for preservation in 1987; total restoration is planned by 1990, with a new steam engine.

TRAVEMÜNDE

STETTIN

Preserved steam icebreaker, occasional passenger sailings
Operator: Förderverein Eisbrecher *Stettin* e V, Travemünde
Built: 1933, Oderwerke, Stettin; 836gt; 51.8m × 13.4m; 100 pass
Machinery: triple expansion; 2200hp; coal-fired
Route: excursions and charters in June/July

Normally moored at Travemünde, the preserved steam icebreaker *Stettin* makes an annual summer trip lasting two or three weeks, with a mixture of public sailings and charters often centred around the Kiel yachting week at the end of June. She made a trip to Hamburg in 1986 for dry-docking.

She is a fascinating steamer, with many steam auxiliary engines for different specialised functions such as moving ballast from bow to stern to help in breaking ice. She originally operated from Stettin and Swinemunde, at the mouth of the Oder, and after the war was based at Hamburg for use on the Elbe, and also the Kiel canal and Baltic. She was withdrawn in 1981, and has been preserved at Travemünde since 1982. An extremely interesting steamer to visit, she is highly recommended. Her oil-fired sister ship *Wal* is still in operation, based at Rendsburg on the Kiel canal, although only in operation very infrequently.

LAUENBURG, RIVER ELBE

KAISER WILHELM*

Preserved paddle steamer
Built: 1900, Dresdner Maschinenbau & Schiffswerft, Dresden-Neustadt;
86t (displ); 57.2m × 4.4/8.4m; 350 pass
Machinery: compound diagonal; 168hp; coal-fired
Route: Lauenburg–Bleckede–Hitzacker; excursions from Lauenburg;
operates about three public sailings monthly in summer

West Germany's last coal-fired paddle steamer is one of those gems of preserved steamers that survive here and there throughout Europe. She was built for service on the river Weser, between Hameln and Hann Münden, through the area known as the Weserbergland. In 1910 she returned to Dresden for rebuilding and lengthening, and in 1954

Opposite: Stern view of *Kaiser Wilhelm*, Lauenberg, 1986

a new boiler was fitted. After withdrawal in 1970, she was purchased for preservation and sailed to Lauenburg under her own steam, and has operated out of Lauenburg ever since, on charters and public sailings upstream along the Elbe to Bleckede and Hitzacker. This stretch of river runs along the East/West border for some way, and one bank is overlooked by watch towers and one side of the river patrolled by East German border guard patrol boats. Occasionally her sailings take her downstream to Hamburg. She is operated by a preservation society, all crew are volunteers, and there is a very friendly atmosphere on board. She has no deck saloons, but a canopy over the after deck, and a small upper deck amidships. The catering is excellent, home cooking by society members. Highly recommended.

Lauenburg was the home for a fleet of excursion paddle steamers until 1961 with *Hugo Basedow* being the last steamer in operation. Relics and models of the Lauenburg are preserved in the excellent Elbe Shipping Museum at Lauenberg. Also on display there is a unique collection of steamer engines: oscillating from the Prague paddler *Hradcany,* which was built in 1880 using engines from an 1855 steamer and sailed until 1968, but was not scrapped until 1981; compound diagonal from the paddle ferry *Bad Schandau I* (1908); and a small upright compound set from the screw-propelled icebreaker *Seelöwe,* built in 1910, but with engines from 1901. Also on display are veteran diesel engines.

The midships section, with engine, boiler and bridge, of *Kaiser Wilhelm's* former runing mate, *Kronprinz Wilhelm* (1881-1967), is preserved at the German Maritime Museum at Bremerhaven.

Steam icebreaker *Stettin*, Travemünde, 1986

Her machinery was oscillating, and she is restored as she would have appeared on the Elbe as *Meissen,* in which guise she ran as part of the Dresden fleet until sold to the Weser in 1907. *Meissen's* engines were built in 1857 by John Penn of Greenwich.

KÖLN, RIVER RHINE

GOETHE

Paddle steamer
Operator: Köln-Düsseldorfer Deutsche Rheinschiffahrt (KD), Köln
Built: 1913, Sachsenberg, Köln; 522t (displ); 83.0m × 8.2/15.7m; 1600 pass
Machinery: compound diagonal, Sachsenberg, Rosslau (Elbe); 750hp; 15km/hr upstream, 23km/hr downstream
Route: various sailings between Köln and Mainz

Goethe, now KD's only paddle steamer, originally had only an aft deck saloon and a small upper deck, with an open foredeck, possibly for goods, but was rebuilt with a large upper deck saloon in 1925. Sunk in a bomb attack on Oberwinter in 1945, she was completely rebuilt and lengthened, given a modern funnel, and re-entered service in 1952 in her present form, with conversion from coal to oil-firing in 1955. In 1979 saw the present colour scheme was applied, and *Goethe* has been the only operational paddle steamer in the fleet since 1982. Unusually, her sailings are not specially marked in the timetable, and she takes her part in a 3-4 day roster along with some of the motor vessels, covering both the scenic Rhine gorge between Koblenz and Mainz, and the less well-known stretch linking Köln, Bonn, the Siebengebirge, and Koblenz. Her passenger accommodation is similar to that of the motorships, with large passenger saloons, excellent catering and even company-

bottled wines. While KD have realised some of the nostalgia potential of a paddle steamer, her long-term future may not be ensured, and there is only a small enthusiast organisation to lobby KD for her retention. Details of sailings can be obtained a few days beforehand from KD booking offices at the various landing-stages. She is enjoyable to sail on, if lacking some of the character of the smaller preserved steamers such as *Kaiser Wilhelm*.

BODENSEE

HOHENTWEIL

Paddle steamer, undergoing restoration
Owner: Internationales Bodenseeschiffahrtsmuseum
Built: 1913, Escher Wyss, Zürich; 378t (displ); 56.9m × 6.5/13.0m;
formerly 850 pass
Machinery: compound diagonal; 950hp

The last surviving Bodensee paddler, and last to be built before 1914, *Hohentweil* has for a number of years been the subject of preservation plans which at last seem to be coming to fruition. She was built as a half-saloon steamer for use out of Friedrichshafen by the Königlich Württembergische Dampschiffahrt, (Royal Württemburg Steamships), coming under control of the Deutsche Reichsbahn in 1920. She was rebuilt from 1933 to 1935 with a fore saloon and new bridge. Withdrawn after the 1962 season, she was sold in 1963 for use by a sailing club at Bregenz as a clubhouse, and remained there until late 1986, when she was towed to nearby Hard to be slipped and restored. Plans are for her to come into use as a museum, and to be rotated on an annual basis between different towns on the Bodensee,

in all three bordering countries. Plans did not originally include the restoration of the engine to steam, as this would be too costly, but for the paddler to be towed between the different places on the lake. However, the news that two new boilers have been ordered, and that the engine will be overhauled by Escher Wyss, must give hope that she will actually return to service. It is planned to restore her completely to original condition by spring 1989, a job estimated to cost over £800,000, and half the funds have been put up by the various town and cantonal authorities around the lake.

WEST BERLIN

SIEGFRIED

ex *Kaiser Friedrich III* 1918
Twin screw steamer, laid up, planned for restoration
Owner: Museum für Verkehr & Technik, Berlin
Built: 1889, Möller & Holberg (later Stettiner Odewerke); 31.2m ×
5.1m; formerly 291 pass

Berlin's last steamer, *Siegfried* has been laid up at Spandau since 1968. She was built for the Stern company as a Type II steamer, one of a series of six, and operated for them until sometime between the wars. In 1965 she was back on charter for Stern & Kreisschiffahrt, until withdrawn. The new Berlin Museum for Transport and Technology has long-term plans to save her and restore her to service as the last Berlin steamer, although the engines and boiler have been removed. She may well return to service as a motorship, though in original external condition, but it is to be hoped that they will be able to preserve this last example of a once numerous type of steamer.

Goethe leaving Koblenz, 1984

SWITZERLAND

SWITZERLAND IS PROBABLY the best-known European ountry for steamers, with the gleaming white paddlers of lakes Lucerne, Brienz, Geneva, and Zürich. The surviving paddle steamers are of broadly similar design, having come in the main from two builders, Escher Wyss and Sulzer. All have a small deck saloon forward and large first class dining saloon aft on the main deck, normally with elaborate decor in the dining saloon. There is often a small smoking saloon below the bridge on the upper deck, and the upper deck is reserved for first class ticket holders. The lake Geneva paddlers are more substantial than the others, as lake Geneva is more open, and storms can blow up quickly. An earlier paddler design with a half-saloon (that is, with the dining saloon raised half a deck) is only represented in Switzerland by the preserved steamers *Neuchâtel* and *Major Davel*, although half-saloon paddlers survive in steam on lake Como.

With so many steamers it is difficult to pick out a special one, but *La Suisse* more than any other paddler gives a sense of grandeur and power, more even than *Waverley*, while *Unterwalden* is probably the finest of the Lucerne paddlers, and *Lötschberg* runs along the lake with the most spectacular scenery.

La Suisse, lake Geneva, 1977

LAKE GENEVA

*LA SUISSE**

Paddle steamer
Operator: Compagnie Générale de Navigation sur le Lac Léman (CGN), Geneva
Built: 1910, Sulzer, Winterthur; 518t (displ); 73.8 m × 8.5/15.9 m; 1200 pass
Machinery: compound diagonal, by builders; 1400hp; 29.1km/hr; new boiler 1971
Route: Lausanne–Evian–circuit of upper lake–Montreux–Lausanne

Flagship of the lake Geneva fleet, *La Suisse* is one of Europe's finest paddle steamers. She was converted to oil-firing in 1960, and a new boiler was fitted in 1971, and at the same time she received a major overhaul including a new wheelhouse. Based at Lausanne, her regular roster includes a lunch cruise to Evian, and an anti-clockwise circuit of the eastern half of the lake in the afternoon, with an additional evening crossing to Evian. The dining room is furnished in Belle Epoque style, and like all lake Geneva steamers, she has her own restaurateur. Of all European paddle steamers, she is the one that most gives a sense of power as one watches the long cranks turning. If you sail on no other steamer on lake Geneva, sail on *La Suisse*.

Simplon in mid-lake, 1983

Dining saloon on *La Suisse*

LAKE GENEVA

*SAVOIE**

Paddle steamer
Operator: CGN, Geneva
Built: 1914, Sulzer, Winterthur; 367t (displ); 63.0 m × 7.2/14.3m; 1000 pass
Machinery: compound diagonal; 900hp; 27.4 km/h; new boiler 1967
Route: Lausanne–Thonon; Lausanne–circuit of upper lake–Montreux–Evian–Lausanne

avoie was the first of the lake Geneva fleet to be retained in steam, to undergo a major refurbishment, and to be fitted with a new boiler. Previous major overhauls had seen the steam engine replaced by diesel power in the various paddlers as their boilers came due for replacement. At that time *Savoie* received a rather incongruous U-shaped bar in the dining saloon, which, however, retains its Louis XVI style furnishings. A new galley in this area in place of the original one over the sponsons has meant, however, that the dining saloon has lost its earlier grandeur. She is little changed externally since building, with an aluminium canopy over the upper deck, fitted in 1928. *Savoie* was laid up from 1962 to 1966, awaiting the fitting of the new boiler. In 1987 she was again showing the need for a major refurbishment with patches of rust and chipped paint and a rather tatty and un-Swiss feel. Work planned for the 1987-8 winter included a major overhaul and the restoration of the dining saloon to original condition.

LAKE GENEVA

SIMPLON

Paddle steamer
Operator: CGN, Geneva
Built: 1920, Sulzer, Winterthur; 483t (displ); 73.8m × 8.5/15.9m; 1500 pass
Machinery: compound diagonal: 1400hp; 29.4km/hr; new boiler 1967
Route: reserve steamer at Lausanne–Ouchy; often substitutes for *Savoie*; used on charters.

uilding of *Simplon* started in 1914, and she was launched in 1915, but not completed until 1920. She is the largest steamer in Switzerland, with a dining saloon decorated in neo-classical style, and was completely restored at a major refit in 1966-67. She is little changed from building, having had an aluminium canopy fitted in 1928, and the small upper deck smoking saloon modernised in 1961.

LAKE GENEVA

RHÔNE

Paddle steamer
Operator: CGN, Geneva
Built: 1927, Sulzer, Winterthur; 364t (displ); 62.5 × 7.2/14.3m; 850 pass
Machinery: compound diagonal; 900hp; 27.4km/hr; new boiler 1969
Route: Geneva–Evian–Lausanne–Montreux–St Gingolph

he last steamer to be built for lake Geneva, *Rhône* has an unusual engine with oil-hydraulic valves which make the eccentrics redundant, and automatic oiling, which means that the cranks have to be totally enclosed, and so the passenger

can only see this cover, and not the cranks moving. These engines show the direction steamer engine design could have taken had steam not been supplanted by diesel. She is economical to operate and is usually on the long day-return trip along the lake from Geneva. She was built to replace the *Bonivard* (1868) which had burnt out in 1925. Because of the urgency of construction for a large wine festival in 1927, her dining saloon was not as elaborately decorated as those of some of the other steamers, and is characterised by dark wood marquetry panelling.

LAKE BRIENZ

LÖTSCHBERG

Paddle steamer
Operator: BLS, Interlaken
Built: 1914, Escher Wyss, Zürich; 260t (displ); 55.6m × 6.8/12.8m; 900 pass
Machinery: compound diagonal; 450hp; 25.8km/h
Route: Interlaken–Brienz

The only paddle steamer on the very scenic lake Brienz, *Lötschberg* is an impressive steamer, full of character. She sails twice daily from Interlaken to Brienz, lower terminus of the steam-powered Briener Rothorn railway. She was distinguished from other Swiss paddlers from 1967 until 1979 by a pink hull, and before that by a green one, but how has the white hull of the others. She was converted to oil-firing in about 1967, and the midships section of the upper deck was glassed-in during the seventies. Because she sails astern down the river Aare from the lake to Interlaken East station, she is fitted with a bow rudder, and a second wheel aft.

Rhône leaving Evian, 1983

LAKE THUN

BLÜMLISALP

Paddle steamer, laid up
Owner: Vaporama, Thun
Built: 1906, Escher Wyss, Zürich; 294t (displ); 60.5m × 6.8/13.1m; formerly 1000 pass
Machinery: compound; 600hp, 26km/hr; coal-fired

Flagship of lake Thun fleet, *Blümlisalp* was Switzerland's last coal-fired paddler when withdrawn in 1971. She is a saloon paddle steamer, of typical Escher Wyss design. In 1975 she was sold to an organisation known as Vaporama, who intended to use her as centrepiece of a steam museum in Thun. Many problems have stood in the way of this, and the steamer has been laid up in a remote spot on the lake since then, and is now very rusty and run down, with an uncertain future. It has been stated that restoration would cost around 8.3 million francs (around £3.3 million) probably an unrealistically high estimate.

LAKE LUCERNE

Uri approaching Lucerne Transport Museum pier, 1987

URI*

Paddle steamer
Operator: Schiffahrtsgesellchaft des Vierwaldstättersees (SGV), Lucerne
Built: 1901, Sulzer, Winterthur; 293.6ft (displ); 61.8 m × 6.8/14.0m;
800 pass
Machinery: compound diagonal; 650hp; 28.2km/hr
Route: Lucerne–Alpnachstad; Lucerne–Vitznau

Oldest of the five operating Lucerne paddlers, *Uri* was refurbished in about 1980, with the work spread over a number of winters. She was rebuilt in 1960-61 with a hydraulically operated telescopic funnel, masts and wheelhouse, to be able to pass under the then new Acheregg bridge, and up the arm of the lake to Alpnachstad, lower terminus of the Pilatus rack railway. The first class dining saloon is in neo-baroque style, designed by the Italian artist Cassina, with outstanding carving on the wood panelling. Like all Lucerne paddlers, she has a second class tearoom in the small fore-saloon on the main deck. She was converted to oil-firing in 1949. The unusual aluminium awning on the upper deck is to prevent soot falling on passengers when the funnel is down.

LAKE LUCERNE

UNTERWALDEN

Paddle steamer
Operator; SGV, Lucerne
Built: 1902, Escher Wyss, Zürich: 294t (displ); 62.0m × 6.8/13.5m;
800 pass
Machinery: compound diagonal; 650hp; 27.4km/h
Route: Lucerne–Flüelen; Lucerne–cruise around historic places on the
lake; evening dance cruises

Unterwalden on a special cruise, 1987

Pride of the lake Lucerne fleet, *Unterwalden* was only saved from scrapping a few years ago by enthusiast pressure. She was withdrawn in 1977, having already been replaced by a motor vessel also named *Unterwalden*, which later had to be renamed *Europa*. *Unterwalden* was totally renovated from top to bottom between 1982 and 1985 at a cost of around £1 million.

Her return to service in May 1985 was marked by great festivities, and really set the seal on much hard work and lobbying by Lucerne enthusiasts, who only a few years before had been faced with the planned withdrawal of the entire fleet by the mid-eighties. Her dining saloon is in neo-rococo style, and has been restored to original condition, while a panorama restaurant on the upper deck was fitted during her recent refit. Like *Uri*, she was refitted to pass under the Acheregg bridge in 1961. She is a beautiful steamer to sail on, and lake Lucerne, surrounded by the Alps, is one of the most scenic steamer haunts anywhere in Europe.

Schiller on lake Lucerne, 1977

LAKE LUCERNE

SCHILLER

Paddle steamer
Operator: SGV, Lucerne
Built: 1906, Sulzer, Winterthur; 319.9t (displ); 63.0m × 7.2/14.3m;
900 pass
Machinery: compound diagonal; 700hp; 28.5km/hr
Route: Lucerne–Flüelen

First of the Lucerne paddlers to have a recent major refurbishment, *Schiller* was refitted in 1977, and normally operates one return trip from Lucerne to the other end of the lake, with eight to 12 intermediate stops, including Vitznau, at the foot of the rack railway up the Rigi. Once a fortnight in summer special steam trains are run on this, and a 'full steam ahead' package, including steamer Lucerne to Vitznau and back, and entry to the Swiss transport museum at Lucerne, is organised. Her dining saloon is in Jugendstil decor, one of the few remaining examples of the this geometric style, with light wood trimmed with mother of pearl, and bronze fittings. A new parquet floor fitted in 1977 has helped to show this off. She still has canvas awnings on her upper deck, whereas many Swiss paddlers have had these replaced with aluminium or the upper deck glassed in. In 1986 gold leaf was applied to her name and bow carving.

Typical Swiss bow ornamentation on *Schiller*

STADT LUZERN

Paddle steamer
Operator: SGV, Lucerne
Built: 1927 Sachsenberg, Rosslau/Elbe, Germany; 427t (displ); 63.5m × 7.8/15.2m; 1200 pass
Machinery: three cylinder diagonal, Sulzer, 1929; 1120hp; 26.3km/h
Route: Luzern–Flüelen

Flagship of the Lucerne fleet, *Stadt Luzern* shows her German ancestry by her large upper deck saloon. Ordered from Sachsenberg because of a lower price, she disgraced herself when her engine completely broke down on trials, and a new engine had to be ordered from Sulzers, who had lost out on the order in the first place. Her present engine is a Unaflow type, similar to that formerly in *Helvétie* on lake Geneva, and features oil-hydraulic gearing and automatic lubrication. This meant that the cranks were formerly totally enclosed, but following enthusiast pressure, the metal covering was replaced in 1981 by a transparent perspex cover, enabling passengers to see the motion of the engine. She has a place in Swiss history, having in 1940 taken the Swiss commander-in-chief, General Guisan, to a historic meeting with his army commanders at Rütli, a meeting which determined Switzerland's armed neutrality in World War II. This is commemorated by a plaque at the foot of the main staircase. In 1980 Queen Elizabeth II made a trip on the steamer. She was the last of the steamers to undergo major refurbishment; this

Gallia leaving Treib, 1984

started in the 1985-6 winter. She has a first class dining saloon forward on the upper deck, so the aft saloon on the main deck is open to all passengers.

GALLIA*

Paddle steamer
Operator: SGV, Lucerne
Built: 1913 Escher Wyss, Zürich; 328.9t (displ); 62.9 × 7.2/14.5m; 850 pass
Machinery: compound diagonal; 1085hp; 31.5km/h
Route: Lucerne–Flüelen

Known as the Flyer of lake Lucerne, *Gallia* is the fastest steamer on the Swiss lakes. Her dining saloon is in neo-empire decor, with larger windows than in some other paddlers. She was refurbished over a period from 1977 to 1979, and was converted to oil-firing, like the other paddlers, in the early fifties. Like all the Swiss paddlers, a joy to sail on, with gleaming machinery and polished brass in the engine room, brass name plates on every step of the main staircase, and spotless cleanliness throughout.

Stadt Luzern arriving at Treib, 1984

Stadt Zürich at Zürich Wollishofen yard, 1987

LAKE ZÜRICH

STADT ZÜRICH

Paddle steamer
Operator: Zürichsee-Schiffahrtgesellschaft (ZSG)
Built: 1909, Escher Wyss, Zürich; 291t (displ); 59.1m × 7.0/13.5m;
850 pass
Machinery: compound diagonal; 500hp; 27km/hr
Route: Zürich–Rapperswil; occasionally to Schmerikon

Stadt Zürich is a typical Swiss paddle steamer, renovated in 1980; she is normally only in use in good weather. She was converted to oil-firing in 1951. She has a bright dining saloon with large windows, but no classical decoration as on most other Swiss paddlers. Like her sister, she was fitted with a telescopic funnel in 1981 for the extension of excursion sailings to Schmerikon. It is to be hoped that she will follow *Stadt Rapperswil* in being re-boilered.

LAKE ZÜRICH

STADT RAPPERSWIL

Paddle steamer
Operator: ZSG
Built: 1914, Escher Wyss, Zürich; 249.3t (displ); 59.1m × 7.0/13.5m;
850 pass
Machinery: compound diagonal; 500hp; 27.2km/hr
Route: Zürich–Rapperswil; occasionally to Schmerikon

The subject of a major refurbishment, including a new boiler, in 1986, *Stadt Rapperswil* has been excellently restored, with a lot of attention to details such as the brass name-plates on each step of the staircase, and round brass 'Escher Wyss' plates at the end of each step. She even has a reconstructed dining saloon in classical style. She, like her sister, normally sails only in good weather, or at least when the weather at the beginning of a day is good, though steamer sailings have been increased in recent summers. Lake Zürich is situated in countryside, with rolling hills surrounding it; the Alps are visible in the distance, but the passengers are more likely to be locals on a day out then international tourists intent on seeing the glories of the mountains.

Opposite: Stadt Rapperswil at Rapperswil, 1977

Greif before restoration to steam (Anton Räber)

LAKE GREIF

GREIF

Screw steam launch, ex motor launch 1987, ex steamer 1916
Operator: Schiffahrtsgenossenchaft für den Greifensee (SGG), Maur
Built: 1895, Escher Wyss, Zürich; 9.5t (displ); 13.4m × 3.0m; 50 pass
Machinery: compound; 10hp
Route: lake Greif; Maur–Uster (east of Zürich)

Amazingly, the original engine of this small passenger launch has remained in existence on land from 1916 to the present day. It is currently being refitted to *Greif* to provide Switzerland's only operating screw steamer, expected to be in steam by 1988.

AUSTRIA

VETERAN PASSENGER VESSELS in Austria are divided between those on a number of lakes throughout the country and those on the river Danube. Traditionally lake services were maintained by fairly small steamers which were easily converted to diesel. Two of the steamers, however, have survived, and both have been restored in recent years; the beautiful paddle steamer *Gisela* on the Traunsee, and the relatively unknown screw steamer *Thalia* on the Wörthersee at Klagenfurt. There also remain a number of very old ex-steamers. On the Danube, the major operator before the partition of the Austro-Hungarian empire following World War I was the DDSG (First Danube Steamship Co), and although their fleet and services are only a shadow of those days, they do have, in *Schönbrunn*, probably Europe's finest river paddle steamer.

GMUNDEN, TRAUNSEE

GISELA*

Preserved paddle steamer
Operator: Traunsee-Schiffahrt Inhaber Karl Eder, Gmunden
Owner: Freunde der Stadt Gmunden
Built: 1871, Ruston, Wien-Floridsdorf; 187.5t (displ); 52.0m × 4.95/9.35m; 300 pass
Machinery: oscillating compound, Prager Maschinenfabrik, 1870; 120hp; new boiler 1975; coal-fired
Route: Gmunden–Ebensee; evening cruises from Gmunden

One of preservation's great success stories of recent years, *Gisela* has been completely restored, the engine even being removed and taken to Linz for total restoration. She re-entered service in 1986, and in 1987 saw regular service in good weather twice weekly, on Thursdays and Sundays, with two return trips daily, also Friday evening cruises and charters.

Gisela was built by Englishman Joseph Ruston for his own service on the lake, and ownership passed later to his nephew John Ruston, who was interned as an alien during World War I. Ownership then passed to Rudolph Ippisch, then to his son in 1953, and on his death to the Eder family in 1976.

Gisela is not too different from when she was built, although in early years she had tiller steering, a figurehead, and a tall, thin funnel. By the late 1970s she was used very infrequently, about half a dozen times a year for charters, although she had had her second new boiler in 1975.

It looked as if she would follow in the footsteps of her sister *Elisabeth* (1858-1969) and be scrapped, but after her withdrawal in November 1980, local enthusiasts started moves to preserve her. They acquired her in mid-1982, by which time she was on land awaiting overhaul. Work progressed slowly at times, and she was unfortunately not ready for the planned 1985 summer season, although she did take part in a flower festival at Gmunden in that summer. In 1986 she returned to steam, and also a small aft saloon was built to house a cafeteria counter, with a small open passenger deck on the upper deck aft of the bridge. Her restoration has been very thorough, and she now bears the bridge telegraphs from *Elisabeth*, manufactured by Stephen and Struthers, Glasgow. Highly recommended; it is worth a trip to Austria to sail on her alone. Her sailings criss-cross the lake, which nestles beneath high mountains, particularly at the southern end.

Gisela at Ebensee, 1987

KLAGENFURT, WÖRTHERSEE

THALIA

ex *Klagenfurt* 1939, ex *Thalia* 1925
Screw steamer, under restoration
Operator: Klagenfurter Stadtwerke, Klagenfurt-See
Built: 1909, Dresdner Maschinenfabrik & Schiffswerft Übigau, Dresden;
132t (displ); 38.5m × 5.5m; 400 pass
Machinery: compound; 150hp; new boiler 1964
Route: Klagenfurt-See–Maria Wörth–Pörtschach–Velden (planned from summer 1988)

Austria's last operating screw steamer, and indeed one of only a couple in central Europe, *Thalia* has been programmed for a complete restoration since 1982, although major work did not start until December 1986. Summer 1987 saw her stripped to main deck level in the company's dry dock at Klagenfurt-See. She is of not dissimilar design to the Achensee's *Stadt Innsbruck*, with large fore and aft saloons, and canopied open upper decks fore and aft. Diesel engines were ordered for her in 1946, but never installed, and instead the steam engine

was overhauled. Later, in 1964, she was fitted with a new oil-fired boiler. A large, ugly, modern wheelhouse was fitted in 1966. Withdrawn at the end of the 1974 season, she lay rusting for a number of years until a local initiative got restoration started. Her owners were taken over in 1913 by Klagenfurt Town Council, and ran the lake steamers along with the tramway and later bus systems. Present services on the route along the lake are maintained by four modern, rather ugly motorships, but it is planned that *Thalia* will take her place in the service again from summer 1988, and also as a 'nostalgia' steamer for charters, following her restoration. It is planned to restore her to original condition, with restoration work at Klagenfurt in 1987 and an engine rebuild underway at the SGV yard at Lucerne, Switzerland, and to use her all the year round; the waters of the Carinthian lakes are much warmer than the other Alpine lakes, being to the south of the mountains. The lake is long and narrow, surrounded by low hills.

VIENNA, RIVER DANUBE

*SCHÖNBRUNN**

Paddle steamer
Operator: Erste Donau-Dampfschiffahrts Gesellschaft (DDSG), Vienna
Built: 1911, Schiffswerft Budapest; 556t (displ); 74.6m × 8.0/15.6m; 250 pass (900 until 1985)
Machinery: compound diagonal; 710hp; 25km/hr downstream
Route: Vienna–Budapest (sold as package with hotel); Vienna–Passau

Recently totally refurbished for 'Oldtimer' sailings at highly inflated prices, *Schönbrunn* is a unique survivor of the once numerous fleet of DDSG paddlers. The company has operated on the Danube since 1830, and by 1892 had 192 steamers, both passenger ships and tugs, in service, and 858 goods barges.

Thalia before restoration (F Schilcher, Klagenfurt)

Thalia undergoing restoration at Klagenfurt, 1987

Schönbrunn in the Wachau section of the Danube, 1984

Right: Mid-section of *Schönbrunn*, Passau, 1979

Services were maintained as far as the Black Sea until 1939, a section now only traversed by cruises, and today regular services are operated from Vienna to Grein, with a more intensive service through the scenic Wachau part of the river, from Krems to Melk. Until 1985, a daily service was operated from Vienna to Passau, with overnight stops in each direction at Linz, using *Schönbrunn* and the two diesel-electric paddlers *Stadt Wien* and *Stadt Passau*. Prior to 1976 the downstream run was made in a single day, but the construction of a number of hydro-electric schemes involving passage through locks, and also slowing the current, made this impossible.

The paddler has impressive fore and aft dining saloons on the main deck, and small saloons on the upper deck which have been added over the years. Her funnel is hydraulically hinged in order to pass underneath bridges. She was modernised at Linz in 1954, when she re-entered service after World War II, and again in 1974 and 1985. Nineteen cabins were provided, but these have not been used since 1985.

Twice-weekly Budapest trips started in 1986, along with a Sunday excursion to Dürnstein, returning by steam train, and in 1987 a full service, on a weekly basis, from Vienna to Passau, with a weekly Vienna to Budapest service only operated on demand. Most of the Budapest sailings have been sold as a package by Mondial Travel, with hotel, sightseeing trips, and coach return. Part of the return trip from Budapest is overnight, and passengers are

normally bussed from Budapest to Komarom, with steamer from there back to Vienna. Prices are exorbitantly high, around £170 for the trip including hotel, bus, and some meals, and a day single from Vienna to Linz around £49. *Schönbrunn* is a beautiful steamer to travel on; one only wishes the fares were more realistic.

THE NETHERLANDS

WITH ITS MANY CANALS and the great ports of Rotterdam and Amsterdam, The Netherlands is an area one would imagine to be rich in veteran steamers. In fact, although there are a number of interesting vessels, the only operating passenger steamer has been recently imported.

A further 23 operating steam tugs are, however, preserved in The Netherlands and many occasionally carry passengers at steam rallies and other special events. Brief details follow:

Name	Date Built	Length	Engine	Fuel	Place Built	Based
CHRISTIAAN BRUNINGS	1900	31.2m	Comp	Coal	Haarlem	Amsterdam
JACOB LANGENBERG	1902	27.0m	Tr Ex	Coal	Elbing	Amsterdam
ex Von Botticher						
ROSALIE	1889	19m	Comp	Coal	Kinderdijk	Amsterdam
ex Willem IV, ex Jacoba, ex Nieuwe Zorg						
HUGO HEDRICH	1929	16.6m	Comp	Coal	Groningen	Zaandam
SCHEELENKUHLEN	1927	21.4m	Comp	Coal	Hamburg	Zaandam
ADELAAR	1925	20.7m	Tr Ex	Coal	Haarlem	Beverwijk
ex Botlek, ex Adelaar						
GABRIELLE	1903	19.5m	Comp	Coal	Brandenburg	Hoorn
ex Amelie, ex Odette, ex Rachael, ex Willy						
BIELENBERG	1927	21m	Comp	Oil	Hamburg	Enkhuizen
ROEK	1930	20.2m	Tr Ex	Coal	Vlaardingen	Enkhuizen
ex Jacomien						
SUCCES I	1897	38.4m	2 Tr Ex	Oil	Bolnes	Enkhuizen*
ex Success, ex Sleipner						
NOORDZEE	1922	22.5m	Comp	Coal	Hamburg	Medemblik
ex Nordsee, ex Taucher Sivers IV, ex B & V XII						
TENIERS	1909	21.5m	Tr Ex	Coal	Rotterdam	Zwolle
ex Antwerpen I						
HENDRINA II	1913	14.3m	Comp	Coal	s'Gravenhage	Leeuwarden
ex Mariette, ex Snel						
MAARTEN	1926	19.4m	Tr Ex	Coal	Deest	Leeuwarden
ex Ido II, ex Luise, ex Hollænd, ex Cor-Adri						
DOCKYARD V	1941	25m	2 × Comp	Oil	Rotterdam	Rotterdam
DOCKYARD IX	1946	25m	2 × Comp	Coal	Rotterdam	Rotterdam*
EPÉE	1949	41.5m	Tr Ex	Coal	Cherbourg	Rotterdam*
FINLAND	1921	22.5m	Tr Ex	Coal	Rotterdam	Rotterdam
ex Delfshaven, ex Hercules, ex Arabe, ex Finland						
VOLLHARDING I	1929	20.2m	Tr Ex	Coal	Hardinxveld	Rotterdam
ex Harmonie VI						
PIETER BOELE	1893	26m	Tr Ex	Oil	Bolnes	Bolnes
ex Speculant, ex Wacht am Rhein VIII, ex Direktor Johann Knipscher, ex Mathilde						
HERCULES	1915	20.3m	Comp	Coal	Martenshoek	Schiedam
ex Fremad II, ex Fremad, ex Gebrs Bodewes II						
FURIE	1916	30.3m	Tr Ex	Oil	Martenshoek	Maasluis
ex Holmvik, ex Holmen III, ex Gebrs Bodewes VI						
GEBR BEVER	1941	25m	Comp	Oil	Rotterdam	Dordrecht
ex Dockyard III						
SUCCES	1909	21.5m	Tr Ex	Oil	Dordrecht	Maasbracht

* Undergoing restoration

JOHANNES

ex *Schill* 1945
Screw steamer, ex tug
Operator: Thalassa Travel, Amsterdam
Built: 1908, Wollheim, Breslau; 15.7 × 4.4m; 34 pass
Machinery: compound; 120hp; coal-fired
Route: Westzaan–Haarlemmermeer (Cruquius Steam Pumping-engine Museum)

Holland's only operating passenger steamer, *Johannes* worked for most of her life as a tug in the eastern part of Germany, being originally owned by Berliner Lloyd, and coming under DDR control after 1945. She was sold to Holland in 1973, and a small passenger cabin has been built aft. Her passenger sailings are only on Saturdays in July and August.

BELGIUM

No operating steamers; *see Part Two.*

FRANCE

No operating steamers; *see Part Two.*

SPAIN

No operating steamers; *see Part Two.*

PORTUGAL

No operating steamers; *see Part Two.*

Piemonte, Arona shipyard, 1983

ITALY

ITALY'S VETERANS ARE rather scattered, with a few surviving paddlers on the northern lakes and a handful of other veterans scattered around the country. *Patria* and *Concordia* are half-saloon paddle steamers, a type now extinct in Switzerland.

Venice, of all cities in Europe the most dependent on water transportation, has a number of veteran vessels, although they are externally indistinguishable from more modern ones. No operating steamers remain in Venetian waters, however; *see Part Two.*

LAKE MAGGIORE

PIEMONTE

ex *Regina Madre* 1946
Paddle steamer
Operator: Navigazione Lago Maggiore (NLM), Arona
Built: 1904, Escher Wyss, Zürich; 273t (displ); 51.2 × 6.2/11.6m; 500 pass
Machinery: compound diagonal; 440hp; 22km/h; new boiler 1974
Route: very occasional excursions on lake

Very much a neglected asset, *Piemonte* is restricted by the NLM management to a few sailings a year, mainly evening cruises in the mid-August holiday week. She is kept in good condition, and had a major overhaul from 1961 to 1965

Patria on lake Como, 1983

and again in 1973-4. She operated excursions from Locarno, at the Swiss end of the lake, for a few years in the late seventies. A completely glassed-in upper deck and overly large wheelhouse rather detract from her appearance. She is of typical Escher Wyss design.

PATRIA

ex *Savoia* 1943
Paddle steamer
Operator: Navigazione Lago di Como (NLC), Como
Built: 1926, N Odero, Sestri Ponente; 286t (displ); 53.7m × 6.4/11.6m; 900 pass
Machinery: triple expansion diagonal; 600hp; 25km/hr
Route: Como–Bellagio–Colico

*P*atria is an interesting paddle steamer, used more in recent years than for some time; she is normally, however, only on Sunday service, except at the height of the season in early August. She is a half-saloon steamer with plush red leather settees in her lower saloon. Catering, however, is rather basic with only a small bar in one of the sponsons. She was refurbished in 1973-4, and a new tall black funnel with one white ring was fitted in 1983, to replace a dumpy white one with red rings that had been fitted when she was converted to oil-firing in 1951. The engines of both Como paddlers have Caprotti valve gear, as on some later Italian steam locomotives. She is a comfortable steamer to sail on, and full of character.

CONCORDIA*

ex *28 Ottobre* 1943
Paddle steamer
Operator: NLC, Como
Built: 1926, N Odero, Sestri Ponente; 286t (displ); 53.8m × 6.4/11.6m; 900 pass
Machinery: triple expansion diagonal; 600hp; 25km/hr; new boiler 1977
Route: Como–Bellagio–Colico (Sunday lunch cruise); Saturday evening cruises from Lecco

*B*uilt as a sister of *Patria*, *Concordia* can be distinguished by the two rings on her funnel, and by an additional saloon on top of her half-saloon, added in a major rebuild lasting from 1973 to 1977. This saloon, which is in keeping with the character of the steamer, enables her to be used for special 'lunch-inclusive' cruises on Sundays, although ordinary passengers are also carried on these sailings. The trip from Como to Colico takes 3½ hours in each direction and the lake is situated in interesting mountainous scenery. The lake is Y-shaped, and the sector from Bellagio to Lecco is visited by *Concordia* on a Saturday evening dance cruise from Lecco. Of the three major Italian lakes, Como is the only one on which the steamers are treated properly; *Piemonte* is cosseted far too much on lake Maggiore, and the two steamers on lake Garda have had diesel engines fitted. Both Como paddlers can be highly recommended, and have an atmosphere very different from Swiss paddlers of similar size.

Concordia, Como Tavernola Shipyard, 1979

Cruise steamer *Albatross*, now *Betsy Ross* (A Duncan)

MALTA

No operating steamers; *see Part Two.*

GREECE AND CYPRUS

GREECE HAS ALWAYS had a reputation for buying old, second-hand ships from other countries, particularly in northern Europe, and it is rather a surprise to find practically no veterans there. There are a number of reasons:

a) Shorter routes which have seen older vessels retained in other countries are generally, in Greece, the preserve of locally-built wooden-hulled passenger boats and landing-craft type car ferries.

b) Second-hand larger vessels have, in the main, a relatively short life in Greek waters; the past twenty or thirty years have seen a trend from the use of older steamers, sometimes ex-yachts or naval craft, to immediate post-war classic passenger-only steamers and motorships, to first generation, and now, second generation, car ferries from northern Europe and Japan.

c) Greece lacks an excursion trade (most passenger ships are ferries or larger ships sailing to various islands, and a day excursions are scaled-down cruise operations rather than the more basic day trips seen in other countries).

d) There are frequent bankruptcies amongst Greek operators.

In addition to the few ships mentioned here, Chandris Lines operate the veteran cruise liners *Victoria* (ex *Dunnottar Castle*-1936/11,541gt) and *Britanis* (ex *Lurline*, ex *Matsonia*, ex *Monterey*-1932/15,412gt in the Caribbean and *Romanza* (ex *Aurelia*, ex *Beverbrae*, ex *Huascaran*) in the Mediterranean on cruises from Venice to the Greek Islands; Epirotiki operate ex-yacht *Argonaut* (1929/4007gt) on luxury charters to travel agencies in both

Europe and the Americas; and a further cruise steamer is *Betsy Ross* noted below, a former cross-channel steamer.

BETSY ROSS

ex *Albatros* 1987, ex *Najla* 1982, ex *Leda* 1979
Twin screw turbine cruise steamer
Operator: American Star Lines
Owner: Anro Marine
Built: 1953, Swan Hunter & Wigham Richardson, Newcastle; 6471gt;
133.0m × 17.4m; 496 pass
Machinery: 4 geared turbines, Wallsend Slipway; 13,000shp; 20kt
Route: cruises from Piraeus to Greek islands (1987)

This vessel operated until 1974 from Newcastle to Stavanger and Bergen as Bergen Line's *Leda* then, after a spell laid up, was used as an accommodation ship under the name *Nalja* or *Najla*, including a spell at Stornoway 1979-80. She was sold to Greece in 1981; after extensive conversion work, she eventually entered service as a cruise liner in 1985. In 1985 she was renamed *Allegro* for two months only for a South American operation which never materialised. She was reported in 1987 to have been sold and renamed *Betsy Ross*, but this could a pseudonym for an American-based charter in the winter months; she may return to her old name when she returns to Europe in the summer months.

Corinthia, Brindisi to Patras service, 1987 (Antonio Scrimali)

PIRAEUS

CORINTHIA

ex *Neptunia* 1987, ex *Duke of Argyll* 1975
Twin screw turbine steamer, car ferry
Owner: Scanmed Shipping Co, Malta
Operator: Hellenic Mediterranean Lines
Built: 1956, Harland & Wolff, Belfast; 4843gt; 114.6m × 17.5m;
800 pass
Machinery: two geared turbines; 10,500shp; 21kn
Route: Brindisi–Corfu–Patras (summer 1987)

Built for the British Railways Heysham to Belfast route as a sister of the *Duke of Lancaster*, (see *Duke of Llanerch-y-Mor*), *Corinthia* was similarly converted for car ferry use. She was sold to Libra Maritime in 1975, and used on the Brindisi-Patras route for a while, but by 1981 was operating an Ancona-Piraeus-Rhodes-Haifa service. Later she was available for charter, and was used by the British organisation Schools Abroad Ltd for a year or two, as well as other charter work. Possibly used on the Brindisi-Piraeus-Izmir route in 1986, she returned to Hellenic Mediterranean in 1987 on charter after they had encountered major financial problems following the disastrous summer of 1986 when the usual American tourist influx to Greece was decimated by terrorism, and their more recent ships had been seized by the bank. She is the last operating cross-channel turbine steamer in Europe.

PIRAEUS

QUEEN M

ex *Rangatira* 1986
Turbo-electric steamer, car ferry
Operator: Marlines, Piraeus (Cyprus registered)
Built: 1972, Swan Hunter Shipbuilders, Newcastle upon Tyne; 9387gt;
152.6m × 21.6m; 1600 pass
Machinery: turbo-electric; 21kn
Route: Ancona–Igoumentisa–Patras–Heraklion–Kysadasi

Originally on the Union Steamship Company of New Zealand's route from Wellington to Lyttelton, linking the North and South Islands of New Zealand, she was built to replace *Wahine*, tragically lost in a storm in 1968 off Wellington harbour. The Union company had long favoured turbo-electric propulsion, but the high cost of fuel and a lack of confidence in the route by passengers following the *Wahine* disaster made the service uneconomic, and *Rangatira* was withdrawn in 1976 and returned to England to be laid up at Falmouth. She was used for a while as a floating hostel at Loch Kishorn for workers at an oil rig yard, but eventually returned to Falmouth until sold to her present owners in 1986.

Opposite: Foredeck view of *Guzelhisar*, 1986

TURKEY

FOR THE STEAM ENTHUSIAST, Turkey must be the closest place to paradise. Until the mid-eighties, the majority of ferries over the Bosporus at Istanbul were steamers, many coal-fired. Unfortunately, many of these have been displaced by modern diesels, partly due to a local mayor who, in an endeavour to clean up the city, has focussed public attention on the damage done to the stonework of the mosques by coal smoke from the ferries.

With eight steamers set to continue for a good number of years yet, and a further eleven still in service in 1987 but under threat of withdrawal (all in commercial service rather than preserved) it can be seen that Istanbul has a very special place in the heart of the steamer enthusiast.

Before describing the routes, I should point out that the city of Istanbul, on the western, or European, shore of the Bosporus,

is served by many dormitory suburbs on the Asian shore. The population of these has greatly increased in recent years as many thousands of country people come into the city for work, and thus the building of a suspension bridge has not lessened the demand for the ferries to any great extent. Moreover, the vast majority of Turks do not own a car, and, in any case, the bridge seems to be a perpetual traffic jam. A second bridge is under construction, and a new service by Norwegian-built catamarans started in 1987 in competition with the steamers; time will tell how these will affect the ferries. Istanbul itself is cut in two by the Golden Horn, an inlet of the Bosporus which has a number of shipyards on its banks. The Galata bridge crosses the Golden Horn in the centre of the city, and the centre part of this is opened in the small hours of the morning to allow access for shipping.

Three groups of routes are operated in the Istanbul area by Türkiye Denizcilik Kurumu: Şehir Hatlari İşletmesi; (Turkish Maritime Lines, City Lines Administration)

Kuzgunck, Tegmen Ali Ihsan Kalmaz and *Burgaz*, Karaköy, 1986

1. Across the Bosporus:
   a) From Karaköy, on the north side of the Galata bridge, to Haydarpaşa, the railway terminus on the Asian shore, and Kadiköy, a major local bus terminal. This route is generally operated by the larger ferries such as the 1961 Fairfield class. Peak hour services serve the two Asian terminals independently, but in off-peak hours they are both served by the same sailing. A ten to fifteen minute frequency is offered for most of the day.
   b) From Eminönü, south of the Galata bridge, to Kadiköy, with some rush hour services extended further south-east to Moda and Bostanci.
   c) From Eminönü to Üsküdar, a mile or so further north on the Asian shore, and another urban bus terminal.
   d) From Şirkeci, adjoining Eminönü, to Harem, the long-distance bus terminal on the Asian shore; a car ferry route.
   e) From Kabatas, a mile or so north of Karaköy, to Üsküdar; also a car ferry route.
   f) From Besiktaş, half a mile north of Kabatas, also known as Barbaross Hayrettin Pasa, and serving the commercial area

around Taksim Square, to Üsküdar; operated by older steamers in the rush hours, but as an extension of route 1c in off-peak hours.

g) Two routes across the upper Bosporus, not normally operated by steamers.

2. Routes up and down the Bosporus:

a) Commuter routes from various piers on both Asian and European sides to Eminönü, city-bound in the morning, outwards in the evenings; weekdays only, about 12 services in each direction, originating from different piers. Up until the opening of the Bosporus bridge, this service was operated all day.

b) A tourist service twice a day in summer (more often on Sundays) from Eminönü right down the Bosporus to Rumeli Kavagi, on the European shore, ('Rumeli' having its origins in 'Roman'), and Anadolu Kavagi on the Asian shore) 'Anadolu' meaning Anatolian, or Asian); an interesting trip, with the Asian shore of the waterway lined by traditional wooden-built *yalis* (villas), and a lot of shipping interest, including a number of ship repair yards on the European shore at Istinye,

where, in a hidden bay, one can see the Bosporus steamers dry-docked in a floating dock, and at Büyükdere. Anadolu Kavagi is on the edge of a military zone, and there is no access beyond the village, which is famous for its fish restaurants. There is a regular bus service back to the city on the European shore for any enthusiast who takes the one-way evening commuter sailings up the Bosporus.

c) A Sunday and public holiday service from Eminönü to Berleybeyi and Çengelköy, a short way beyond the bridge, operated on a two-hourly frequency by the steamer *Sarayburnu* in 1984, although now probably operated by a diesel.

3) From the inner side of the Galata Bridge up the Golden Horn, past the shipyards, to Eyüp, a service which is now completely in the hands of modern motor launch operators and which now continues under the bridge and across to Üsküdar.

4) Sea of Marmara routes:

a) From Şirkeci to the Princes Islands, a group of islands in the Sea of Marmara, about an hour's sailing time away. Calls are made at Kadiköy, and at the islands of Kinaliada, Burgazada, Heybeliada, and Büyükada, not necessarily at all

islands by all sailings. The islands are a very popular day trip destination, particularly in summer, and there are greatly increased services on summer weekends, when the high capacity of the Fairfield 1961 steamers is required.

b) An express service from Şirkeci in winter and Kabataş in summer, to Büyükada, with occasional calls at the other islands, and onwards to Yalova on the southern shore of this arm of the sea of Marmara, with bus connection to Bursa; long the preserve of the -bahçe class of classic diesel ferries.

c) A car ferry service from Kartal directly across to Yalova. No steam in recent years.

d) A service from Bostanci, on the Asian shore, and served by train from Haydarpasa, to the Princes Islands. Not normally steam.

The shuttle passenger service across the mouth of the Gulf of Izmir, from Hereke to Karamürsel, and two car ferry services in the Dardanelles, are operated by the same section of the national shipping company.

The steamers are of similar basic design, with twin screws, saloons forward and aft on main and upper decks, and the engines in full view. Some of the older steamers have an open foredeck with a framework for an awning, others have this area covered, but open at the sides. The same basic design of ship has been continued to the present day, with the large Sehit class little changed. The Fairfield 1961 steamers also have a third passenger deck at bridge deck level, with a covered deck open at the sides, originally known as a 'winter garden'. A feature of all the steamers are the narrow alleyways outside the saloons at main deck level. Generally one saloon, previously first class, has upholstered seats, and the others basic wooden slatted benches. The Fairfield 1961 group also has one small, former deluxe, saloon with armchairs.

Catering is from a buffet, run independently, and an interest-

ing feature of the steamers are the tea boys, who come around with trays full of glasses of tea, freshly squeezed orange juice, or bottles of soft drinks. On the Bosporus tourist route, a speciality is fresh yoghurt brought on board at Kanlica, whose claim to fame is apparently that it is the yoghurt capital of Turkey. The yoghurt is thicker than British yoghurt, and is sweetened with icing sugar. The buffets themselves vary, some being obviously a source of pride to their operators, with much polished brass and chrome, others being rather basic.

Most of the steamers have two whistles, a chime whistle and a siren, and the older vessels had two sets of triple expansion engines, although the 1961 group have two sets of compound engines connected in tandem on each shaft.

Major operator in the past was Şirketi Hayriye, who gave its ships both numbers, (used in Lloyds Register, as Bosporus No 66, etc) which were marked on the funnel and later on plates on the side of the bridge wing houses, and names, which were not recognised by Lloyds until 1954, but were always in use. Şirketi Hayriye merged in 1944 with two other companies, the Haliç company, which operated small numbered (Haliç 1 . . .) launches, all long since scrapped, on the Golden Horn, and the AKAY company, which operated to the southern part of the Asian shore, and to the Princes Islands, and from whose fleet the remaining three pre-1939 steamers came.

A considerable group of ferries were withdrawn from 1984 to 1987, and while some have been sold, there is often no confirmation of further service. Withdrawn steamers lie at a breakwater at the western end in the large shipbuilding and repair yard at Pendik. There is no public access, but I have personally photographed them by obtaining access to the garden of a neighbour-

Burgaz, Kadiköy, 1984

ing villa, courtesy of the gardener and maid, who seemed happy to let me in to take photos, if rather puzzled.

In addition to all the steamers, there are the three large diesels of the -bahçe class, eight Dutch and Turkish-built post-war diesels, (some now being withdrawn), fourteen modern motorships of the Sehit class, six larger motorships of the Maltepe class, similar to the Fairfield 1961 steamers, and four small launches on the Golden Horn service. All except the latter are impressive vessels, with an immediate post-war trend to ugly designs halted, and most of the recent vessels being of reasonable appearance. There are also some fifteen diesel car ferries, including those on the Dardanelles services.

The current fate of the recently withdrawn steamers is rather uncertain; a number were sold in 1986 and 1987, and others were up for sale, and may have been sold, though the sale has not yet been reported. Those vessels still in steam or being restored are listed in Part One, while those undergoing conversion or whose future is uncertain are listed in Part Two.

Suvat, Üsküdar, 1986

route 1b in 1984 and on a variety of routes in group 1 in 1986. She was originally listed in Lloyd's Register as *Bourgaz* but this is merely the difference between the French and English transliteration of the old Ottoman script, which was in use until about 1933. The steamer has a very well kept buffet. She is distinguished, like all the older generation of steamers, by wooden panelling in her main and upper deck saloons.

ISTANBUL

SUVAT
ÜLEV

Twin screw steamers
Built: 1938, Atlas Werke, Bremen, Germany; rebuilt 1965; 637gt;
62.4m × 10.3m; 1626 pass
Machinery: two triple expansion, Burmeister & Wain
(*Suvat*)/Christiansen & Meyer, Hamburg (*Ülev*); 850hp
Route: 1a; 4a; 1f

ISTANBUL

BURGAZ*

Twin screw steamer
Built: 1912, Ateliers & Chantiers de Provence, Port Bouc, France;
697gt; 61.3m × 9.4m; 1445 pass
Machinery: two triple expansion by builder's Marseilles yard; 790hp
Route: 1f; 1b; 1a

The last pre-1914 steamer in service, *Burgaz* is recognisable by a tall funnel, with a short extension pipe. She was converted to oil-firing and her engines rebuilt (with new builder's plate) at the Halic yard in 1961. She operated on

Originally similar to the earlier steamers, but rebuilt in 1965 with a modern funnel, these two vessels now appear as slightly smaller versions of the 1961 steamers, without the topmost passenger deck. They are often used as relief vessels on other routes, including those to the Princes Islands.

Fairfield-built *Ataköy*

Büyükdere approaching the Bosporus bridge, 1986

Büyükdere, Eminönü pier, 1986

YALOVA*
BÜYÜKDERE

Twin screw steamers
Built: 1948, Verschure, Amsterdam; 561gt; 54.4 × 10.9m
(*Yalova*)/8.3m (*Büyükdere*); 1041 pass
Machinery: two triple expansion by builders; 680hp;
Route: 2a; 2b; 1f

Last survivors in steam of a sextet of Dutch-built steamers which came from a consortium of builders and engine builders, these vessels are of basically similar design to the earlier ferries; these two can be distinguished from the remainder of the sextet by domed tops to the funnels, and by being oil-burners, although it is unclear whether they were built as such or converted later.

Opposite top: Yalova leaving Beşiktaş, 1986

Opposite bottom: Yalova off Beşiktaş, 1986

HARBIYE†
PENDIK†
ATAKÖY (ex Genclik 1961)*
KUZGUNCUK
TEGMEN ALI IHSAN KALMAZ (ex Ihsan Kalmaz)
INKILAP
TURAN EMEKSIZ
KANLICA

Twin screw steamers
Built: 1961, Fairfield, Glasgow; 781gt; 69.9m × 13.6m; 1952 pass
Machinery: two compound in tandem on each shaft, by builder to Christiansen & Meyer design (except† - by Christiansen & Meyer, Hamburg); 1600hp; 13kn
Route: 1a; 3a

The final culmination of Clyde-built steam ferry design, these vessels can be distinguished in appearance from similar, locally built, motorships by taller, but still modern, funnels. Mainstay of the Karaköy to Haydarpasa and Kadiköy routes, where their high passenger capacity is probably frequently exceeded, they operate a very intensive service, every ten minutes at peak periods, on the twenty-minute crossing of the Bosporus. Loading and unloading is by both main and upper decks, and by gangways both fore and aft of the engine room, although few Turks wait for the gangway to be put in place; the macho thing is to jump off as soon as the ship touches the pier. Even so, it takes five to ten minutes to clear a load of passengers in the rush hours. This group are also used for summer weekend service to the Princes Islands.

HURRIYET

Double-ended screw steamer (one screw each end), car ferry
Built: 1960, Haliç, Istanbul; 894gt; 58.2m × 16.0m; 480 pass
Machinery: two triple expansion, Klawittwer, Danzig, 1914; 640hp; 8kn
Route: 1d, 1e

This steam car ferry is fitted with engines from one of a group of three ferries, *Kinalida*, *Maltep*, and *Pendik*, built by Klawitter in 1914 and scrapped in the early sixties, and is probably next in line for withdrawal. The vessel is named after Istanbul's main newspaper. Of seven similar car ferries, two were scrapped in 1987, and the remainder may be scrapped or converted to diesel. All these steam car ferries are true double-enders, and have no passenger accommodation on the car deck, only fairly spartan saloons on the upper deck. An eighth steam car ferry, *Karamürsel*, was built with a unique system of propulsion, one set of paddle wheels at each end. The engines were second-hand from the then recently scrapped paddle steamers *Bagdad* and *Basra*, which had been built in 1904 by Howaldtswerke of Kiel. Built in 1956, *Karamürsel* must have been difficult to manoeuvre, and only lasted a few years. She may have subsequently been used as a pontoon, but I have no definite knowledge. Clearly, if she is still in existence, and the engines are still in her, they will be of considerable historic importance.

Kuzguncuk with Costa Lines' *Enrico C* behind, 1986

ORHAN ERDENER

Double-ended screw steamer (one screw each end), car ferry
Built: 1962, Haliç, Istanbul; 1198gt; 67.2m × 20.0m; 738 pass
Machinery: two triple expansion, by builder; 740hp; 9kn
Route: 1d; 1e

*O*rhan Erdener is typical of a group of seven locally-built car ferries, all in operation until 1986 in the city, but possibly with previous service on the Dardanelles and Kartal-Yalova routes. Her engines are listed as being built by the Halic yard, but they may have been reconstructed from engines from scrapped steamers of that time; gauges, etc, seem to be have been interchangable, with some from Dresden and some from Clydeside in the same engine room.

HÜSEYIN HAKI

Double-ended screw steamer (one screw each end), car ferry
Built: 1964, Haliç, Istanbul; 1072gt; 67.2m × 20.0m; 738 pass
Machinery: two triple expansion, Simons, Renfrew; 750hp; 9kn
Route: 1d; 1e

*H*üseyin Haki is a steam car ferry, built with engines from the salvage vessel *Imroz I*, ex *HMS Salvage Duke*, which had been lost in 1959, but the engines salvaged. Like all the Istanbul car ferries except *Kartal* (now scrapped), her boilers were new buildings by Ottenser Eisenwerke, Hamburg-Altona. I have no record of her vehicle capacity, but around 24 cars can probably be carried.

Semsipaşa in mid-Bosporus (Selim San)

SEMSIPAŞA

Double-ended screw steamer (one screw each end), car ferry
Built: 1966, Haliç, Istanbul; 1072gt; 67.2m × 20.0m; 738 pass
Machinery: two triple expansion by builder; 740hp; 9kn
Route: 1d, 1e

A similar car ferry to *Orhan Erdener*, with a similar history. Sister ship *Sirkeci* was withdrawn and sold in 1987, and *Kartal* and *Kabatas* were scrapped.

Car ferry *Hüseyin Haki* detail

Guzelhisar leaving Beşiktaş, 1986

GÜZELHISAR

ex *Güzelhisar/Bosporus No 68*
Twin screw steamer
Owner: Sehir Hatlari Isletmesi
Built: 1911, Hawthorn Leslie, Newcastle upon Tyne; 453gt; 46.4 ×
7.9m; 903 pass
Machinery: two triple expansion, Wallsend Slipway, Tyneside; 440hp;
coal-fired

Last of the former Sehit Hatlari steamers to remain in service, *Güzelhisar* was withdrawn in December 1986, but retained by the company for use as a museum ship, and possibly for future operation on charter for making films. One of a group of 14 large twin screw ferries, two of which were sunk in World War I, two scrapped in the late sixties, and all but one of the remainder of which survived in service until major withdrawals started in the early eighties, an amazing testimony to the skills of British and French shipbuilders. All were steamers of great character, with tall funnels, wooden-sided saloons and open foredecks. They operated in their last years on the Bosporus commuter runs and the Besiktas to Üsküdar ferry, the route that *Guzelhisar* served in her last year in service.

Boğaziçi as a restaurant steamer, 1984

KALENDER

ex *Kalender/Bosporus No 67*
Twin screw steamer
Owner: Denizciler Sendikasi
Built: 1911, Hawthorn Leslie, Newcastle upon Tyne; 453gt; 46.4 ×
7.8m; formerly 853 pass
Machinery: two triple expansion, Wallsend Slipway, Tyneside; 440hp,
coal-fired

Sister of *Güzelhisar*, *Kalender* was withdrawn in 1984, and reportedly sold in 1986 to Denizciler Sendikasi (Turkish Seamen's Union) for use as a training ship. The similar *Küçüksu*, built in 1910 by Ateliers & Chantiers de France, Dunkirk, was withdrawn in 1974, but reinstated by 1981 after protests in view of her important war record in World War I at Gallipoli. By the time she was finally withdrawn in early 1986 she was the penultimate steamer of this class in service.

BOĞAZIÇI

ex *Boğaziçi/Bosporus No 66*
Twin screw steamer, undergoing restoration
Owner: Ufuk Denizcilik
Built: 1910, Fairfield, Glasgow; 434gt; 46.8 × 7.9m; formerly c900 pass
Machinery: two triple expansion by builders; 455hp; coal-fired

Halas under restoration, Büyükdere, 1986

Withdrawn in about 1981, *Boğaziçi* was taken to Marmaris, on the Aegean coast and used as a floating restaurant. She returned to Istanbul in 1984 and was extensively refitted, work which included extending the upper deck aft saloon right to the sides of the steamer and the fitting of an executive office on the bridge, with an astro-turfed passenger deck created aft of the bridge with deck chairs. *Boğaziçi* was fitted with very plush restaurant fittings, with the flock wallpaper common in Indian restaurants in the UK, and a diesel generator was installed in her engine room (perhaps from a former truck engine); in spite of all that she still a steamer of character. She commenced service from Kabatas is summer 1984 on meals-inclusive cruises to the Princes Isles or on the Bosporus by day, and up the Bosporus in the evening. Burnt out in September 1984, the ship is now hauled up on a slipway at Tuzla for eventual rebuilding.

ISTANBUL

HALAS

ex *Halas/Bosporus No 71*, ex *HMS Waterwitch* 1921, laid down as
Reşit Paşa/Bosporus No 73
Twin screw steamer
Built: 1915, Fairfield, Glasgow; 584gt; 46.7 × 7.9m; formerly 911 pass
Machinery: triple expansion by builders; 700hp; coal-fired

Laid down as a sister to *Sarayburnu* and *Boğaziçi*, but requisitioned while on the stocks by the Royal Navy as a despatch steamer, *Halas* was finally sold to Şirketi Hayriye in 1923, possibly having been based at Istanbul prior to that. She was originally to be numbered 73, but numbers 71 and 72 had been ordered from Hawthrorn Leslie and cancelled during the war, so *Halas* bore the number 71. Refurbished and used in the seventies on tourist excursions, she was withdrawn in 1984, sold and converted for use on restaurant cruises. She was seen May 1986 looking very smart, almost ready for service, with a white hull and pale buff funnel; I have had no reports as to whether she actually entered service. When she originally entered service in Turkey she was also known as *Kurtuluş*, meaning 'deliverance' and was seen as a sign of the fresh beginnings in the country after the end of the civil war which saw the triumph of Kemal Atatürk, and the beginning of the westernisation of Turkey.

EAST GERMANY
(German Democratic Republic)

EAST GERMANY IS PROBABLY one of Europe's richest and most varied countries as far as veteran steamers and motorships are concerned. The highlight must be, of course, the fleet of paddle steamers on the Elbe at Dresden, which includes a number of centenarians, but there are also interesting ex-steamers both at Berlin and on the Baltic Coast. The DDR as a country has a healthy interest in transport history, and veterans are often well documented, with a number preserved as 'technological monuments'.

Almost all Fleets are state-owned, and excursion boat operations are known as Weisse Flotte (White Fleet), followed by the name of the area.

It should be noted that hotel or campsite reservations have to be made before an entry visa is issued, except for East Berlin where a day visa from West Berlin is available, although this latter prohibits travel beyond the city limits. Once inside the country, travel is not generally restricted, with a rail network like Britain's before Beeching. I personally have travelled in the Dresden and Berlin areas without restriction, but there may be some restriction on the movement of Westerners and on photography in certain parts of the Baltic coast area, for example at Wolgast.

The Dresden paddlers are unique in Europe, and indeed in the world, with a whole fleet of pre-1900 oscillating-engined steamers in service. While a few have been withdrawn in recent years, one major encouraging sign for the future of the steamers is that while, for a number of years, second-hand tug boilers were utilised when the original boiler wore out, in more recent years new boilers have been built for the older steamers. One would imagine that the present fleet is comparatively safe for the future.

The steamer routes from Dresden pass through interesting and varied scenery along the river Elbe. Details are given for peak season operations, but sailings start at Easter and continue until the end of October. Some four services operate upstream from Dresden to Bad Schandau or Schmilka on the Czechoslovakian border, each morning, returning in the afternoon, with a further Bad Schandau-based roster giving an afternoon upstream departure from Dresden, and a further Pirna-Bad Schandau-Pirna roster. The route upstream first passes through the suburbs of Dresden, then passes Pillnitz Palace, then reaches the area known as 'Saxon Switzerland', where the river flows through a rocky gorge.

There are also sailings to from Dresden to Decin, and from Bad Schandau to Usti, in Czechoslovakia, and two-day trips from Dresden to Usti, but these two latter trips are under the auspices of the Deutsches Reisebüro and have to be pre-booked. There may be visa problems for Westerners on these trips, and the two day trip would entail missing a night already paid for at a Dresden hotel. In 1985, the first two trips were by one of the diesel-electric paddlers, and the Usti trip was worked by two modern motor vessels working in tandem.

Downstream, the Elbe passes through pastoral countryside to the cathedral city and porcelain centre of Meissen, and on to Riesa. One sailing daily goes to Reisa, and another to Meissen certain days of the week. There are also local cruises at Dresden, including coffee cruises, and evening cruises.

Three Elbe paddlers other than those listed here survive in static use elsewhere in East Germany, as does the centre section of *Meissen* (1881), on service on the Elbe until 1907, then until 1967

on the Weser as *Kronprinz Wilhelm,* preserved in the (West) German Maritime Museum at Bremerhaven.

Two further Dresden paddlers have been scrapped in recent years; *Bad Schandau* (1892) in 1978, and *Einheit* (1873) in 1983. The latter had been withdrawn in 1974, and saw two years in use as a restaurant ship at Dresden before a long lay up period.

The last paddle steamer at Magdeburg, *Hermes* (1878), was scrapped in 1979 after 11 years out of service. The steam paddle tug *Württemberg* (1909) has been preserved on dry land at Magdeburg since 1975. She is a typical two-funnelled Elbe tug of a type which were once numerous.

The waters around Berlin, with the rivers Spree, Havel and Dahme and a number of connecting lakes and canals, have seen the operation of a large fleet of steamers and motorships down through the years, although no operating steamers survive. In 1928 there were 230 passenger vessels in operation in the city, 82 steamers and 148 motorships. Partition of the city has led to the division of the cruising areas between West Berlin and East Berlin.

The Berlin steamers evolved as a distinctive type; twin screw steamers with tall funnels, and main and upper deck saloons. On dieselisation, the funnels were invariably removed because of the many bridges, and so a lot of their character was lost. From 1889 to 1911 some 28 steamers of four standard classes were built at Stettin, and a number of these survive as motorships.

The East Berlin routes are probably the more scenic, and the most popular route is the five-hour trip 'round the Müggelberge', starting from the Weisse Flotte's base at Treptow park, sailing along the Spree to Köpenick, then on a circular route including a crossing of the large open Müggelsee lake, followed by a section along the canalised Müggelspree, a picturesque narrow section with overhanging willow trees which is lined by very western-looking holiday homes with attractive gardens running down to the canal. On this section there is often a sudden commotion, as a photographer races up a strange wooden scaffolding tower at the water's edge and takes a photograph with an antique plate camera of the passengers on the foredeck of the vessel as it passes. Copies of these photos are available by the time the trip returns to Treptow. The route then follows another, wider canal, crosses a couple of other lakes, and returns to Köpenick by the river Dahme. This trip is offered six times daily, with one trip continuing along a further industrialised canal to the pretty village of Woltersdorf, terminus of an antique interurban tramway connecting with the main railway line. At Woltersdorf there is a large lock, giving access to further lakes and canals. The lock is surmounted by a footbridge, which makes an excellent viewing platform. Woltersdorf is half a mile outside the Berlin city area covered by the 24-hour visa, but there seem to be no controls on the boats.

There are many longer excursions available, one even going as far as Bad Saarow, a six and a half hour single journey each way from Grünau (near Köpenick) halfway to the Polish border through a succession of lakes and canals. There is also a regular service, as distinct from excursions, from Friedrichshagen, on the Müggelsee, to Woltersdorf and Alt-Buchhorst. Tickets are cheap, but seat reservations are compulsory on the excursions.

Lowering the funnel and masts on *Stadt Wehlen*, 1985

In 1945 the DSU was founded, and gradually took over the vessels of the private owners in the Russian sector of Germany. In 1956 the Weisse Flotte Berlin took over operations in Berlin, although private owners remained, one as late as 1980, chartering their ships to the Weisse Flotte.

Most of the more popular excursion services in East Berlin are operated by modern motorships, and the few veterans that survive are often used on charter duties.

The river Havel flows south into Berlin, drawing its waters from a myriad of lakes reaching almost as far as the Baltic coast. From Berlin, the Havel flows on through Potsdam and Brandenburg before meandering across country to join the Elbe near Wittenberge. Passenger services operate at Potsdam, Brandenburg and Rathenau on the lower Havel, and at Fürstenberg, Rheinsberg and Lychen on the upper Havel, also at Kyritz, (river Dosse and Dosse lake), Neuruppin (Ruppiner See), Templin (Röddelinsee), Mirow and Waren (Müritz-Havel Kanal and Müritz See), and at Plau (Plauer See) on the Havel and its tributaries. Other services in the area on lakes which do not drain into the Havel are on the Kummerower See at Malchin and Demmin, on the Tollensesee at Neubrandenburg, on the Ücker See at Prenzlau, on the Krakower See at Krakow, and at Schwerin on the Schweriner See.

DRESDEN, RIVER ELBE

STADT WEHLEN*

ex *Mühlberg* 1962, ex *Dresden* 1926
Paddle steamer
Operator: Weisse Flotte Dresden
Built: 1879, Werft Blasewitz, Dresden; lengthened 1895; 56.4m × 5.2/10.4m; 802 pass
Machinery: compound oscillating, Ruston & Co, Prague, 1857; reconstructed 1915; 180hp; coal-briquette fired; new boiler 1979
Route: Dresden–Bad Schandau–Schmilka; Dresden–Riesa

Oldest steamer in the Dresden fleet, *Stadt Wehlen* is a typical Elbe paddler with a long narrow hull and the oscillating engines which were fitted to all the pre-1914 paddlers. The lower part of her machinery is original from 1857, having been fitted in an earlier *Dresden* of that year, but the upper part dates from 1915, when the original simple expansion machine was converted to a compound. An upper deck was added in 1950, and a second new boiler and major overhaul in her centenary year of 1979 have seen her fit for many more years' service. As on all the steamers, her engines and boiler are visible, and she is recognised as a historic vessel, details of her history being prominently placed on board. The funnel is cranked down by hand in order to pass under bridges.

Meissen at Riesa, 1985

DRESDEN, RIVER ELBE

DIESBAR

ex *Pillnitz* 1927
Paddle steamer
Operator: Weisse Flotte Dresden
Built: 1884, Werft Blasewitz, Dresden; 50.1m × 4.7/9.6m; 584 pass
Machinery: simple oscillating, 1857, John Penn & Son,
Greenwich; 110hp; coal-briquette fired; new boiler 1959
Route: museum ship at Dresden, expected to re-enter service 1988

Last of an earlier generation of steamers, *Diesbar* was restored in order to function as a museum ship at Dresden for the 150th anniversary of the Elbe steamers in 1986. She is distinguished by having no upper deck, merely a canopy over the after deck, and a taller, thinner, funnel, now painted black rather than the silver of the remainder of the steamers. Her engines are the last simple, non-compound oscillating set in operation, probably anywhere in the world, and were originally in *Pillnitz*, ex *Stadt Meissen*, of 1857. She is little changed since building; a wheelhouse and steam steering gear, rather than tiller steering at the stern, were added in 1928, and the roof on the after deck as late as 1963. In 1976 she was chartered for one summer season on the Czechoslovak section of the river, but was subsequently used as a reserve steamer only, being laid up from 1980 onwards. It is to the management's credit that they realised her historic significance, and repaired her at their own works at Laubegast. She was opened to the public at the 150th anniversary celebrations of the Elbe paddle steamers in June 1985, with an exhibition in her fore saloon on the lower deck, and it is planned to complete the second stage of the renovation and to restore her to steam by the 1988 season.

DRESDEN, RIVER ELBE

MEISSEN

ex *Sachsen* 1928, ex *König Albert* 1898
Paddle steamer
Operator: Weisse Flotte Dresden
Built: 1885, Werft Blasewitz, Dresden; lengthened 1928; 60.7m × 5.6/11.3m; 1042 pass
Machinery: compound oscillating, ÖNWDG, Dresden; 230hp; coal-briquette fired; new boiler 1985
Route: Dresden–Bad Schandau–Schmilka; Dresden–Riesa

Meissen, fitted in 1985 with a new large fore-saloon, normally takes her place along with *Weltfrieden*, *Dresden* and *Leipzig* on the busy morning departures from Dresden. She had had an earlier fore-saloon, to a different design, built in 1959, and an upper deck and aft deck saloon added in 1928. Her engines, originally similar to *Diessen*, were compounded in 1914. She re-appeared in her centenary year after a major refit with a new boiler, the new narrower fore deck saloon replacing the previous one which looked as though a shed had been placed on the deck, and an extended after deck saloon, also with centenary motifs on her paddle boxes, which, as on all the Elbe paddlers, have no vents. A feature of the steamers are the crests on the paddle boxes, often that of the town after which the steamer is named; *Weltfrieden* has a globe and dove of peace.

WELTFRIEDEN

ex *Pillnitz* 1952, ex *Diesbar* 1927, ex *Köningin Carola* 1919
Paddle steamer
Operator: Weisse Flotte Dresden
Built: 1886, Werft Blasewitz, Dresden; lengthened 1927; 60.5m × 5.6/11.2m; 603 pass
Machinery: compound oscillating, ÖNWDG, Dresden; 230hp; coal-briquette fired; new boiler 1983
Route: Dresden–Bad Schandau–Schmilka; Dresden–Riesa

Renamed in 1952 in the cause of world peace, *Weltfrieden*, like *Meissen*, has been reconstructed in recent years with a fore saloon, and takes her place on the busier services, where restaurant service is offered. Her engine was rebuilt and compounded in 1912, and she narrowly escaped conversion to a cargo ship in 1923. In 1927 she was lengthened, and an aft deck saloon and upper deck were built, while the fore deck saloon was added in 1967. In 1943 she was used to transport evacuees during the bombing of Hamburg. She was used in the 1978 season for the two-day Usti excursions, and then underwent a major overhaul from 1979 to 1983, when she was fitted with new fore and aft deck saloons, a new boiler and funnel, a steel upper deck in place of the wooden one, and a new wheelhouse. As on many of the paddlers, engine and boiler parts and even steam pipes are labelled for the interest of passengers.

Weltfrieden at Stadt Wehlen pier, 1985

KURORT RATHEN

ex *Bastei* 1956
Paddle steamer
Operator: Weisse Flotte Dresden
Built: 1896, Werft Blasewitz, Dresden; 55.5m × 5.4/10.3m; 752 pass
Machinery: compound oscillating, Kette, Dresden-Übigau; 145hp; coal-briquette fired
Route: Dresden–Bad Schandau–Schmilka; Dresden–Riesa

Kurort Rathen is similar to *Stadt Wehlen*, with a small upper deck fitted in 1928. Her engine was built as a compound type. Like all the Dresden paddle steamers, she has a hinged funnel, which is hand-cranked. Another feature of these river steamers is the long pole which is used to steady the vessel when she stops at a pier. Because of the strong current in parts of the river, on reaching the pier when approaching from down-stream the engine is reversed and a long pole, kept handy on the foredeck, is swung by a crew member and stabbed into the riverbed; the crewman then hangs on grimly until the steamer is stationary and the gangplank can be out ashore. Spare poles are kept stored on the foredeck for the frequent occasions when the poles break.

Kurort Rathen at the Laubegast yard, Dresden, 1985

Below: Pirna leaving Blasewitz for Dresden, 1985

DRESDEN, RIVER ELBE

PIRNA*

ex *König Albert* 1919
Paddle steamer
Operator: Weisse Flotte Dresden
Built: 1898, Werft Blasewitz, Dresden; 56.1m × 5.0/10.4m; 740 pass
Machinery: compound oscillating, Kette, Dresden-Übigau; 145hp; coal-briquette fired
Route: reserve steamer at Dresden Laubegast

Currently used as a reserve steamer, *Pirna* is of the same pattern as *Stadt Wehlen*. She was used as a floating office at the Junkers factory in Dessau in 1943-44, and had a coal-bunker fire in 1972, but resumed service the following season. A replacement boiler, probably second hand, was fitted in 1974-5.

DRESDEN, RIVER ELBE

JUNGER PIONIER

ex *Sachsen* 1951, ex *Karlsbad* 1946
Operator: Weisse Flotte Dresden
Built: 1898, Werft Blasewitz, Dresden; 56.1m × 5.0/10.3m: 740 pass
Machinery: compound oscillating, Kette, Dresden-Übigau; 145hp; coal-briquette fired
Route: Dresden-Bad Schandau-Schmilka; Dresden-Riesa

Sister of *Pirna*, *Junger Pionier* received a second-hand tug boiler in 1978. She was the last ship built at the Blasewitz yard before it was replaced by the present Laubegast yard. She is a fast steamer, with slightly wider paddle floats than the other steamers, and was fitted with steam steering from building; most earlier steamers were built with tiller steering at the stern. Refitted and out of service in 1985, she returned to service in midseason in 1986, and was reserve steamer in 1987. The Dresden fleet annually carries some 1,500,000 passengers, from a peak of 3,630,351 in 1898, and currently runs around 80,000km per year.

DRESDEN, RIVER ELBE

DRESDEN

Paddle steamer
Operator: Weisse Flotte Dresden
Built: 1926, Werft Laubegast, Dresden; 68.7m × 6.9/12.7m; 1363 pass
Machinery: compound diagonal, WUMAG, Dresden-Übigau; 275hp; coal-briquette fired
Route: Dresden-Bad Schandau-Schmilka

One of only two survivors with conventional diagonal engines, *Dresden* is of a much more modern type than the older steamers, and was built with an aft deck saloon and an upper deck. She also has twin rudders, of a type used on Rhine steamers. She is used on the more important sailings, such as the mid-morning departure from Dresden. She is also used for charters, and in 1984 carried Presidnet Kim Il Sung of North Korea, who was so impressed that he ordered an exact replica to be built for service in North Korea. This entered service in 1986, named *Pyongyang No 1,* apparently identical in every detail with *Dresden*, and is reckoned to be the first of a fleet of steamers at Pyongyang, operating from the city to a nearby amusement park. *Dresden* was damaged by fire in 1946, and thus escaped being requisitioned by the Russians, not re-entering service until 1949, when a fore deck-saloon was added. She received a major overhaul in 1979-80.

Leipzig heading upstream from Dresden, 1985

Dresden on the Elbe, 1985

Stadt Wehlen Bastei at Stadt Wehlen, 1985

DRESDEN, RIVER ELBE

LEIPZIG*

Paddle steamer
Operator: Weisse Flotte Dresden
Built: 1929, Werft Laubegast, Dresden; 69.7m × 7.0/12.8m; 1487 pass
(see below)
Machinery: compound diagonal, WUMAG, Dresden-Übigau; 325hp;
coal-briquette fired
Route: Dresden–Bad Schandau–Schmilka

Similar to *Dresden*, but very slightly larger, *Leipzig* represents the final stage of paddle steamer development on the Elbe. She was used as a hospital ship between 1942 and 1944, and was bombed and sunk in 1945, but rebuilt and returned to service in 1949; unlike her sister, she did not receive a fore deck saloon until 1978. Although listed as carrying 1487 passengers, a notice seen on board in 1985 showed only 890, which may indicate a general cut-down on certificated capacity. Catering, as on all the Elbe paddlers, is rather unusual with meals and even drinks being served by waiters who come round the decks at certain times with certain items; for example, they may come first with a tray of beer glasses, then with orange squash, and an hour or so later the saloon may be set with coffee and cakes. It seems almost impossible to obtain anything other than at those times, which can lead to a hungry trip for the enthusiast who has not come prepared. There are shops on most of the steamers, selling souvenirs, postcards, and chocolates, but on some they are below decks in the galley area, although still open to the public. Postcards are also sold by the purser's office, often in sets; these are inexpensive and generally come with the steamer's stamp on the back. Passenger loads are high, with many East Ger-

mans and also tourists from many of the eastern bloc countries. Fares are very low, around 75p for the three or four hour single trip to Schmilka.

STADT WEHLEN, RIVER ELBE

STADT WEHLEN BASTEI

ex *Pötzscha-Wehlen-Bastei*, ex *Specht* or *Helene*
Screw steamer
Operator: VEB Binnenreederei
Built: 1927, Werft Laubegast, Dresden; 14.5m × 3.5m; 78 pass
Machinery: compound, Maschinenfabrik Übigau; 45hp; coal-fired
Route: Elbe ferry at Stadt Wehlen, reserve steamer

This is a small steam passenger ferry, usually lying at Stadt Wehlen, but used to replace the normal ferry when the water is very high, or when the river is icy; the normal ferry is unusually driven by a cable connected to a wire crossing high above the river. There are a number of similar passenger ferries along the stretch of the Elbe from Pirna to the Czech border, but all the others are diesel, and I have no historical details. The engines of the last paddle ferry, *Bad Schandau I* (1908), which was scrapped in 1972, are preserved in the Elbe Shipping Museum at Lauenberg (see West German section). The privately preserved steam tug *Sachsenwald* (1914) usually lies in a backwater of the Elbe opposite Königstein, between Stadt Wehlen and Bad Schandau.

BRANDENBURG, RIVER HAVEL

NORDSTERN

Steam tug, ex passenger steamer tug
Owner: L Bischoff, Brielow
Built: 1902, Wiemann, Brandenburg; 26.0m × 4.8m
Machinery: triple expansion; 260hp

Built for combined passenger service from Brandenburg to Berlin, and also for use as a tug, *Nordstern* is still in steam, and in commercial operation as a tug. She is probably of the same type as *Johannes* (see The Netherlands); a tug with a small canopy aft for occasional passenger use. She now has no permanent passenger accommodation.

WOLGAST, BALTIC SEA

STRALSUND

Steam train ferry
Operator: Deutsche Reichsbahn
Built: 1890, Schichau, Elbing; 37.5m × 9.8m; 3 rail carriages
(no passengers)
Machinery: 2 × 112.5hp
Route: Wolgast–Usedom

This amazing survivor is classed as a 'technological monument', and thus is believed to be safe from scrapping. She was built for the train ferry from Stralsund to Altefähr on the island of Rügen, on the main rail route from Berlin to Sweden, but in 1901 she was transferred to a service at Peenemunde, near Wolgast, home of the German rocket bases in World War II. She operated here until taken to the present route in 1950. She was rebuilt in 1987, when both engines were taken out of the steamer and taken to Dresden for rebuilding; a new boiler was provided, and she is still in steam. She has twin funnels, with a small bridge atop a metal inverted 'V' structure. For some time prior to rebuilding she had been powered by a tug tied alongside, as her engines were out of order. Wolgast is a naval base, and photography is believed to be strictly forbidden.

POLAND

AS FAR AS is known, there are no veteran steamers in operation in Poland; however, a few paddle steamers survive in static use, including possibly one ex British paddler. The major area of operation was on the river Vistula from Gdansk to Warsaw. One other steamer of note is the steam training ship, former trawler *Jan Turlejski*, built at Gydnia in 1953, with triple expansion engines by Rankin & Blackmore of Greenock, makers of *Waverley*'s engines. She was withdrawn in late 1985, and is now used as a stationary boiler. *See Part Two.*

Steam train ferry *Stralsund* at Wolgast, 1984 (Claus Rothe, courtesy World Ship Society)

CZECHOSLOVAKIA

THE MAIN ATTRACTION for the enthusiast in Czechoslovakia is the group of four paddle steamers in operation on the Vltava, a tributary of the Elbe, from Prague. They are fascinating, and subtly different from the Dresden paddlers, although of similar basic design. One other interesting survivor is the hull of the last stern-wheel paddle tug in existence, *SL-4*, in use as a static workboat at Decin. She was built at Stettin in 1895, and was operated as *Preussen* for a Stettin owner until 1932, then by Czech owners, renamed *CSPO IX*, and later *Rip*. She was withdrawn in about 1953, then used as workshop ship at Hamburg for some time before coming back to Czechoslovakia. Lying at Prague, and planned for eventual preservation is the small paddle tug *A Lanna 1* (1890), an interesting small single funneled steamer, withdrawn in about 1960.

PRAGUE, RIVER VLTAVA

DĚVÍN*

ex *T G Masaryk* 1952, ex *Karlstein* 1945, ex *Antonín Švehla* 1942
Paddle steamer
Operator: Osobní Lodní Doprava v Praze (OSD), Prague
Built: 1938, Ústecka Lod, Ústí (Aussiger Schiffswerft, Aussig); 62.0 × 5.6/10.5m; 885 pass
Machinery: compound diagonal, CKD, Prague; 220hp
Route: Prague–Slapy Dam, river Vltava

*D*ěvín was intended when built for service on the Elbe, in connection with the Dresden paddlers *Leipzig* and *Dresden*, but, with her sister *Vyšehrad*, she was hurriedly pulled back to Prague when Germany annexed the Sudutenland in 1938, and never operated on the Elbe in passenger service. In 1944 she was used as a floating soup kitchen in bombed Dresden. She had a major rebuild in 1961, and was converted to oil-firing in 1979. Services are normally upstream to Slapy, on a varied route passing through the industrial outskirts of Prague and on past a deep gorge section of the Vltava (named Moldau in German). The river has been damned in a number of places for hydro-electric power, and a notable feature are the very deep modern locks. The final section is quite spectacular, on a steep-sided lake behind a dam; the section from Štěchovice to the foot of the large Slapy Dam has only been navigable since completion of locks in 1955. Modern motor vessels operate on the lake above the Slapy Dam. *Děvín* and her sister differ from the other two Prague paddlers in having an upper deck open to passengers, probably only a feature since the 1961 rebuild, although this is cleared when the steamer passes under low bridges, and in having a hydraulically operated funnel-lowering mechanism; the two smaller paddlers have hand-cranked funnels. Sailings are twice daily in summer to Slapy, and catering is rather basic.

Opposite: Vyšehrad and *Labe* at Prague, 1985

Děvín at the Slapy terminus, 1985

PRAGUE, RIVER VLTAVA

VYŠEHRAD

ex *Dr Edvard Beneš* 1952, ex *Wischerad* 1945, ex *Labe* 1942, ex
Dr Edvard Beneš 1939
Paddle steamer
Operator: OSD
Built: 1938, Ústecka Lod, Ústi (Aussiger Schiffswerft, Aussig); 62.0 ×
5.6/10.5m; 885 pass
Machinery: compound diagonal by CKD, Prague; 220hp
Route: Prague–Slapy Dam, river Vltava; charters; evening cruises in
Prague

Vyšehrad has a similar history to *Děvín*; she was rebuilt in
1959, converted to oil-firing in 1980, and underwent
major refurbishment, including the addition of restaurant seating in her main deck saloons, in 1983-4. Her 1985 sailings were charters to Cedok travel agency, evening cruises
including a typical Czech meal, which were marketed to foreign
tourists. This was an innovation, because the Prague steamers
are not usually 'sold' in this way; in fact the tourist information
office in the city is hard pressed to come up with any information at all about them. These cruises are operated up and down
the river within Prague itself.

PRAGUE, RIVER VLTAVA

VLTAVA

ex *Moldau* 1945, ex *Vltava* 1941
Paddle steamer
Operator: OSD
Built: 1940, Ústecka Lod, Ústi (Aussiger Schiffswerft, Aussig), com-
pleted at Praga yard, Prague; 54.0 × 5.1/9.1m; 650 pass
Machinery: compound diagonal, CKD, Prague; 150hp
Route: Prague–Slapy Dam, river Vltava

Vltava was built as the prototype for a class of six sisters,
but in the event only one further steamer, *Labe,* was built.
Her upper deck was added in 1960, but removed in 1961
because of stability problems. She was converted to oil-firing in
1979. In appearance she is a smaller edition of *Vyšehrad* and
Děvín.

PRAGUE, RIVER VLTAVA

LABE*

Paddle steamer
Operator: OSD
Built: 1940-1949, Praga yard, Prague; 53.1m × 5.1/9.1m; 500 pass
Machinery: compound diagonal, CKD Prague; 150hp; coal-fired
Route: Prague–Slapy Dam, river Vltava

Last coal-fired steamer of the fleet, *Labe* is in regular
service to Slapy. She is a steamer of character, with an open
bridge and a hand-cranked collapsible funnel to pass under
some extremely low bridges. Her engines, unfortunately, cannot
be seen to great advantage from the passenger deck, unlike most
paddle steamers. She was planned to carry the name *Morava,*
but building was halted by the war and she was not completed
until 1949. Her open after deck was made into a saloon in a 1977
rebuild. She can be distinguished by a black funnel with a red
band, where as the other Prague paddlers have silver funnels with
a red band.

HUNGARY

HUNGARY WAS THE MOST recent area in Europe to give up steamer
operation, when *Budapest* was withdrawn in 1986. Veterans
include static vessels on the Danube at Budapest (and one former
Danube paddler elsewhere), and the old motorships and a further static vessel on lake Balaton. *See part two.*

BULGARIA

BULGARIA'S ONLY VETERAN passenger vessels are on the Danube,
as far as I know; little is known about the vessels, apart from
Radetsky, which was built to commemmorate an important event
in the country's history.

RIVER DANUBE

RADETSKY

Paddle steamer, ex tug
Built: 1954, Budapest; rebuilt 1964; 57.4m × 7.5/17.5m
Machinery: compound diagonal; 400hp
Route: cruises on Danube for members of state youth movements

Radetsky was built as a paddle tug, but reconstructed in 1966
as a replica of the DDSG paddle steamer *Radetsky* of 1851,
which was hi-jacked in 1876 on the Bulgarian section of
the river. Some 200 men came on board dressed as peasants,
then produced guns and took over the ship. The captain was
forced to put them ashore at the village where they had planned
to begin their struggle, and when he had done so, he was given
a statement by the men, witnessed by the passengers, to show
that he had acted under duress, and thus to preserve him from
trouble with the DDSG management. This action by Bulgarian
freedom-fighters marked a major step in the direction of an
independent Bulgaria. Building of the present steamer in 1966
was marked by a re-enactment of this event and a trip to Vienna.
The original tug on which the replica was built was one of around
100 of the Type 732 class built at Budapest in the mid-fifties,
mainly for service on Russian rivers.

RUMANIA

PASSENGER STEAMER SERVICES in Rumania are operated in the
Danube delta region, an area with many channels and islands
and abundant rare wildlife, and on the Danube itself. A fascinating trio of veterans are listed in this book; the oldest passenger
steamer in the world, the first Austrian paddler on the Bodensee, and a turbine steamer that changed the history of Britain.

In the early seventies, at least two further paddlers were in use
in the Danube delta; both are believed scrapped, but could possibly still be extant and laid up. They were *Chiele Bicazului*, ex
Basarab (1893), a former paddle tug converted to passenger use
in 1945; and *16 Februarie*, ex *Brancoveanu* 1951, ex *Vasarheley*
1931, built as a Hungarian paddle tug in 1892 at Budapest, sold
to Rumania in 1931, and converted to a passenger steamer in
1951.

RIVER DANUBE

TUDOR VLADIMIRESCU*

ex *Grigore Manu* 1944, ex *Sarmizgezuta* 1920, ex *Croatia* 1918
Paddle steamer, ex paddle tug 1958
Operator: NAVROM
Built: 1854, Altofen yard, Budapest; rebuilt in present form 1958;
65.8m × 8.0/14.4m; 391 pass
Machinery: compound oscillating, Escher Wyss, Zürich; 600hp
Route: Danube delta; excursions from Tulcea and Galati

Tudor Vladimirescu was long believed to have been built in 1874, and this is stated on the builder's plate, but research shows her to have been built as far back as 1854 for the DDSG, which even at that time had a fleet of 71 steamers. She was used as a tug, and her original 520hp oscillating engine was rebuilt to a compound in 1867. In 1918 she was given to Rumania as war reparations, and continued to operate as a tug until 1958, when she was extensively rebuilt, emerging as a modern two-funneled passenger paddler. As far as is known, she continues to sail, and her original engines are still in operating. A photgraph of similar *Achilles* (1857) shows her original condition to be a flush-decked tug, with a clipper bow, two tall funnels fore and aft of the paddle boxes, and much less in the way of deckhouses than the preserved paddle tug *Ruthof*. A 1939 list of Rumanian vessels shows her as a passenger steamer, so she may have carried some passengers in the pre-war years, but her present condition would appear to date definitely from 1958. This list also shows another *Grigore Manu*, built as DDSG's *Vindobona* in 1898; however, she did not have Escher Wyss engines, and so was probably a different steamer. While *Tudor Vladimirescu* is very historic, with her modern rebuilding she is clearly not as special as *Skibladner*, now dethroned from her position as the oldest passenger steamer in the world.

USSR

THE SOVIET UNION IS the only really unknown country as far as steamers are concerned; there are many river navigations in the country, and quite probably some with veteran river steamers, though much traffic has been placed in the hands of hydrofoil operators in the past twenty years or so. Westerners are not allowed to travel beyond city boundaries without permission, although cruises were offered, through Intourist, prior to the Chernobyl nuclear accident in 1986 on the river Dnieper from Kiev to Odessa, with occasional cruises also taking in part of the Danube, and are currently offered on the Volga, from Kazan to Volgograd. These utilise modern East German built cabin passenger ships.

Long-distance passenger services are operated on these rivers, and also on the river Moscow, which runs into the Volga, thus offering a service south from Moscow to Volgograd, and onwards via the Volga-Don canal to the river Don and the Black Sea (the Volga flows into the Caspian Sea). A service possibly also exists northwards by the Volga-Baltic canal to Leningrad and even to the Arctic through a further canal, also northwards as far as Perm on the Volga. Services are believed to operate in Siberia, on the rivers Yenisei north from Krasnoyarsk, Ob north from Omsk, and Lena north from Yakutsk.

About 500,000km of waterways in the USSR are reckoned to be suitable for navigation or timber floating, with 123,000 used for passenger or cargo traffic: the Volga itself is 3700km long. Many rivers have been tamed and their power harnessed by hydro-electric dams. The Siberian rivers are ice-bound for eight to nine months, and the European for four to six months, although periods when the rivers are passible have been extended in recent years by the effective use of icebreakers.

Records of vessels used are practically non-existent; a large class of cabin passenger paddle steamers, however, was built at Budapest in the 1950s for Russian river service, and it must be assumed that many are still in operation:

1948	S JSEZ LENYIR
NOVOSIBIRSZK	V GUSEV
PERM	VL ARSENIKEV
1949	1956
PETROZAVIDZSK	A KORNEYCHUK
	E BOGRIKY
1952	DOSTOYEVSKY
MAXIM GORKY	G GRENSKY
VLADIVOSTOK	J GALON
	MATROS
1953	S ROUPAK
MAYAKOVSKY	V STAVSKY
NEKRASOV	
PRAVLENKO	1957
SERAFIMOVICH	DOBROLYUBOV
TURGENEV	DZHAMBUL
V SHISHKOV	LESKOV
VS VISHNEVSKY	M SIBIRIAK
	NIKITIN
1954	PISHYEMSKY
A AFINOGENOV	POMYLAVOVSKY
BOGDAN	PRISHVIN
KHMELINITSKY	ZHUKOVSKY
BOR GERBATOR	
DEMS BEDNY	1958
GEN KIRSANOV	BARNAUL
IVAN FRANKO	BIYSK
J KRILOV	KAZAN
J PETROV	RYBINSK
K TRENTOV	SVERDLOVSK
PAV BAZHOV	TOMSK
Z PRIDAVOLIN	UFA
1955	1959
A MAKARENKO	BLAGO VESHENSKY
A MALYSHKIN	KHABAROVSK
AL POLESAY	IRKUTSK
ARK GUJDOR	KRASNOYARSK
H VISHNEVSKY	OMSK
S ALIMOV	

All type 737 paddle steamers
Built: Budapest; 71.4m × 8.25/15.4m; 250 pass
Machinery: compound diagonal; 450hp

Most have a single low funnel, but later examples have two funnels side by side; these include Hungary's *Budapest*, which is of the same class, as is the now scrapped Czechoslovakian paddler *Bratislava* (1958). The steamers have two full length decks and cabin passenger accommodation for the long hauls on the Russian rivers.

PART TWO

CONVERTED AND STATICALLY PRESERVED
STEAM SHIPS

SCOTLAND

RENFREW

RENFREW FERRY

ex *Erskine* 1971, ex *Renfrew* 1962
Steam chain ferry, undergoing restoration at
Renfrew
Owner: Renfrew District Council
Built: 1935, Fleming & Ferguson, Paisley; rebuilt
1962, J Lamont, Port Glasgow; 68ft × 48ft
Machinery: triple expansion driving chain across
river bed; 16hp

In service across the River Clyde from
Renfrew to Yoker until 1952, then a spare
ferry until 1962, when she was rebuilt to
take 20 cars rather than 12 and placed on
the service from Erskine to Old Kilpatrick.
Replaced by Erskine Bridge in 1971, spare
at Renfrew until vehicle ferry service ceased
in 1984, then taken over by Renfrew

District Council. Presently being restored
for exhibition at Glasgow Garden Festival
1988, then as maritime museum at
Renfrew, housing ship models, etc from the
Renfrew shipyards of Simons and Lobnitz,
as well as from her builders and other
Paisley yards.
The diesel-electric Renfrew ferry of 1952 is
presently being rebuilt for use as a
restaurant in Glasgow City Centre.

PORT GLASGOW

COMET

Replica of 1812 paddle steamer, monument at Port
Glasgow
Built: 1962, G Thomson, Buckie/Lithgows Ltd, Port
Glasgow; 21.5t (displ); 44.9ft × 11.4/15.9ft
Machinery: single cylinder side-lever; Lithgows Ltd;
10hp

Replica of Henry Bell's *Comet*, Europe's first
commercial passenger steamer, which

entered service in 1812 from Glasgow to
Helensburgh. Rapid expansion of the Clyde
steamer fleet over the next few years
displaced her to West Highland service
where she was wrecked on Craignish Point
in 1820. Her engine was salvaged, and is
now in the Science Museum, London.

Replica was built for the 150th
anniversary celebrations, made a few
sailings in that year, then lay in Lithgow's
yard for some years, eventually ending up
in her present position surrounded by a
high fence in the centre of Port Glasgow.
Interior and engine not accessible to the
public

LOCH NESS AND CALEDONIAN CANAL

SCOT II

Motor vessel, ex steamer 1960, combined
tug/icebreaker/inspection vessel/passenger vessel
Operator: British Waterways Board
Built: 1931, Leith; 57gt; 75ft × 15.1ft; 70 pass
Route: cruises Inverness–Caledonian Canal–Loch
Ness; three sailings daily

Built for use as an ice-breaking tug on the
canal, converted to passenger use and
dieselised in 1961; still also used as
inspection vessel on Canal.

Opposite top: Comet replica, Port Glasgow
town centre

Opposite bottom: Scot II, Inverness, 1978

Left: Renfrew Ferry at Erskine, 1971, a few
days before withdrawal

Maid of the Loch when still in service

Wingfield Castle awaiting restoration, Hartlepool, 1986

Below: Lincoln Castle, Hull Corporation pier, late 1960s

ENGLAND

GATESHEAD

CALEDONIAN PRINCESS

Also known as *Tuxedo Princess*
Restaurant and nightclub ship at Gateshead, river
Tyne, ex turbine cross-Channel car ferry steamer
Owner: Quadrini Group
Built: 1961, Wm Denny & Bros, Dumbarton;
4042gt; 353ft × 57.2ft; formerly 1400 pass
Machinery: two Pametrada steam turbines by
builder; 4960shp

Built for British Railways crossing from
Stranraer to Larne. Stern-loading only, and
when superseded by bow and stern loaders
saw service from 1970 onwards on routes
from Fishguard to Rosslare, from
Weymouth to the Channel Islands, and as
general relief steamer on Sealink services.
Operated for one season in 1981 on the
Dover to Calais service, as the English
Channel's last turbine steamer in operation.

Withdrawn at the end of that season,
purchased by her present owners and
converted, with major changes in passenger
accommodation, to present role as
nightclub/bar/restaurant. There are plans to
move her to Glasgow.

RIVER TYNE

SOL EXPRESS

ex *Earl Siward* 1981, ex *Dover* 1977
Turbine cross-Channel car ferry steamer, laid up on
river Tyne; proposed conversion to
restaurant/nightclub ship
Owner: Quadrini Group
Built: 1965; Swan Hunter & Wigham Richardson,
Newcastle; 3641gt; 369ft × 57.2ft; formerly 3602
pass
Machinery: two Pametrada steam turbines,
Wallsend Slipway; 10,350shp; 20kn

Built for British Rail's Dover-Boulogne
service, later used from Holyhead to Dun
Laoghaire. Renamed *Earl Siward* in 1977
following refurbishment, and spent a
further period based at Dover, also being
used as relief ferry on other Sealink routes
until withdrawal in 1981.

Purchased by Cyprus based Sol Ferries for
service from Piraeus to Cyprus, but laid up
after a year or two because of the high cost
of operation of a steamer. Brought back to
the Tyne in 1986. It is planned that after
rebuilding she will replace *Caledonian
Princess* at her Gateshead berth.

HARTLEPOOL

WINGFIELD CASTLE

Paddle steamer (car ferry), undergoing restoration
as museum ship at Hartlepool, Cleveland
Owner: Hartlepool Museums
Built: 1934, W Gray & Co, Hartlepool; 556gt;
209.7ft × 33/57ft; formerly 1200 pass, 20 cars
Machinery: triple expansion diagonal, Central
Engineering Works, Hartlepool; 1200hp, coal fired,
13kn

Operated on Humber ferry service from
Hull to New Holland with occasional
excursion sailings until withdrawal in 1974.

Then moved to the Thames, and later
Swansea for possible use as a restaurant
ship, but no plans came to fruition. Brought
back to her birthplace in 1986 for full
restoration as a museum and memorial to
local shipbuilding. Work done on her will
use the work-force that has successfully
restored *HMS Warrior*.

HARTLEPOOL

DUKE OF YORK

Semi-derelict ex houseboat, ex screw steam launch,
at Hartlepool
Built: 1894, Thames Electric and Steam Launch Co,
Twickenham; 80ft × 13.5ft

Built as private steam launch on Thames
for Andrew Pears (of Pears Soap fame);
later ran as passenger steamer until 1941,
when the engines were removed for scrap
to help the war effort, and she was
converted to a houseboat. Now lying on top
of quay at Hartlepool, near *Wingfield Castle*.
Interesting design with fore and aft saloons
with clerestory roofs.

SCARBOROUGH

REGAL LADY

ex *Oulton Belle* 1954
Motor vessel, ex steamer 1954
Operator: T Machin & K Garside, Scarborough
Built: 1930, Fellows & Co, Great Yarmouth; 75gt;
84ft; 222 pass
Route: excursions from Scarborough

Built as a double-ended steamer for the
route from Yarmouth to Lowestoft, to
similar design to *Yarmouth*. Veteran of
Dunkirk, and rebuilt after the war as a
single-ended steamer, sold to Scarborough
owners in 1954, when she was renamed
and dieselised, and used there until 1970.
Then based at Norwich until her return to
Scarborough in 1987.

GRIMSBY

LINCOLN CASTLE

Restaurant ship, ex paddle steamer (car ferry), at
Grimsby
Owner: C Jackson, Cleethorpes
Built: 1940, A & J Inglis Ltd, Pointhouse, Glasgow;
598gt; 208.8ft × 33.1/55.5ft; 1200 pass; 20 cars
Machinery: triple expansion diagonal, Ailsa
Shipbuilding Co Ltd, Troon; 850hp, 13kn

Last paddle steamer on the Hull-New
Holland ferry service, withdrawn in 1978
following failure of a boiler survey. Differs
from *Wingfield Castle* and *Tattershall Castle*
in having her funnel and boilers forward of
the paddles rather than aft. Used as a
restaurant on the shore at Hessle until
c1986, when moved to Immingham for
refitting before starting a similar role at
Grimsby under new ownership.

BINFIELD, ISLE OF WIGHT

RYDE QUEEN

ex *Ryde*
Restaurant ship at Binfield, River Medina, Isle of
Wight, ex paddle steamer
Owner: unknown
Built: 1937, Wm Denny & Bros, Dumbarton; 566gt;
223ft × 29/52.5ft; formerly 1011 pass
Machinery: triple expansion diagonal; 14kn

Traditional paddle steamer used on
Portsmouth to Ryde ferry service by the
Southern Railway, later British Railways,
and on excursions on the Solent.
Withdrawn 1969, moved to present
location 1972 after lay up. Damaged by fire
1977, but later repaired.

The engines are still in place, but the
boiler has been removed and a disco dance
floor built in the former boiler area. New,
at present un-named, owners, a property
development company, were reported to
have bought her in late 1987. They plan to
restore her and keep her in her present
static role.

SOUTHAMPTON

CALSHOT

ex *Galway Bay* 1987, ex *Calshot* 1964
Twin screw motor vessel, ex steam tug/tender
1964, undergoing restoration at Southampton
Owner: Southampton Museums
Built: 1930, J L Thornycroft, Southampton; 702gt;
147ft × 33.1ft; 422 pass (at Galway)

Built for Red Funnel Steamers as a
combination vessel to be used both as a tug
and to tender liners at anchor in the
Solent, *Calshot* also undertook excursions
down Southampton Water to see the liners
such as *Queen Mary* sail. Sold in 1964 to a
subsidiary of Holland America Line, who
had then introduced calls at Galway, she
undertook excursions to the Aran islands,
and continued on these for CIE for many
years after the liner calls had ceased. A
daily summer service to Inishmore was
maintained until 1986, and she was sold at
the close of that season to Southampton for
restoration as a museum ship.

GOSPORT

VADNE

Yacht club, ex screw steamer 1965
Owner: Gosport Cruising Club, Weevil Lake,
Gosport
Built: 1939, Vosper, Portsmouth; 75gt; 73ft × 19ft
Machinery: compound

Used on Portsmouth to Gosport ferry until
service 1965, latterly as reserve steamer. No
recent information.

PLYMOUTH

SOUTHERN BELLE

ex *Shuttlecock* 1947
Motor vessel, ex screw steamer 1947
Built: 1928, Rogers, Cremyll; 26gt; 66ft; 159 pass
Route: excursions from Plymouth including river
Tamar and Yealm

On River Dart for a short while c1983 but
normally based at Plymouth; can be
distinguished from her sister *Northern Belle*
by having two masts.

PLYMOUTH

NORTHERN BELLE

ex *Armadillo* 1945
Motor vessel, ex screw steamer 1945
Operator: Tamar Cruising and Cremyll Ferry
Built: 1929, Rogers, Cremyll; 25gt; 66ft; 174 pass
Route: Plymouth–Cremyll Ferry

Sister of *Southern Belle*, originally fitted with
private cabin for use of Earl of Mount
Edgecumbe and his family, the Mount
Edgecumbe Estate being owners until 1945;
on same route all her life.

FALMOUTH

PRINCESSA

Motor vessel, ex steamer 1950s
Operator: G H & W G Pill, Falmouth
Built: 1921; 48gt; 65ft; 125 pass
Route: excursions from Falmouth to Helford river
and River Fal

Former Portsmouth–Gosport ferry; later in
service for Blue Funnel Cruises on local
excursions from Southampton from mid
fifties to c1985.

TRURO

COMPTON CASTLE

Restaurant ship, ex paddle steamer, at Truro
Owner: D Worlledge
Built: 1914, Cox, Falmouth; 97gt; 108ft × 17.5/28ft
Engine removed, now in museum at Blackgang
Chine, Isle of Wight

Former River Dart paddler, fleetmate of
Kingswear Castle, withdrawn 1962;
restaurant at Kingsbridge 1964-1978. At
Looe for planned restoration to steam
1978-1982, by which time the plans had
not come to fruition, and she was rotting
away. Her present owner has considerably
altered her for the worse, and she bears
little resemblance to her condition as a
steamer.

LLANERCH-Y-MOR, DEE ESTUARY

DUKE OF LLANERCH-Y-MOR

ex *Duke of Lancaster*
Restaurant, nightclub and market ship, ex turbine
cross-channel steamer, at Llanerch-y-Mor, Dee
Estuary
Owner: Empirewise Ltd
Built: 1956, Harland & Wolff, Belfast; 4450gt;
376.1ft × 57.4ft; formerly 1200 pass, 105 cars
(from 1970)

Built for British Railways Heysham to
Belfast service, but undertaking a number of
cruises in her earlier years. Converted from
a passenger-only steamer to a car ferry
steamer in 1970, but unfortunately this
conversion did not give enough headroom
for commercial vehicles; the service became
uneconomic and was withdrawn in 1975.

Then used as relief steamer at Holyhead
until 1978; used in present role since 1980
with market on car deck, amusement
arcade, shops, etc. Berthed on mud in Dee
estuary remote from other shipping.

PRESTON

MANXMAN

Restaurant and nightclub ship, ex turbine cross-
channel steamer
Owner: Manxman Leisure
Built: 1955, Cammell Laird, Birkenhead; 2495gt;
325ft × 47ft; formerly 2301 pass
Machinery: two Pametrada steam turbines; 7500hp;
20kn

Last to be built, and only survivor, of a
group of six similar classic passenger cross-
channel steamers operated by the Isle of
Man Steam Packet Co; operated until 1982
on services from Douglas to Liverpool,
Llandudno, Dublin, Belfast, Ardrossan, and
Fleetwood. The last surviving classic (i.e.
passenger only) cross-channel turbine
steamer in northern Europe. Following her
withdrawal from service she had a film
role, disguised as the Russian steamer
Moskva, before moving to her final berth at
Preston. Radically remodelled inside for use
as a nightclub, with two discos, three
restaurants and eight bars. Engines have
been retained in situ. Traditional colours
replaced by a rather garish new colour
scheme.

Manxman as a nightclub, Preston, 1987

Swift on Windermere, 1981

MARYPORT

FLYING BUZZARD

ex *Harecraig II* 1987, ex *Flying Buzzard* c1960
Museum ship, ex screw steam tug/tender
Owner: Maryport Maritime Museum
Built: 1951, Ferguson Bros, Port Glasgow; 261gt;
114.9ft
Machinery: compound

Tug built for the Clyde Shipping Co with
small saloon and certificate for 150
passengers for attending ships on trials.
Later at Dundee, now open as a museum
ship at Maryport.

At nearby Whitehaven is Britain's last
working harbour steamer, the dredger
Clearway (1927).

LAKE WINDERMERE

TERN

Twin screw motor vessel, ex steamer 1958
Operator: Windermere Iron Steamboat Co
Built: 1891, Forest, Wivenhoe, Essex; 120gt; 140.3ft
× 18.1ft; 608 pass
Route: Lake Windermere, excursions from
Bowness on Windermere; also Christmas cruises

Built for the Furness railway's service on
Windermere; an attractive vessel with a
canoe-like hull. Continued under railway
ownership until Sealink was privatised in
1984. New owners resurrected present
company name, used from 1848 to 1858 by
a steamer operator on the lake. There has
been talk of a possible return to steam for
Tern, but this is probably unlikely at the

present time. Her current colour scheme
with white hull and yellow funnel with
black top is probably the most suitable of a
number of recent liveries. Her present route
was new in 1987, previously she had taken
her place on the Lakeside–Bowness–
Ambleside service.

LAKE WINDERMERE

SWIFT

Twin screw motor vessel, ex steamer 1957, laid up
Owner: Windermere Iron Steamboat Co
Built: 1900, T B Seath & Co, Rutherglen; 203gt;
150ft × 21.1ft; 724 pass

Built for Furness Railway, and used until
the early eighties; now laid up at lakeside.
More traditional design than the canoe-like
Tern.

ULLSWATER

LADY OF THE LAKE

Twin screw motor vessel, ex steamer 1935
Operator: Ullswater Navigation & Transit Co Ltd
Built: 1877, T B Seath & Co, Rutherglen; 45gt; 97ft
× 14.7ft; 220 pass
Route: Glenridding–Howtown

The smaller of the two veterans on
Ullswater, *Lady of the Lake* can be
distinguished by a shorter saloon. Badly
damaged by fire 1965, she did not re-enter
service until 1979, when she was fitted
with new engines. Normally used on a
high-season extra service from Glenridding
to Howtown.

LAKE WINDERMERE

DRAKE

Diesel chain ferry, ex steamer 1960
Built: 1954, Lytham Shipbuilding & Engineering Co;
70gt; 65ft
Route: car ferry across Windermere

ULLSWATER

RAVEN

Twin screw motor vessel, ex steamer 1935
Operator: Ullswater Navigation & Transit Co Ltd
Built: 1900, T B Seath & Co, Rutherglen; 58gt;
112.3ft × 15ft; 284 pass
Route: Glenridding–Howtown–Pooley Bridge

Veteran with uneventful career on
Ullswater; now on her second set of diesels,
fitted in 1964. The very scenic route passes
the foot of some of England's highest
mountains, and is very popular with
walkers.

DEWSBURY, CALDER & HEBBLE CANAL

MAY QUEEN

Motor launch, perhaps ex steamer
Owner: Robinsons Hire Cruises, Dewsbury
Built: 1922; 58ft; 80 pass
Route: cruises on Calder & Hebble Navigation,
Dewsbury

Operated at Chester to 1980, then briefly at
Sheffield and Newark, before coming to
present owner in 1985. The present owner
hopes to restore her to steam.

NEWARK, RIVER TRENT

SONNING

Motor vessel, ex steamer 1947
Operator: Greens Passenger Launches, Newark-
on-Trent
Built: 1902, Salter Bros, Oxford; 38gt; 85ft; 196
pass
Route: Excursions on River Trent from Newark,
occasionally to Nottingham

Formerly in Salters fleet on Thames, sold to
Newark 1983; classic Salters ex-steamer
with half-saloon aft.

LONDON, VICTORIA EMBANKMENT

QUEEN MARY

ex *Queen Mary II* 1976, ex *Queen Mary* 1935
Former triple screw turbine excursion steamer,
undergoing conversion to restaurant ship
Owner: Bass Charrington Ltd
Built: 1933, Wm Denny, Dumbarton; 1014gt;
252.5ft × 35.1ft; formerly 1820 pass
Machinery: three direct-drive turbines by builders

Final development of the Clyde turbine
steamer, and direct descendant of *King
Edward* (1901), first commercial turbine
steamer in the world, *Queen Mary* sailed for
most of her life from Glasgow's city centre
Bridge Wharf to the resorts of the Clyde
Coast. Renamed in 1935 to free the name
for the Cunarder *Queen Mary*, she operated
the Gourock to Dunoon ferry service during
the war years, and was reboilered and
converted to oil-firing in 1957, receiving
one large funnel in place of her two small
ones. From 1970 onwards she was based at

Gourock on a variety of Clyde excursion
sailings, and was withdrawn at the end of
the 1977 season.

After two years laid up at Greenock
having been bought by Glasgow District
Council for use as a museum ship, she was
sold for use on the Clyde as a restaurant
ship, but stayed at Greenock. In 1981 she
was purchased by a Chinese restaurateur
and moved to the Thames. Her turbines
and boiler were removed, two turbines
being presented to the Science Museum and
the other being placed on deck as the
planned centrepiece of a restaurant. Work
progressed slowly on conversion while she
was berthed at Tilbury.

In 1987 she was sold to the brewers Bass
Charrington, who had previously operated
the Clyde paddler *Caledonia* (1934) in a
similar role as *Old Caledonia* until she was
destroyed by fire in 1980. She was then
towed to Chatham Historic Dockyard and
dry-docked. It is planned to renovate her
there, and to have her towed into position
as a restaurant on the Victoria Embankment
in central London by mid-1988. It is to
Glasgow District Council's disgrace that
they did not preserve *Queen Mary*, and it is
to be hoped that what remains of her can
be finally used again as a restaurant.

Queen Mary II approaching Millport Keppel
pier

LONDON, ST KATHERINE'S DOCK

YARMOUTH

Restaurant and museum ship, ex double-ended
screw steamer
Owner: Taylor Woodrow Ltd, St Katherine's Dock,
London
Built: 1895, T Bradley, Great Yarmouth; 56gt; 74ft
× 16ft; formerly 180 pass
Machinery: compound, Crabtree & Co, Great
Yarmouth; 70hp

Double-ended ferry built for Yarmouth to
Gorleston service, although she spent a few
years after World War I on the
Southampton to Hythe run, and was latterly
on excursion services from Yarmouth.
Withdrawn in 1969, moored at
Woodbridge, Essex until taken to London
under her own steam in 1973. On display
on the top of the quay at St Katherine's
Dock since 1976.

LONDON, THAMES EMBANKMENT

TATTERSHALL CASTLE

Restaurant ship, ex paddle steamer
Owner: Chef & Brewer Ltd
Built: 1934, W Gray & Co, Hartlepool; 556gt;
209.6ft × 33/54.7ft; formerly 1200 pass, 20 cars
Machinery: triple expansion diagonal, Central
Marine Engineering Works, Hartlepool; coal-fired

Sister of *Wingfield Castle*, even launched on
the same day. Operated Hull to New
Holland ferry service across the Humber
until 1972, then moored on Thames in
central London at the Embankment,
initially as an art gallery, and from 1982 in

her present role as pub and restaurant. Well maintained, engine still in situ, but car deck partially decked over to provide a covered walkway from the gangplank to the saloon entrance.

LONDON, RIVER THAMES

QUEEN ELIZABETH

Motor vessel, ex steamer 1947
Operator: Westminster Party Boats, London
Built: 1924, Salter Bros, Oxford; 93gt; 110ft × 16.7ft; 275 pass
Route: Westminster to Thames flood barrier at Woolwich

Sister of *Abercorn*; one of few Thames vessels to retain funnel; operated by Mears, and later Thames Launches, on up-river service for many years; tunnel stern.

LONDON, RIVER THAMES

VICEROY

Motor vessel, ex steamer 1929
Operator: Catamaran Cruisers, London
Built: 1902, Gosport; 62gt; 70ft; 207 pass
Route: Charing Cross to Tower Pier and Greenwich; charters

Former Portsmouth harbour ferry, used on Thames since 1929; recently had saloon added on upper deck.

LONDON, RIVER THAMES

ABERCORN

Motor vessel, ex steamer 1948
Operator: Catamaran Cruisers, London
Built: 1925, Salter Bros, Oxford; 107gt; 110ft × 16.7ft; 276 pass
Route: Charing Cross to Tower Pier and Greenwich; charters

Like many Thames veterans, has been much altered over the years, with a new upper deck saloon in 1986. Has tunnel stern to reduce draft, like many Salters-built vessels. Owned by Mears, Richmond, and used on upstream services prior to World War II.

LONDON, RIVER THAMES

VISCOUNT

Motor vessel, ex steamer 1948
Operator: Thompsons Launches, Westminster
Built: 1908, Salter Bros, Oxford; 75gt; 100.6ft × 16.6ft; 275 pass
Route: Westminster to Tower Pier and Greenwich

Used until 1948 by Mears, Richmond, then by Thames Launches until they gradually sold their fleet in the seventies; altered from original appearance.

LONDON, RIVER THAMES

HURLINGHAM

Motor vessel, ex steamer 1947
Operator: Tidal Cruises, London
Built: 1915, Salter Bros, Oxford; 114gt; 101.3ft × 16.5ft; 249 pass
Route: Westminster to Tower Pier and Greenwich

Similar history to *Viscount*; tunnel stern.

LONDON, RIVER THAMES

MARCHIONESS

Motor vessel, ex steamer 1953
Operator: Tidal Cruises, London
Built: 1923, Salter Bros, Oxford; 46gt; 85.5ft × 14.5ft; 152 pass
Route: Westminster to Tower Pier and Greenwich

Similar History to *Viscount*. She is one of the few remaining 'little ships' which took part in the Dunkirk evacuation in 1940, and, like all these, carries a commemorative plaque on board.

LONDON, RIVER THAMES

VISCOUNTESS

Motor vessel, ex steamer 1945
Operator: Tidal Cruises, London
Built: 1926, Salter Bros, Oxford; 116gt; 110.3ft × 16.6ft; 255 pass
Route: Westminster to Tower Pier and Greenwich

History similar to *Viscount*; tunnel stern vessel; new steel saloon 1983.

LONDON, RIVER THAMES

FERRY PRINCESS

Motor vessel, ex steamer 1968
Operator: Woods River Services, London
Built: 1948, Gosport; 74gt; 73ft; 256 pass
Route: Westminster to Tower Pier and Greenwich

Former Portsmouth to Gosport ferry, included here, although post-war, as she was built as a steamer.

LONDON, RIVER THAMES

ROYALTY

Motor vessel, ex steamer 1948
Operator: George Wheeler Launches
Built: 1913, Salter Bros, Oxford; 110gt; 101.2ft; 249 pass
Route: Westminster to Tower Pier and Greenwich

Also operated by Mears and Thames Launches; recently had new wheelhouse added.

Viscount between Tower Bridge and Greenwich, 1980

LEIGH ON SEA

FERRY PRINCE

Motor vessel, ex steamer 1967, laid up
Owner: Thames Pleasure Craft Ltd
Built: 1939, J Thornycroft, Southampton; 70gt; 72ft; 230 pass

Former Portsmouth Harbour ferry, sold 1967 for London services; currently laid up at Leigh on Sea.

LONDON, RIVER THAMES

CONNAUGHT

Motor vessel, ex steamer 1951
Operator: S A Metcalf, Westminster
Built: 1911, Salter Bros, Oxford; 77gt; 106ft × 16.6ft
Route: Westminster to Kew and Hampton Court (summer); Westminster to Greenwich (winter)

Probably the best preserved of the traditional Thames vessels with half-saloon aft, *Connaught* is expertly turned out with a blue hull and white, black-cowled funnel with crest. A tunnel stern boat, she has run on up-river services from London most of her life. New engines fitted 1983.

LONDON, RIVER THAMES

HENLEY

Motor vessel, ex steamer 1958
Operator: J J Shearing, London
Built: 1896, E Clarke & Co, Brimscombe, Thames & Severn Canal; 36gt; 80ft; 149 pass
Route: Westminster to Kew, Richmond, Hampton Court

Part of Salters fleet until 1976 when sold to present owners, in near-original condition, appearance spoiled by a bright blue hull in 1987.

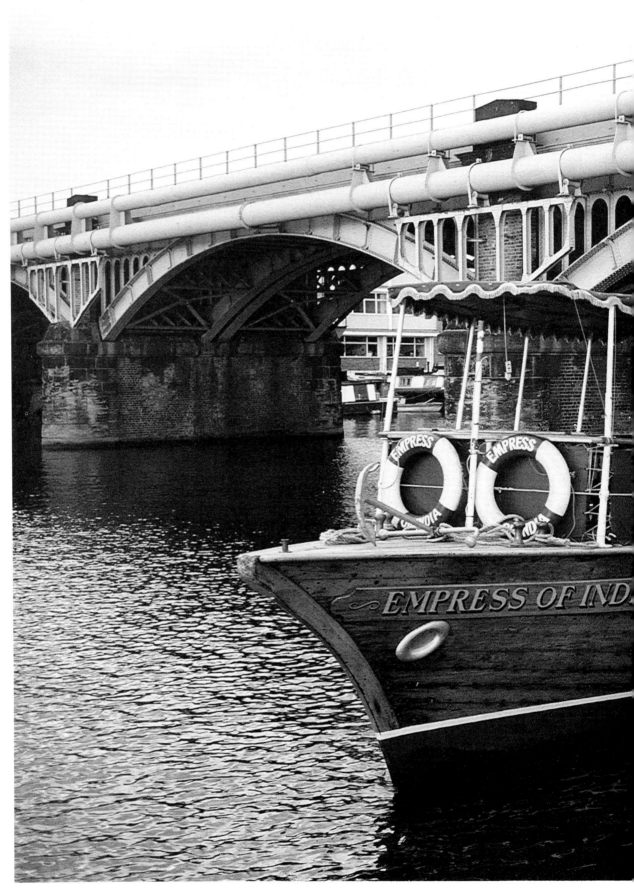

Empress of India, restored but diesel-powered

LONDON, RIVER THAMES

THE KING

Motor vessel, ex steamer 1948
Operator: Thames Tripping, Westminster
Built: 1902, H Tagg, Hampton Court; 50gt; 81 ft ×
14.5ft; 196 pass
Route: Westminster to Kew, Richmond, Hampton
Court

Built by original owner, used by him until
1915, then by Mears, Kingston, for about
30 years; since then by various owners;
traditional design.

LONDON, RIVER THAMES

KINGWOOD

Motor vessel, ex steamer 1950
Operator: C H Wyatt, Westminster
Built: 1915, Salter Bros, Oxford; 71gt; 101.2ft ×
16.5ft; 225 pass
Route: Westminster to Kew, Richmond, Hampton
Court

Tunnel stern vessel; formerly Mears, then
Thames Launches; like a number of others,
used as a hospital launch on the Thames
during World War II; saloon rebuilt after
fire 1976.

KINGSTON, RIVER THAMES

EMPRESS OF INDIA

Motor vessel, ex steamer c1952
Operator: Turks Launches, Kingston
Built: 1898, Bond Boat Building Co, Maidenhead;
53gt; 71ft; 75 pass
Route: executive charters from Kingston

Attractive vessel with varnished hull;
operated on excursions from Maidenhead
1898-1921, Windsor 1921-1976, and at
Kingston 1976-1986. Recent refurbishment
for the de-luxe charter market has included
the fitting of a dummy funnel and return to
'Victorian' appearance, and she now
operates meal-inclusive charter cruises;
traditional design with half-saloon aft.

KINGSTON, RIVER THAMES

NEW WINDSOR CASTLE

Motor vessel, ex steamer
Operator: Turks Launches, Kingston
Built: 1923, Jacobs Ltd, Windsor; 85gt; 94ft; 175
pass
Route: Kingston to Hampton Court; charters

Traditional vessel with aft half-saloon and
varnished hull; operated for builder at
Windsor until 1972, then at Kingston.

KINGSTON, RIVER THAMES

EM

Motor launch, probably ex steamer
Operator: G H F Parr, Kingston
Built: c1900; 44.6ft; 59 pass
Route: Kingston to Hampton Court

Attractive small varnished-hull launch of
unknown origin, in service at Windsor
1933-1955, since then from Kingston.

KINGSTON, RIVER THAMES

YARMOUTH BELLE

Twin screw motor vessel, ex steamer
Operator: F & B Boat Co, Kingston
Built: 1892; 28gt; 60ft; 153 pass
Route: Kingston to Hampton Court

Very ugly conversion of old vessel,
probably formerly based at Great Yarmouth
for Norfolk Broads trips; on Thames from
c1948 onwards, operated by Thames
Launches 1956-1971.

RUNNYMEDE, RIVER THAMES

HURLEY

ex *Phoenix*, ex *Caucase*
Motor vessel, ex steamer
Operator: French Bros, Runnymede
Built: 1914; 27gt; 66ft; 96 pass
Route: Runnymede to Windsor; Runnymede to
Hampton Court

Rebuilt 1924 from a fire-damaged private
launch, operated by Salters until 1931.
Operated at Evesham along with *Gaiety*
from the late twenties until the sixties, and
was derelict by the early seventies, when
she was purchased by her present owners,
returned to the Thames, and rebuilt in
modern form.

RUNNYMEDE

NUNEHAM

Motor vessel, ex steamer c1960, undergoing
restoration
Operator: French Bros, Runnymede
Built: E Clarke & Co, 1898; 37gt; 85ft; 150 pass

Typical Salters steamer, but with smaller aft
saloon than most, in their fleet until 1971,
used on Westminster to Hampton Court
route 1971-81, acquired by present owners
1982; on land awaiting major restoration.

RUNNYMEDE, RIVER THAMES

GAIETY

ex *Oxford* 1922
Motor vessel, ex steamer c1929
Operator: French Bros, Runnymede
Built: 1889, E Clarke & Co, Brimscombe (Thames
& Severn Canal); 21gt; 66ft; 141 pass
Route: Thames from Runnymede

Salters' second steamer, operated on their
Thames services until 1929, when she
moved to Evesham by the Kennet and
Avon canal and River Severn. Sold to
French Bros, Runnymede and planned to be
taken back by road late 1987. A white-
hulled, large open launch with no cabin
accommodation; it is possible that the new
owners will take some time to restore her.

BOULTERS LOCK, RIVER THAMES

BELLE

Motor launch, ex steam launch 1950s
Operator: The Maidenhead Steam Navigation Co
Built: Kingston, 1894; 76ft; 80 pass
Route: Charters from Boulters-on-the-River Hotel,
Boulters Lock

In service at Worcester from building till
the mid-seventies; brought back to the
Thames and restored for luxury charter
work; small aft deck saloon; excellently
restored but rather spoiled by the
misleading marketing claim to be 'the
Steamship *Belle*'.

RIVER THAMES

READING

Motor vessel, ex steamer 1949
Built: 1901, Salter Bros, Oxford; 37gt; 80ft; 171
pass

STREATLEY

Motor vessel, ex steamer 1959
Built: 1905, Salter Bros, Oxford; 39gt; 80ft; 182
pass
Laid up in 1987

GORING

Motor vessel, ex steamer 1952
Built: 1913, Salter Bros, Oxford; 47gt; 84.7ft; 199
pass
Laid up in 1987

WARGRAVE

Motor vessel, ex steamer 1950s
Built: 1913, Salter Bros, Oxford; 46gt; 80ft; 199
pass

OXFORD

Motor vessel, ex steamer 1950s
Built: 1922, Salter Bros, Oxford; 44gt; 85ft; 199
pass

HAMPTON COURT

Motor vessel, ex steamer 1950s
Built: 1923, Salter Bros, Oxford; 47gt; 85ft; 199
pass

MAPLEDURHAM

Motor vessel, ex steamer 1959
Built: 1927, Salter Bros, Oxford; 75gt; 105ft; 345
pass

CLIVEDEN

Motor vessel, ex steamer 1966
Built: 1931, Salter Bros, Oxford; 79gt; 105ft; 276
pass
Built: 1930, Salter Bros, Oxford; 40ft; 61 pass
Operator of all the above: Salter Bros
Routes: short cruises from Oxford;
Oxford–Abingdon; Reading–Henley; Henley–Marlow
(high season only); Marlow–Windsor;
Windsor–Staines

Salter Brothers have maintained a service
on the Thames from 1888 until the mid-
seventies, from Oxford right through to
Kingston, and thereafter on the currently-
served stretches of river. They pioneered
the traditional Thames design with a half
saloon aft, and their boats are kept to

Cliveden leaving Windsor, 1987

traditional appearance, with none of the ungainly extra saloons many veterans lower down the Thames have gained. Diesel engines were fitted in the fifties and early sixties.

Daniel Adamson, Boat Museum, Ellesmere Port, 1987

RIVER THAMES

MARLOW

Motor vessel, ex steamer 1956
Built: 1902, Salter Bros; 85ft; 250 pass

Withdrawn from Salters fleet c1974, later moved to Willen Lake, Milton Keynes, to serve as a café; disused for some time, she was moved away in 1987, possibly back to the Thames.

KIDDERMINSTER

BEATRICE

ex steamer 1952, undergoing restoration
Owner: *Beatrice* Preservation Society, Stourport
Built: c1875

Withdrawn 1972 after many years' service; privately owned at Pershore, but purchased by preservation society in 1986, and moved to Kidderminster for restoration on land. Similar to *Belle* at Maidenhead with small aft saloon. History uncertain.

ELLESMERE PORT

DANIEL ADAMSON

ex *Ralph Brocklebank* 1936
Museum ship, steam tug/tender/inspection steamer
Owner: Port of Manchester Authority
Built: 1903, Tranmere Bay Development Co; 173gt; 110ft × 24.5ft; 100 pass
Machinery: compound, J Jones & Sons, Liverpool

Built for the Shropshire Union Canal Co as a passenger-carrying tug, operating a ferry service across the Mersey until 1915. Purchased by Manchester Ship Canal Co in 1920, and used as their tender and inspection steamer. Rebuilt with improved passenger accommodation 1936; gradually used less and less for towing, and used as inspection steamer on the Ship Canal up to early eighties. Now at the Boat Museum at Ellesmere Port, and can only be viewed externally at present.

WATERFORD, RIVER SUIR

CRYSTAL ROSE

ex *Solent Queen* 1984 ex *Ferry King* 1960s
Motor vessel, ex steamer; probably laid up
Built: 1918, Camper & Nicholson, Gosport; 49gt;
64ft; 176 pass

Built for Portsmouth to Gosport ferry
service; sold to Blue Funnel Cruises,
Southampton, dieselised and rebuilt late
fifties; sold to Waterford c1984, and used
on local cruises for a year or two. These
appear to have ceased. No recent
information.

NORWAY

FREDRIKSTAD, OSLOFJORD

HVALER

Preserved motor vessel, ex steamer 1948
Owner: Østfold Maritime School
Built: 1892, Fredrikstad Mek Verksted; 87gt; 83ft ×
16.7ft; formerly 194 pass

In service from building right up to 1979
on local route from Fredrikstad to the
Island of Hvaler. Saved from scrapping by
enthusiasts and preserved, but probably
only sails on charters. She has probably
more in common with the Swedish
steamers than with most Norwegian, which
were designed to operate in more exposed
waters.

FREDRIKSTAD, OSLOFJORD

ALFEN

Motor vessel, ex steamer 1952, probably laid up
Built: 1893, Kristiansand; 133gt; 88ft × 17.3ft

Operated Kristiansand-Arendal until 1934,
in Bergen area 1934-1963, Strömstad-
Fredrikstad until c1980. Typical local
passenger/cargo steamer, dieselised and
lengthened 1952, and rebuilt as passenger
vessel, more to Swedish pattern, after
arrival at Fredrikstad. No recent
information.

SANDEFJORD, OSLOFJORD

STAUPER

ex *Tungenes*, ex *Rogaland*
Repair ship, ex passenger motor vessel, ex steamer
1950
Owner: Nika AS, Sandefjord
Built: 1929, Stavanger Stoberi & Dock; 851gt;
177.2ft × 31.2ft

Coastal steamer used on express route from
Stavanger to Bergen, and also on the Bergen
to Oslo express service; dieselised 1950;
withdrawn 1964 and rebuilt as a special
ship for sandblasting. Sister *Kronprinsesse
Martha*, built at Danzig, now *Sport Rover*,
operated for a short while in the West
Indies as a small cruise ship with an
emphasis on water sports such as
windsurfing, and was then laid up at
Harlingen in Holland for a number of years

before being sold to Californian owners for
proposed conversion to a luxury cruise
vessel to operate out of Barbados.

STAVANGER

RISKAFJORD II

ex *Olava* 1927, ex *Särö* 1884, ex *Byelfen* c1883, ex
Wittus 1881, ex *Sylfid* 1879, ex *Löfstad* 1870s, ex
Oldevig 1870, ex *Särö* 1867
Motor vessel, ex steamer 1952
Operator: 1864, A Keiler & Co, Göteborg; 88gt;
82ft × 14ft; 160 pass
Route: Stavanger-Hommersak

Norway's oldest coastal passenger ship, this
much rebuilt ship has been on this service
since 1927. Originally operated in Sweden
from Göteborg to Särö until 1867, from
Karlstad to Kristinehamn until c1870, and
on a variety of routes on the Baltic coast
until sold to Frederikshald, near Halden,
Norway in 1884 for service to Hvaler island
and over the Swedish border to Strömstad;
used there until 1927. After deck enclosed
in 1934, diesel fitted and new
superstructure built 1952; new engine 1960.

VERDAL, TRONDHEIMSFJORD

VÆRDALEN

Motor vessel, ex steamer 1950s, undergoing
restoration to steam
Owner: Olaf Engvig, Rissa/Verdal
Veteranbåtforening
Built: 1891, Trondhjems Mek Verksted; 49gt; 77.6ft
× 16.6ft

Built as an engines-aft passenger-cargo
steamer for operation on the inner
Trondheimsfjord from Trondheim to
Verdal; later operated in 1930s on route
from Trondheim to Levanger. Sold 1948 to
Kristiansund owners, and later to a number
of different owners, at Trondheim and in
the Vesteraalen islands. Owners in
Vesteraalen converted her to cargo
motorship in early fifties. Purchased for
preservation 1980, and moved to
Trondheim in 1981. She was later moved
to Verdal for restoration, but her owner has
been involved in the restoration of
Hansteen, and so has had little time so far
for *Værdalen.* It is planned to restore her to
steam, and to operate her as a passenger
steamer on the Trondheimsfjord.

SKIEN, BANDAK CANAL

VICTORIA

Motor vessel, ex steamer 1953
Operator: AS Turist Trafikk, Skien
Built: 1882, Akers Mek Verksted, Oslo; 152gt;
96.5ft × 18ft; 150 pass
Route: Skien to Dalen via Bandak canal; daily in
summer

Operated on this service as a passenger-
cargo steamer until 1956, having been
dieselised in 1953, *Victoria* was rebuilt and
returned to service for the tourist trade in
1963. Her route is one of the most varied
scenic routes in Europe. Starting from the
industrial town of Skien, *Victoria* sails up a
lake between rolling hills, then passes
through a staircase of locks on the Bandak

canal, where passengers can walk from one
lock to the next, and pick wild strawberries
on the way! Later the journey crosses long
lakes with high mountains each side.
Recent years have seen some sailings
curtailed at Kviteseid, and a second ship,
Vildanden (1942), was placed on the route
from 1986. This enabled daily sailings to be
given rather than the thrice-weekly in each
direction which had been offered
previously. *Victoria* is an interesting ship to
sail on, if a little lacking in the character
one would expect from a centenarian; this
is made up for, however, by the
magnificence of the scenery.

LAKE FEMUND

FÆMUND II

Motor vessel, ex steamer 1958
Operator: AS Fæmund, Røros
Built: 1905, Ørens Mek Verksted, Trondheim; 81gt;
78.5ft × 17.1ft; 75 pass
Route: lake Femund; Sondervika–Elgå (daily)–
Femundsenden (2 or 3 days per week)

Operating on the little known lake Femund,
on the high fells near the Swedish border,
the veteran *Fæmund II* caters for tourists,
hikers, and even canoeists. When she was
built she was transported to Røros by rail,
and then to the lake by horses. She was
until about ten years ago the only transport
for the isolated communities on the lake
shore, and she is a good sea-boat on a lake
which can be rough at times. In the early
years she was also used as a tug. In 1959
the steam engine was replaced by a 160hp
Volvo Penta diesel, and 1980 a major
change in appearance occurred with the
building of a saloon on the main deck. She
is still the only link with civilisation other
than by four-wheel drive vehicle for a
handful of local inhabitants, and makes a
number of stops at small jetties on the 2¾
hour trip from Søndervika (also known as
Sørvika) to Elgå. There are bus connections
from Røros to Søndervika for her sailings,
and a sail on *Fæmund II* through one of
Europe's last wilderness areas is a
fascinating experience.

Norway also has many veteran coasters,
and a number of these have been converted
from passenger steamers. In most cases
only the hull has remained of the old
steamer. The list below is not exhaustive,
but indicates some important vessels.

ALFRED JENSEN ex *Lyngen*; ex steamer
(1931/474gt); passenger/cargo ship until
1966 for Troms Fylkes Co, then rebuilt to
fishing vessel.

HAMO, ex *Askheim* 1968, ex *Bergum*
1964, ex *Aalvik* 1963; (1929/181gt);
Mjellem & Karlsen, Bergen; former HSD
passenger/cargo steamer, steam version of
Granvin; sold and rebuilt 1962. Purchased
by present owners, Statlandverftet AS, Nord-
Statland, for possible rebuilding 1982. No
recent information.

INLAND, ex *Nessvaag* 1986, ex *Oksnevaag*
1975, ex *Inland* 1956; ex steamer (1876,
122gt); Built; Lindholmen Verft, Göteborg,
Sweden; used as passenger steamer on the
Göteborg to Marstrand route until 1882,
then on Telemark canal up until 1956,

Victoria, Bandak canal, 1985

Below: Fæmund II, Elgå pier, 1985

when she was rebuilt to a coaster. New engine 1966; Lloyd's Register gives speed as 4 knots!

KILORAN, ex *Alverstrømmen* 1973, ex *Alversund* 1966; ex steamer (1926/187gt); passenger/cargo service in Bergen area till 1966, when sold and converted to cargo vessel following boiler failure.

MIRA, ex *Blaaøy* 1971, ex *Hamre* 1951, ex *Tinfos* 1926; (1910//158gt); ex passenger steamer, formerly on Indre Nordhorland Co routes from Bergen, but built for owners at Skien, and in service at Kristiansund 1916-1925, and at Oslo for one year in 1926; diesel coaster from 1950.

NIBETA, ex *Gerlaug* 1967, ex *Lindaas* 1961; ex steamer (1909/123gt); used as passenger/cargo steamer on Bergen local routes until 1960, then converted to coaster.

TAMBURFJELL, ex *Grotting* 1966, ex *Tambur,* ex *Lagatun* 1962 (1914/164gt). Operated at Trondheim until 1962; then converted to diesel coaster.

TUNGHOLM, ex *Helvig* 1954, ex *Bratsberg* 1905, ex steamer (1884/104gt); Passenger/cargo service on Telemark canal until 1905, rebuilt 1954 to cargo ship. No recent information.

VAKA, ex *Oster* 1964, ex steamer (1908/199gt); used as passenger/cargo steamer for Indre Nordhorland Co at Bergen until 1963; rebuilt 1966 to coaster.

SWEDEN

GÖTEBORG
STYRSÖ

Motor vessel, ex steamer 1953
Operator: Styrsöbolaget
Built: 1907, Eriksbergs Mek Verkstad, Göteborg; 184gt; 30.9m × 6.45m; 212 pass
Route: Göteborg–Marstrand; excursions

Used in Göteborg's southern islands, such as Styrsö, until 1970, subsequently on excursion service. Typical Swedish steamer type, with restaurant on upper deck, and bridge on same deck forward. Fitted with a squat motorship funnel when diesel engine fitted in 1953; new tall 'steamer-type' funnel and mainmast were fitted in 1987, giving her a traditional profile again.

GÖTEBORG
OCKERÖ

ex *Färingsö* 1935, ex *Tor II* 1919
Cargo motorship, ex passenger steamer 1958
Owner: unknown
Built: 1904, Motala; 31.7m × 5.9m

One of a group of *Tor* passenger boats in the Stockholm archipelago service, built as quasi-sister to present *Västan*; rebuilt with icebreaker bow 1907; sold to lake Mälar owners in 1919, and to west coast owners in 1935, operated until 1954. Rebuilt as cargo motorship in 1958 and used on the cargo service from Göteborg to Öckerö and

nearby islands. Ran aground 1983, and sold. No recent information.

MARSTRAND
GAMBRINUS V

ex *Prins Oscar*
Private motor launch, ex steamer
Built: 1866, Lindholmen, Göteborg

Used as ångslup at Stockholm, then cargo boat; now privately owned.

TJÖRN
VESTVÅG II

ex *Wisingsborg* 1980, ex *Bjorn III,* ex *Ellen*
Motor vessel, ex tug, ex steam tug
Operator: Orust Kommun
Built: 1885, Motala Verkstad, Motala; 39gt; 19.2m; 100 pass
Route: spare vessel for service Rönnäng–Åstol (small island off Tjörn)

Built as twin screw tug for use at Svartvik, near Sundsvall, then used at Stenungsund; passenger use in late seventies on Vättern, early eighties at Tjörn.

Soten approaching Smogen, 1982

UDDEVALLA

GUSTAFSBERG

ex *Gustafsberg II*
Motor vessel, ex steamer 1951
Operator: Uddevalla Turisttrafik
Built: 1898, Göteborgs Mek Verkstad; 52gt; 19.88m
× 4.34m; 134 pass
Route: Uddevalla-Byfjorden piers-Stången

Used on local services form Uddevalla since
built, steam engine replaced by diesel 1951.

UDDEVALLA

SUNNINGEN

ex *Frithiof* 1936, ex *Östra Skärgården 3* 1918
Motor vessel, ex steamer 1950s
Operator: Uddevalla Turisttrafik
Built: 1911, Motala Verkstad, Motala; 47gt; 23.5m
× 4.8m; 145 pass
Route: Uddevalla-Byfjorden piers-Stången

Built for use at Blekinge, then at Södertalje
1981-36, where she ran alongside *Ejdern*; at
Uddevalla 1936-date; rebuilt 1965. Like
Gustafsberg, a former ångslup (steam
passenger launch).

ELLÖS, ÖRUST

ELLÖSFÄRJAN

ex *Hakefjord III* 1960, ex *Örnsköldsvik* 1941, ex
Rollo 1918, ex *Nordre Elf* 1917
Motor car ferry, ex steamer
Operator: Lysekil Kommun
Built: 1898, Torskag; 92gt; 29.2m; 90 pass
Route: Ragardsvik-Ellös

Modern car ferry constructed on old hull
1962; formerly a typical Swedish steamer
built for Göta river service from Göteborg,
later a tug at Stockholm and at
Örnsköldsvik in north Sweden, returning to
the west coast in 1941. Motorised 1951.

LYSEKIL

SOTEN

ex *Sodra Skärgården* 1943, ex *Glafsfjorden* 1935,
ex *Vaddö* 1915, ex *Arholma* 1913, ex *Skokloster*
1911, ex *Östhammar* 1900, ex *Enköping* 1883
Motor vessel, ex steamer 1948
Operator: Rederi AB *Soten*, Lysekil
Built: 1868, Oskarshamns Varvet; 108gt; 30.3m;
250 pass
Route: Lysekil-Smögen-Kungshamn

The oldest ship in Lloyd's Register, *Soten* is
a veteran that has been generally
overlooked by maritime historians. She sails
daily in the summer along a rather exposed
stretch of the Bohuslän coast, and, at least
until a few years ago, also ran in winter.
She carries a small amount of cargo on the
foredeck, generally crates of beer from the
government liquor store at Lysekil and
empties back, and is of the traditional
Swedish steamer design with open foredeck
for cargo, a raised 'tween deck with saloon
above on the upper deck, and a small
upper deck above the aft deck. There is a
small cafeteria counter.
    Built for service on lake Mälar, she sailed
in the Stockholm archipelago from 1882 to
1900, but her owners went bankrupt after

she ran aground, and she was back on lake
Mälar 1900-1911, then at Norrtalje
1911-1915, later on lake Vänern. Here she
was rebuilt in 1920, with the traditional
Swedish rounded sides of her 'tween deck
straightened to give more cargo space. In
1935 she moved to Göteborg, and in 1943
to her present area. Dieselised in 1948, she
is a remarkable veteran, and is still in
commercial service rather than enthusiast
preservation. In fact she is so popular that
passengers often have to be turned away
from her sailings, particularly evening
cruises.

LYSEKIL

STÅNGEHUVUD

Motor vessel, ex steamer
Operator: unknown, Lysekil
Built: 1868, Lindholmens Varvet, Göteborg; 36gt;
24.1m; 126 pass
Route: Ellos-Lysekil

Amazingly for such an old vessel her
history seems to be little recorded;
normally on services from Ellös to Lysekil,
from 1984 she has been used as a Savings
Bank boat calling at places between
Fiskebäckskil and Bovallstrand.

SMÖGEN

SOTEFJORDEN

ex *St Erik* 1933
Motor vessel, ex steamer
Operator: Hållötrafik, Smögen
Built: 1880; 25gt; 18.9m; 105 pass
Route: Ferry from Smögen to the island of Hållö,
small island with lighthouse and bathing place;
evening cruises

Former Stockholm fire-boat; to Kungshamn
and converted to passenger use 1933; small
vessel with cabin aft and open foredeck.
Formerly operated by *Soten*'s owners.

GOTTSKÄR

LIBERTY

ex *Dover I* 1965, ex *Brattön* 1964, ex *Östrea*
1945, ex *Edvard Melin* 1920
Motor vessel, ex steam tug
Operator: C E Sären, Gottskär
Built: 1882, Göteborgs Mek Verkstad, Göteborg;
18.8m × 4.8m; 45 pass
Route: angling trips from Gottskär

Converted tug, passenger service from
1945; present owner bought her 1965.

KARLSKRONA

KUNGSHOLMEN

ex *Skeppsholmen* 1970s, ex *Herserud* 1925, ex
Sjuan 1909
Motor ferry, ex steamer 1953
Owner; Swedish navy
Built: 1905; Brodins Varvet, Gävle
Military ferry Karlskrona-Kungsholmen

Classic Swedish ferry design. Former lake
Mälar ferry, sister of *Mälaren 3*. Used as
military ferry from 1925 onwards, serving
Coastal Artillery installations on an island
near the Karlskrona naval base.

STOCKHOLM

VÄSTAN

ex *Nya Svartsjölandet* 1937
Motor vessel, ex steamer 1953
Operator: Waxholms Ångfartygs AB
Built: 1900, Motala Verkstad, Motala; 118gt; 32.5m
× 5.9m; 340 pass
Route: Stockholm-Ornö-Utö (cargo/passenger
service Tuesday to Thursday); various archipelago
destinations (weekends)

Of classic design, but with slightly squatter
motorship funnel, and shorter upper deck
with no restaurant, *Västan* operates a
fascinating cargo run to the islands of the
southern archipelago, calling at many
isolated jetties with cargoes as varied as
planks of wood, crates of beer, and pallets
of fruit and vegetables. All this is dealt with
by a small collapsible crane on the
foredeck. At weekends she does extra runs
to other islands. One of six sisters, she was
was built for service on lake Mälar, and
sailed to the islands of Svartsjölandet and
Munsö, fairly near to Stockholm. Run off
that trade by bus competition, she was
purchased by the Waxholm company in
1937 for cargo/passenger use in the
archipelago. Her upper deck was rebuilt in
1945, and a diesel was fitted in 1953, with
a second new engine in 1966. She has been
on her present service since 1968. She is a
fascinating ship to sail on; her route to
Ornö and Utö is extremely scenic and
interesting, and a trip on *Västan* is a world
removed from the tourist image of, say,
Drottningholm. Her withdrawal was planned
in 1984, but a petition to the company by
enthusiasts has managed to save her for a
further few years at least.

STOCKHOLM

DJURGÅRDEN 4

ex *Nybron 2* 1901
Motor passenger ferry, ex steamer 1973
Operator: Waxholms Ångfartygs AB
Built: 1897, Brodins Varvet, Gävle; 41gt; 20.8m ×
5.4m; 207 pass
Route: Stockholm: Nybron-Djurgården

Operated on Stockholm routes since built;
rebuilt 1976, and again in 1987. Last steam
ferry in regular traffic before diesel fitted in
1973. Classic Swedish ferry design, i.e. not
double-ended, but with passengers boarding
at one end and disembarking at the other,
with hydraulic ramps and gates. Prototype
for modern larger ferries *Djurgården 8*
(1977); *Djurgården 9* (1981), and
Djurgården 10 (1982) which now bear the
brunt of the traffic. Djurgården is a popular
island destination near Stockholm city
centre with a park, open air museum, and
amusement park.

Västan unloading timber, 1985

STOCKHOLM

DJURGÅRDEN 7

ex *Elba 2* 1953; ex *Saltsjöbaden 1* 1938
Motor passenger ferry, ex steamer 1971
Operater: Waxholms Ångfartygs AB
Built: 1893, Brodins Varvet, Gävle; 34gt; 20.5m ×
5.36m; 197 pass
Route: Stockholm: Nybron–Djurgården

Built as a connecting ferry from Stockholm
city centre to the terminus of the
Saltsjöbaden suburban railway, used at
Västerås 1938-1952, then on Djurgården
services. *Djurgården 4* and 7 saved from
withdrawal by same enthusiast campaign
that saved *Västan* in 1984. Built as
prototype for classic Swedish local steam
ferry.

STOCKHOLM

NYBRON 1

ex *Färjan 6* 1969, ex *Lidingofärjan 2* 1927
Motor passenger ferry, ex steamer 1969
Operator: Waxholms Ångfartygs AB
Built: 1907, Brodins Varvet, Gävle; 47gt; 20.6m ×
5.4m; 191 pass
Route: Stockholm: Nybron–Djurgården

Built for ferry from Ropsten to Lidingö, in
the north-west of Stockholm, used across
Göteborg harbour 1927-1966; return to
Stockholm 1969.

STOCKHOLM

GUSTAFSBERG VII

ex *Saxaren 73*, ex *Gustafsberg VII* 1929
Motor vessel, ex steamer 1985
Operator: Ångfartygs AB Stromma Kanal
Built: 1912, Oskarshamns Mek Verkstad,
Oskarshamn; 266gt; 34.7m × 7.1m; 310 pass
Route: Stockholm–Gustavsberg; evening cruises

Sadly dieselised after the 1985 season, in
spite of strong protests by enthusiasts, who
even offered to underwrite losses from
retaining steam propulsion. The protests
were in vain, probably because the diesel
machinery had already been bought.
Gustafsberg VII was built as an icebreaking
steamer for a service to the village of that
name, home of a famous porcelain works,
and sailed on that route until 1929, when
she was sold to the Waxholm company and
renamed. She then took her place on the
Ljusterö route, which became her preserve,
and was converted to oil-firing in 1961, but
withdrawn in 1964 after mechanical
problems. After various changes of
ownership, she was purchased by the
Stromma Canal Co in 1973, and returned
to steam under her original name on a
tourist service on the very scenic route to
Gustavsberg. She remains on this route, and
her appearance was not altered by the
fitting of a diesel, as she retains her tall
funnel and and classic profile.

STOCKHOLM

ÖSTANÅ I

Motor vessel, ex steamer 1985
Operator: Ångfartygs AB Stromma Kanal
Built: 1906, Bergsund, Stockholm; 194gt; 33.3m ×
6.2m
Route: Stockholm–Waxholm; evening cruises

This classic Stockholm steamer was taken
out of service with boiler trouble in 1958,
and lay for many years in the city centre
next to *Blidösund*'s berth. Restoration was
often planned, but other priorities always
came first. Eventually a diesel was fitted
and she was restored to service 1985, to
give a regular shuttle service from the city
centre to Waxholm along with *Björkfjärden*.
Built for the Östanå company's all-year
service to Ljusterö and Lagnö, which she
maintained until the fifties, when more
varied duties beckoned.

STOCKHOLM

KUNG KARL GUSTAF

ex *Karl Gustaf* 1982, ex *Blå Jungfrun* 1980, ex
Götland 1976, ex *Athena* 1957, ex *Stallarholmen*
1955, ex *Argo*, ex *Göteborg*
Motor vessel, ex steamer 1951
Operator: Rederi AB Karl XII
Built: 1892, Bergsund, Stockholm; 125gt; 25.7m ×
4.9m
Route: charters from Stockholm

Rebuilt veteran, one of a number of vessels
in the lucrative charter trade from
Stockholm; operated on Göta canal in
summer months until 1986. Pilot boat at
Göteborg 1892-1894; at Gävle 1894-1949;
converted to passenger vessel on lake Mälar
1950-55; Göteborg 1955-57; Lidingö
1957-60; Göteborg 1960-76; Oskarshamn
1976-80; Uppsala 1980-81; Göta canal
(Motala to Berg) 1982-86; steam engine
replaced 1951; used for luxury day cruises
by Göta Canal Co while based at Göteborg.

STOCKHOLM

ODEN GAMLE

ex *Bebban III*, ex *Oden Gamle*, ex *Ostergyllen*
1977, ex *Kolmården*, ex *Ostergyllen*, ex *Oden*, ex
Essingen I
Motor vessel, ex steamer 1961
Operator: Rederi Stockholms Ström
Built: 1902, Bergsund, Stockholm; 76gt; 29.9m ×
5.3m
Route: charters from Stockholm

Former ångslup restored to near original
appearance but without funnel and still
with diesel engine; used for charters. Built
for lake Mälar service to Stora Essingen.
Operated for many years for Waxholm
company, sold, motorised and operated at
Norrköping in the sixties, later being
privately owned at Stockholm for a period
before coming back into passenger service.

STOCKHOLM

KUNG KARL

ex *Karl XII* 1985, ex *Skurusund* 1970, ex *Express*
1968, ex *Ulriksdal I* c1910, ex *Delfin* 1905, ex
Fama 1903, ex *Rosa* 1894, ex *Sylfid* 1889
Motor vessel, ex steamer 1951
Operator: Rederi *Stockholms Ström*
Built: 1872, Lindholmens Varvet, Göteborg; 32gt;
17.9m × 3.7m; 70 pass
Route: charters from Stockholm

Another former ångslup; used at Gävle until
1903, Stockholm to c1910, then at
Örnsköldsvik in northern Sweden until
1967. Rebuilt 1951 with icebreaker hull,
and again c1968 to 'veteran' appearance.
Used c1984 on Göta canal at Söderköping
for a short period

STOCKHOLM

STOCKHOLMS STRÖM 1

ex *Träpatronen* 1985, ex *Centralfärjan 2* 1976
Motor ferry, ex steamer 1938
Operator: Rederi AB *Stockholms Ström*
Built: 1902, Bergsund, Stockholm; lengthened 1950;
24gt; 17.2m; 131 pass
Route: Stockholm–Fjäderholmarna

Former classic Stockholm harbour ferry,
used on a short ferry route from Gustaf III's
statue to the National Museum until 1935;
then on various routes in Stockholm; low
passenger capacity compared to other
ferries prompted sale to Norrbyskär in
northern Sweden in 1978 after a few years
laid up; returned to Stockholm 1985 for
present service to Fjäderholmarna, an island
only opened to the public in 1985 after
many years of military use

STOCKHOLM

STOCKHOLMS STRÖM 2

ex *Badholmen I* 1986, ex *Djurgarden 6* 1981, ex
Stockholm-Sodra Lindingön 1925, ex *Saltsjöbaden 3*
1913
Motor ferry, ex steamer 1961
Operator: Rederi AB *Stockholms Ström*
Built: 1894, Södra Varvet, Stockholm; 44gt; 22.3m
× 5.4m; 220 pass
Route: Stockholm–Fjäderholmarna

Classic Stockholm harbour ferry, sister of
Djurgården 7; converted to diesel-electric
propulsion 1961; used at Waxholm
1981-1985.

STOCKHOLM

KUNG ERIK

ex *St Erik* 1976, ex *Solö* 1964, ex *St Erik* 1963
Motor vessel, ex steamer 1952
Operator: Rederi AB Sommar & Sol
Built: 1881, Lindholmens Varvet, Göteborg; 235gt;
37.3m × 6.1m; 292 pass
Route: charters from Stockholm

Historic vessel spoiled by a mock-nostalgia
refit in 1979 which gave her two tall
funnels, and an after deck closed in by
perspex windows. Built for Marstrand
Company's Göteborg to Marstrand and
Lysekil passenger-cargo service, and ran on
this until 1963, having been rebuilt with

teak upper deck 1920 to partner *Bohuslän*,
and dieselised, with a modern funnel fitted,
in 1951. Used Byxelbrok-Öland 1963,
Stockholm (lake Mälar) 1964-5; Piteå
(northern Sweden) 1966; then back to
Stockholm; seriously damaged by fire 1976,
then rebuilt in present form. Used for
charters.

GURLI

ex *Trosa* 1897, ex *Lofö* 1885, ex *Åkers Kanal*
1884, ex *Nya Åkers Kanal* 1876
Motor vessel, ex steamer 1964
Operator: Rederi AB Ballerina
Built: 1871, Bergsund, Stockholm; 97gt; 21.9m ×
4.5m; 172 pass
Route: charters from Stockholm

Also used as library boat, calling at many
small places in the archipelago. Built for
service on the Åkers canal, north-east of
Waxholm, but replaced by a larger, more
comfortable steamer in 1884. Used on lake
Mälar from Stockholm to Björkö in the
fifties before dieselisation in 1964.

STOCKHOLM

DELFIN VI

ex *Masen* 1964
Motor vessel, ex steamer 1952, used as offices
Owner: Tourist Sightseeing AB
Built: 1904, Jönköpings Mek Verkstad; 21.4m ×
5.4m

Former Waxholm Co ångslup, used until
1964 (with diesel from 1952). Berthed in
centre of Stockholm, office on hull 1983.

STOCKHOLM

STJERNORP

ex *Fina Fisken* 1970s, ex *Stjernorp* 1964
Privately owned motor vessel, ex steamer, statically
preserved
Owner: unknown
Built: Akers Mek Verksted, Oslo, 1870

Ex steamer of an older generation; in
service on lake Vättern for many years, sold
to Stockholm 1964. Berthed at the back of
Skeppsholm Island in the city centre for
several years

STOCKHOLM

HEBE (diesel)

ex *Maria* 1898
Motor vessel, ex steamer 1911
Built: 1876, Södra Varvet, Stockholm; 18m × 3.8m

Operated from building until 1898 at
Stockholm, then sold to Störsjön at
Östersund, as a freight vessel and tug.
Dieselised and lengthened in 1911
following a major machinery breakdown in
1908. Returned to Stockholm 1982.
Possibly in use on charter work.

WAXHOLM

WAXHOLM III

ex *Skärgården* 1908
Restaurant ship, ex steamer, at Waxholm
Owner: unknown
Built: 1903, Bergsund, Stockholm; 36.00m × 6.8m

Classic steamer in service at Norrköping
until 1908, then on Waxholm Co routes to
the northern archipelago until 1950, and as
excursion and reserve steamer until
withdrawn in 1961. Berthed at Waxholm

since 1964, and restored to original
condition, with engine and boiler removed
but anchor still operated by steam winch.

STOCKHOLM

KUNG RING

Motor vessel, ex steamer 1952
Operator: Allt i Sjötänst
Built: 1902, Bergsund, Stockholm; 40gt; 20.1m ×
5m; 172 pass
Route: Solö–Furusund–Rödlöga (northern part of
archipelago)

Former ångslup with SÅA (Stockholms
Ångslups AB), major ångslup operators, who
operated her until c1970. Built for winter
service with enclosed cabin and ice-
breaking hull.

NORRTÄLJE

NORRTELJE

ex *Express* 1965, ex *Norrtelje* 1961
Restaurant ship, screw steamer, berthed at
Norrtälje
Owner: Stiftelsen SS *Norrtelje*
Built: 1900, Södra Varvet, Stockholm; 359gt; 44.2m
× 8m
Machinery: triple expansion; 800hp; 15kn

Largest and finest of all Stockholm
steamers, *Norrtelje* represented a stage
between the standard steamer and *Bohuslän*,
with the upper deck carried forward over
the foredeck, and bridge and chart-house
on a third deck. Placed in service from
Stockholm to Norrtälje, calling at a number
of places in the northern archipelago en
route, and used here until 1950. Used as an

Ex steam launch *Hebe*, Stockholm, 1985

auxiliary gunboat in World War II; on
excursions from Stockholm and Norrtälje to
Åland 1951-1961, and on the Stockholm to
Sandhamn route in 1962. Used as a
restaurant and sightseeing boat terminal at
Stockholm 1965-67 under the ownership of
travel company Nyman & Schulz, and then
purchased by an enthusiast organisation
and towed to Norrtälje in 1968. Since then
she has been in use as a restaurant, but the
society hopes eventually to restore her to
steam. This would require major work on
the engine and boiler, costing about
£400,000. She was towed back to
Stockholm for a few weeks in May 1987 for
drydocking and use as an exhibition to
promote the Norrtälje area.

WÄDDÖ

WÄDDÖ KANAL

ex *Färja 63/51*, ex *Frånö* 1960s, ex *Stufvaren IV*
1950, ex *Dafne* 1919
Motor vessel, ex steam launch
Operator: P & M Jonasson, Väddö
Built: 1884, Motala Verkstad, Motala
Route: excursions on Wäddö canal, northern
archipelago

Used at Stockholm until 1919, later at
Kramfors, and as ferry at Harnösand.

STOCKHOLM, LAKE MÄLAR

PRINS KARL PHILIP

ex *Bayard* 1980, ex *Hönö* 1968, ex *Bayard* 1947,
ex *Nya Hillersjö* 1931
Motor vessel, ex steamer 1952
Operator: Ångfartygs AB Strömma Kanal
Built: 1901, Bergsund, Stockholm; 221gt; 32.8m ×
5.9m; 347 pass
Route: Stockholm Klara Mälarstrand–Drottingholm
Palace

Looking every inch a steamer, the diesel-
powered *Prins Karl Philip* has been restored
to classic appearance by her owners for the
prestigious Drottningholm service. Built for
service on lake Mälar, used on Göteborg to
Hönö route 1933-1967; dieselised and fitted
with a short motorship funnel in 1952.
Operated at Åskersund, lake Vättern, 1969,
and at Köping at the western end of lake
Mälar 1970-1973. Purchased by present
owners 1974, fitted with a tall ex-dredger
funnel and a new engine in 1978. Placed
on present service after major refit 1982.
Has unusual slightly raised aft saloon on
main deck.

STOCKHOLM

ANGANTYR

Motor vessel, ex steamer 1955
Operator: Ångfartygs AB Strömma Kanal
Built: 1909, Motala Verkstad, Motala; 80gt; 23.2m
× 5.3m; 209 pass
Route: Stockholm–Stora Essingen; also in summer
Stockholm–Millesgården (archipelago side of city)

Angantyr on lake Mälar, 1985

Built as sister of *Drottningholm*, but has
never had full upper deck saloon. Used by
SÅA on service to Stora Essingen for many
years, taken over by Waxholm company
1968, sold to Stromma Canal Co 1978.
Dieselised 1952, when a short, raked,
funnel was fitted. This was replaced by a
taller one in 1980 when a new engine was
fitted. Used on a variety of services, she
had a major refit in 1983 and returned to
her old route on an all-year commuter
charter to Savings Bank Headquarters on
Stora Essingen, with a summer service on
the other side of the city to the Sculpture
Museum at Millesgården.

STOCKHOLM, LAKE MÄLAR

SJÖFRÖKEN

ex *Torsund* 1970, ex *Sjöbuss 2* 1960, ex *Delfin*
1939
Motor launch, ex steamer
Operator: Ångfartygs AB Stromma Kanal
Built: 1875, Motala Verkstad, Motala; 26gt; 17.4m
× 3.6m; 105 pass
Route: excursions in Stockholm through the bridges
of lake Mälar

Former ångslup rebuilt as waterbus, used
for a variety of routes in recent years. Used
on Stora Essingen run when *Angantyr* is on
her summer roster.

VÄSTERÅS, LAKE MÄLAR

ELBA

ex *Elba I* 1952, ex *Elba* 1938, ex *Bomhus I* 1917,
ex *Stadsgården 2* 1900
Motor ferry, ex steamer
Operator: Västerås Kommun
Built: 1897, Brodins Varvet, Gävle; 96gt; 24.8m ×
5.4m; 260 pass
Route: Västerås–Elba

Sister to preserved *Djurgården 3*, at
Stockholm to 1900; at Gävle 1900-1917,
and since then at Västerås. Lengthened
1926, dieselised 1952.

HUDIKSVALL

FORTUNA

ex *Fort Unna*
Steam tug
Built: 1857, England; 16.2m
Machinery: Wennbergs Mek Verkstad, Karlstad,
1915

Included here, although not a passenger
steamer, this little-known veteran steam tug
is probably the oldest tug in the world.
Built from sections shipped from an English
builder, she ran on Dellen lakes,
Helsingland, before being moved to
Hudiksvall in the Gulf of Bothnia in 1878.

HARNÖSAND, HÖGA KUSTEN

KUSTTRAFIK

ex *Turisten* 1938
Motor vessel, ex steamer 1952
Operator: Höga Kusten-Båtarna, Ullånger
Built: 1908, Eriksberg Mek Verkstad, Göteborg;
196gt; 30.0m × 5.45m
Route: excursions on the Höga Kusten (High Coast)

Built as classic steamer for Göta river
service from Göteborg, sold to Umeå 1918,
and to present area 1938 for
passenger/cargo service between Harnösand
and Örnsköldsvik; diesel fitted 1952; this
service ceased in 1961, and she was used at
Luleå 1963-1972. Major rebuild 1967
completely altered her appearance and
disguised her age. On present service since
1972.

KÖPMANHOLMEN

ULVÖN

ex *Tor* 1951 ex *Nätra Express*
Motor vessel, ex steamer 1928
Operator: Örnsköldsviks Kommun
Built: 1915, Motala; 61gt; 22.2m
Route: Köpmanholmen–Ulvön

Built as a tug for Russian owners, but never
delivered. Used at Gävle for many years; on
present route from 1951 after rebuilding.
All year round passenger/cargo ferry to
island of Ulvön

Baltic Star at Skeppsbron quay, Stockholm,
1981

LULEA

DYKAB II

ex *Ålfors* 1978, ex *Mergo* 1967, ex *Britt* 1953, ex
Greta 1945, ex *Brynhild* 1920, ex *Express* 1914
Diving vessel, ex passenger steamer 1935
Owner: AB Nyström & Hellström Dyk- &
Bärgningsservice, Luleå
Built: 1905, Karlstads Mek Verkstad; 19.5m

Used as passenger steamer at Karlstad to
1914; for SÅA at Stockholm to 1920, at
Göteborg to 1935. Sold to Luleå 1935, and
used as a barge, but later an engine was
fitted, and she was used as a coaster
1953-1965, and as a diving vessel from
then. Unrecognisable as former passenger
vessel.

VISBY, GOTLAND

DJURGÅRDEN 5

Restaurant ship, ex diesel-electric ferry 1982, ex
steam ferry 1963
Owner: unknown, Visby, Gotland
Built: 1901, Södra Varvet, Stockholm; 23.1m ×
5.7m; formerly 234 pass

Former Djurgården ferry used as a
restaurant at Visby, Gotland since 1982.
Diesel-electric machinery installed 1962.

SWEDEN

Wilhelm Tham on lake Mälar, 1985

ship, but the food is excellent. *Juno* was rebuilt and dieselised in 1961.

GÖTA CANAL

WILHELM THAM

Motor vessel, ex steamer 1966
Operator: Rederi AB Göta Kanal, Göteborg
Built: 1912, Motala Verkstad, Motala; 308gt; 31.5m × 6.7m; 70 cabin pass, 20 deck pass (formerly 80)
Route: Göteborg-Stockholm (4 days)

Built for a service from Stockholm to Jönköping on lake Vättern, *Wilhelm Tham* was bought by the canal company in 1914, and has been on the service since then. Rebuilt and dieselised 1966.

GÖTA CANAL

DIANA

Motor vessel, ex steamer 1969
Operator: Rederi AB Göta Kanal, Göteborg
Built: 1931, Finnboda, Stockholm; 311gt; 30.5m × 6.8m; 73 cabin pass, 20 day pass (formerly 77)
Route: Göteborg-Stockholm (4 days)

The most recent of the three Göta canal vessels was modernised in 1969. Like the others, her cargo derrick was removed and extra cabin space put in place of the hold.

DALSLAND CANAL

STORHOLMEN

ex *Furesöen* 1933, ex *Bombus II* 1917, ex *Fagerudd*, ex *Döbeln*
Motor vessel, ex steamer
Owner: Storholmens Rederi
Built: 1896; 51gt; 21.6m; 130 pass
Route: Dalsland canal; Köpmannebro-Bengtsfors

Very scenic trip; passes over Håverud aqueduct, where road, rail, and canal all pass over a river. *Storholmen* has operated here since 1938; previously in Stockholm on Stora Värtan, and earlier at Gävle.

MARIESTAD, GÖTA CANAL

SJÖSTJERNAN

ex *Polstjernan*
Motor vessel, ex steamer
Operator: Sea Star Shipping, Mariestad
Built: 1890; 59gt; 12 pass, berthed
Route: charters on Göta canal and connecting lakes

Built as lake Vänern's inpsection steamer, preceding the preserved *Polstjärnan*, motorised and used for excursions and as a cargo vessel for a brewery in Mariestad 1929-1955, then as passenger ferry at Öckerö in Göteborg archipelago until c1977. Present owner has completely rebuilt her with cabin accommodation, and operates her for charter cruises of several days.

STOCKHOLM, BALTIC SEA

APOLLO III

Twin screw motor vessel, ex steamer 1982
Operator: Viking Line
Owner: Rederi AB Slite, Slite, Gotland
Built: 1962, Finnboda, Stockholm; 4898gt; 101.5m × 17.2m; 1250 pass
Route: Stockholm-Mariehamn (Åland)

Former cross-channel steamer; diesel engines fitted 1982. Built for Svea Line's Stockholm-Turku service, sold to Viking Line 1976 for cruises to Mariehamn

STOCKHOLM, BALTIC SEA

BALTIC STAR

ex *Minisea* 1978, ex *Bore Nord* 1978, ex *Birger Jarl* 1973
Twin screw motor vessel, ex steamer 1982
Operator: Ånedin Line, Stockholm
Built: 1951, Finnboda, Stockholm; 1865gt; 92.4m × 14.3m; 918 pass
Route: Stockholm-Mariehamn (Åland)

On similar service to *Apollo III*. Also built for Svea Lines Stockholm-Turku route; sold 1972 to Jakob Lines for route from Skellefteå to Jakobstad; used in 1974 from Turku to Visby, and 1975-1977 as an accommodation ship in Norway after a plan to use her on Great Lakes cruises fell through. Used on current service from around 1980; diesel fitted 1982. Classic Scandinavian. Both she and *Apollo III* were previously engined with quadruple expansion engines with a low-pressure exhaust turbine.

GÖTA CANAL

JUNO

Motor vessel, ex steamer 1961
Operator: Rederi AB Göta Kanal, Göteborg
Built: 1874, Motala Verkstad, Motala; 304gt; 30.3m × 6.7m; 74 cabin pass (formerly 76)
Route: Göteborg-Stockholm (4 days)

Oldest of the three similar canal vessels, *Juno* has been on her service since building. Originally used for cargo and passengers, but when cargo carrying became uneconomic the service almost ceased. In 1956 the three remaining boats were rescued by the Thunbolaget cargo shipping company, and the service geared to tourism. For many years the passage, took three days but in recent years a few trips have taken four days with an overnight stop, passengers still sleeping on board. From 1987 the normal service has taken four days, allowing more sightseeing stops, and occasional trips are scheduled for five days. The number of day passengers carried has been drastically cut in 1987, obviously in pursuit of a more up-market cruise image. The only major traffic flow is day passengers across lake Vättern and occasional cylists who are making the canal towpath trip. The trip is extremely interesting, crosses three large lakes, Vänern, Vättern and Mälar, and also a stretch of the Baltic, and traverses two major canals' in addition to the Göta canal, the Trollhättan and Södertalje canals, as well as one river, the Göta. The cabins are rather small, as dictated by the size of the

Juno crossing lake Roxen, 1985

Below: Diana in Trollhättan canal lock, 1985

KARLSBORG, GÖTA CANAL

SANDÖN

ex *Aurora Borealis* 1970, ex *Bore* 1967
Motor vessel, ex steamer
Operator: Rederi AB Karlsborgs Marina
Built: 1910, Eriksbergs Mek Verkstad, Göteborg;
129gt; 29.8m; 200 pass
Route: Karlsborg–Töreboda

Built for ferry service at Karlskrona for
Swedish armed forces. Sold 1967 to
Stockholm owner; at Karlsborg since 1977.
Classic Swedish steamer design.

KARLSTAD, GÖTA CANAL

RAN II

ex *Elfsnabben* 1963, ex *Mysingebaden*, ex *Elsa* 1939
Motor vessel, ex steamer 1948
Operator: unknown
Built: 1899, Götaverken, Göteborg; 43gt; 15.8m;
80 pass
Route: charters from Karlsborg until 1985, present
location unknown

Originally on Göta river service from
Göteborg, then Marstrand in 1930s, Muskö
(Stockholm's southern archipelago)
1945-63, during which time she was
dieselised and rebuilt; Lysekil 1963-72;
Karlsborg 1972-85; possibly at Arvika 1985.

KARLSBORG

MUNIN

Motor launch, ex steamer, undergoing restoration
at Karlsborg
Owner: Rederi AB Karlsborgs Marina
Built: 1915, Södra Varvet, Stockholm

Former Waxholm company ångslup,
dieselised 1954; sold to Göteborg area
1959, now undergoing restoration by
Sandön's owners.

VADSTENA, LAKE VÄTTERN

VICTORIA AF WADSTENA

ex *Hebe III* 1982, ex *Torsö* 1939
Motor vessel, ex steamer 1956
Operator: Rederi Wetterns Båttrafik, Vadstena
Built: 1915, Wennbergs Mek Verkstad, Karlstad;
38gt; 19.7m × 4.4m; 112 pass
Route: excursions and charters from Vadstena

In service at Mariestad until 1939, then on
ferry service Gränna-Visingsö 1939-1981;
present service since 1982. Diesel fitted
1956; rebuilt and new engine fitted c1973;
rebuilt again 1982 to provide restaurant.

LINKÖPING, KIND CANAL

KIND

Motor launch, ex steamer
Operator: Rederi AB Kind
Built: 1898; 49gt; 22.9m
Route: Kind canal; Linköping–Rimforsa

Launch on Kind canal, an old little-used
canal running south from Linköping; the
7-hour trip passes through 15 locks.

TRANÅS, LAKE SOMMEN

STRÖMSHOLMEN

Motor vessel, ex steamer 1965
Operator: Lars Kallstienius, Tranås
Built: 1884, Ljungströms Verkstad, Kristianstad
Route: excursions on lake Sommen from Tranås

Former ångslup, on Sommen since 1912.
Used until 1958; rebuilt 1960; dieselised
1965; restoration and rebuilding, with a
new funnel (which had been removed some
years ago to get under low bridges), and a
buffet planned 1985 by captain, Lars
Kallstienius. Probably built for use as
harbour tug at Karlshamn.

LAKE SILJAN

GUSTAF WASA

Twin screw motor vessel, ex steamer 1959
Operator: Siljans Båttrafik
Built: 1876, Södra Varvet, Stockholm, rebuilt 1984;
140gt; 29.7m × 5.3m; 150 pass
Route: Leksand–Mora; excursions from Leksand,
Mora, and Rättvik

Interesting survivor, rebuilt 1984 after a
major fire in 1982. The rebuild has given
her a pleasing 'antique' appearance,
although unlike her original condition, and
without much of the atmosphere of a
veteran. She has sailed on the lake since
building, being originally on a
cargo/passenger service. Gradually over the
years various alterations were made,
including straightening of the sides of the
'tween deck, and fiting of an upper deck
aft, and in 1958 she was completely rebuilt
and dieselised, with an upper deck saloon.
Services originally operated also on lake
Orsa, north of Mora, and on the Insjön,
south of Leksand, to Tunsta, and beyond
there on the Österdal river to Gråsta before
the railway opened in the 1880s. As with
many similar operations, the operating
company went into liquidation in the mid-
fifties, when the cargo section of the trade
became uneconomic, and *Gustaf Wasa* was
taken over by another company for tourist
traffic. Her recent rebuild has fitted her
better for present-day traffic and for
evening dance cruises. Sailings are often
fully booked in advance, particularly the
afternoon cruises, which are preceded by a
morning sail up or down the lake from
Leksand to Mora or vice versa. Siljan is
quite a large lake, with generally low
shores.

LEKSAND, LAKE SILJAN

ENGELBREKT

ex *Mora* 1903
Private motor vessel, ex steamer
Built: 1866, Motala Mek Verkstad, Motala; 24.1m
× 4.5m

Former passenger steamer, in use on lake
Siljan from 1866 until 1952. Laid up for
many years, then rebuilt, diesel fitted, and
used as private yacht, based at Leksand. In
poor condition.

ALINGSÄS, LAKE MJÖRN

JERNLUNDEN

ex *Yxingen*
Preserved steam launch at Alingsäs, lake Mjörn,
east of Göteborg
Owner: Mjörns Ångbåtsförening
Built: 1890s; 11.7m × 3.0m
Machinery: single cylinder; 8hp

Built as timber towing tug for lake Yxingen;
used as passenger boat on Kind canal in
20s; laid up 1969; preserved 1976. No
recent information.

STORSJÖN (GASTRIKLAND)

EMMA

Preserved motor launch, ex steamer
Owner: unknown, Sandviken (near Gävle)
Built: 1904, Brodins Varvet, Gävle

Used on Storsjön in Gästrikland (not to be
confused with the Storsjön at Östersund) as
passenger launch. Diesel fitted 1939;
withdrawn 1960s; restored to original
condition 1976-8 at Sandviken, but with
former truck engine fitted. Not known if
passenger trips are operated.

STRÖMSUND

SVANINGEN

ex *Ramsele*
ex steamer, undergoing restoration
Owner: Vattudalens Båtklubb, Strömsund
Built: 1875, Lindberg, Södra Varvet, Stockholm;
20.2m × 4.4m; c120 pass

Originally in service on Faxälv river at
Ramsele, but most of her life operated on
the scenic Ströms Vattudal, in the fells of
northern Jämtland north of Östersund, as
passenger steamer and tug. Service ceased
1956, and steamer used for one further
season purely as a tug. Laid up and used as
summer cottage until taken to Strömsund
for restoration in 1972. Boat club are
restoring her for use as a motor vessel, and
plan to run her on excursions.

FINLAND

TURKU

WINGA

ex *Ragnborg* 1955, ex *Pirkko* 1950, ex *Ålands Express*
Motor vessel, ex steamer
Owner: K Kinnunen, Turku
Built: 1877, Oskarshamn, Sweden; rebuilt 1946, 1955; 196gt; 34.4m × 6.1m

Veteran passenger ship, sixth oldest vessel listed in Lloyd's Register, no further details available.

KIMITO

MAJLAND

ex *Mailand* 1925, ex *Gute* 1919, ex *Söderhamn* 1904, ex *Transit No 3* 1897, ex *Franzén* 1869, ex *Transit No 4* 1857
Coaster, ex barge, ex passenger/cargo steamer 1924
Owner: E Paulin, Kimito
Built: 1856, Motala Verkstad, Motala, Sweden; 223gt; 38.3m × 6.9m

Remarkable survivor, having been built at Motala in the same year and at the same yard as *Skibladner*, although the latter was shipped to Kristiania (now Oslo) in sections, and assembled there. She was built for a short-lived service from Grimsby to St Petersburg via the Göta canal, in order to avoid the tolls on traffic passing through the Öresund. In 1857, these were abolished, and she was sold to Stockholm owners and used on services from Stockholm to northern Sweden, and also to Gotland between 1857 and 1869; then for a number of successive owners on Swedish coastal service, eg 1886-1897 Stockholm-Norrköping-Helsingborg-Göteborg. Purchased by the Gotland Company in 1904, and used on Stockholm-Visby service until 1916; then sold again; in service from Stockholm to Turku 1919-1923, latterly for Finland Steamship Co. Sold for scrapping 1923 and hull converted to barge. Diesel engine fitted 1961; still in service as sand-carrier. Has had a total of 21 owners in her life. Early illustration shows an extremely antique steamer with foresail and very tall funnel, not dissimilar to *Salama* at Savonlinna.

TURKU

ERIKA

ex *Andre* 1927, ex *Kullervo* 1923, ex *Wirumaa* 1916, ex *Stella* 1912, ex *Mariehamn* 1890, ex *Höganäs* 1887, ex *Fredriksborg* 1882
Motor yacht, ex sand carrier 1973, ex barge 1957, ex passenger steamer 1927
Owner: unknown, Turku
Built: 1869, Södra Varvet, Stockholm; 30.5m × 5.4m

Another remarkable survivor, still showing her classic hull lines despite much alteration. Built for Stockholm-Vaxholm service; operated there until 1881; Mölle (north of Helsingborg)-Malmo 1882-1890; Turku-Mariehamn 1890-1911; Tallinn (then

Reval)-Riga 1912-1916; at Vyborg (now Viipuri) c1917. Rebuilt to barge 1925; diesel engine fitted and used as sand carrier 1957; refitted with passenger cabin in cargo space 1973. Visited Stockholm 1977. Possible use as excursion boat but no confirmation received. No recent information.

TURKU

SORA VII

ex *Isak Pollack*
Sand carrier, ex steamer
Owner: T Torkkel, Miami (USA)
Built: 1857, Sweden; rebuilt 1934; 169gt; 36.1m × 7.1m

Further veteran sand carrier in Turku area. No details of history available.

TURKU

VON KONOW

ex *Untamo*
Coaster, ex passenger steamer
Owner: Oy Hinaus, Turku
Built: 1901, Björneborgs Mek Verkstad, Pori; rebuilt 1932, 1951; 111gt; 30.5 × 5.5m

Coaster, built as traditional local passenger steamer.

TURKU

MESSINA I

ex *Korsholm II* 1962, ex *Viola* 1955, ex *Frederick Wilhelm* 1913
Coaster, ex naval staff ship 1967, ex passenger steamer 1962
Owner: Laivanisännistöyhtiö *Messina I*, Turku
Built: 1893, W Rosenlew & Co, Pori; rebuilt 1955, 1968; 214gt; 40m × 7m

Built as coastal steamer; used by builders on route from Pori right around to Vyborg (Finnish to 1945); sold 1897 and on the following services: Vaasa-Stockholm 1897-1902; Pori-Vyborg 1902-1913; Helsinki-Tallinn for EFFOÅ 1913-1940; Turku-Mariehamn 1941-1955; Umeå-Vaasa 1955-1962; then 1962-1967 naval staff ship. Sold for scrapping 1968, but hull resold and converted to diesel-engined sand carrier. Succeeded as naval staff ship by *Korsholm III*, now *Öland* (see Denmark section).

HELSINKI

J L RUNEBERG

ex *Helsingfors Skärgård* 1937
Motor vessel, ex steamer 1966
Owner Verustamo Oy *J L Runeberg*, Porvoo
Built: 1912, AB Sandvikens Skepps, Helsinki; 138gt; 28.8m × 6.7m; 220 pass
Route: Helsinki-Porvoo; Helsinki-Loviisa

Traditional steamer design, but with open upper deck, operating four days weekly from Helsinki eastwards to Porvoo, calling at Haikko manor house restaurant, and all-inclusive lunch trips are offered here. Has kept tall funnel and steamer appearance since dieselised 1966. Purchased by present owners in 1986, but retained on the Porvoo

route which she has served since 1937, with the exception of a few years after 1945 when she was on local Helsinki harbour service. Recent years have seen a new route operated once weekly from Helsinki to Loviisa.

HELSINKI

CHRISTINA

ex *Nautilus* 1978
Motor vessel, ex steamer 1981
Owner: Luottorengas Oy, Helsinki
Built: 1903, Sandvikens Skeppsdocka, Helsinki; 161gt; 29.8m × 6.1m

Former survey steamer, converted to passenger motor vessel c1981. No news of any service; probably based at Helsinki.

HELSINKI

KRISTINA REGINA

ex *Borea* 1987, ex *Bore* 1977
Twin screw motor vessel, ex steamer 1987
Operator: Rannikkolinjat (Kristina Cruises), Helsinki
Built: 1960, Oskarshamn Varvet, Oskarshamn, Sweden; 3878gt; 99.8m × 15.3m; 1120 pass(to be reduced)
Route: cruises from Helsinki to Tallinn, Leningrad, etc

This impressive two-funneled steamer was the last steam ferry in the Baltic. A side-loading car ferry, *Bore* was built for Silja Line's service from Stockholm to Turku. In 1977 she was sold to Jakob Lines for their service across the north of the Gulf of Bothnia from Skellefteå to Pietarsaari; then had a spell from 1982 to 1984 as an accommodation ship in Algeria. Brought back to the Baltic in 1984 for a luxury service on her original route for Aure Lines; this failed after a few months and she was laid up at Turku. Reportedly sold to an American company for rebuilding as a luxury cruise liner named *Vanderbilt*; the sale was never finalised, and in 1987 she was sold to Kristina Cruises for conversion to a diesel mini cruise liner to run alongside ex naval patrol vessel *Kristina Brahe*. Her steam engines were of an unusual quadruple expansion type with an exhaust turbine, built on a turbo-compressor system.

TAMPERE, LAKE NÄSIJÄRVI

PYYNIKKI

ex *Jatko*
Motor vessel ex steamer
Operator: Runoilijan Tie Oy (Poets Way Ltd), Tampere
Built: 1873; rebuilt 1962; 29gt; 17.7m × 3.3m; 61 pass
Route: Tampere-Maisansalo

Modernised veteran launch used since 1962 on local route running north from Tampere; originally on service on Pyhäjärvi, south of Tampere.

TAMPERE, LAKE NÄSIJÄRVI

KRINOULA

ex *Metsä*, ex *Längelmäki*
Motor vessel, ex steamer, laid up
Built: 1916

Former passenger steamer, also used as tug for a time, rebuilt in sixties; this appears to be a home-made job with two bus bodies mounted on the old hull. Possibly in use as youth club; no recent information.

TAMPERE, LAKE NÄSIJÄRVI

TERVALAHTI

ex *Lokki*
Preserved screw steamer, in use as children's playground
Built: 1900, Oy Sommers, Tampere

Traditional passenger steamer used on lake Näsijärvi until 1963, then used as children's playground at Nalkalantori. No recent information.

TAMPERE, LAKE NÄSIJÄRVI

LÄNSI-TEISKO

Privately owned motor vessel, ex passenger steamer
Owner: A Löfblom, Tampere
Built: 1907, Oy Sommers, Tampere; 72gt; 23.5m × 4.8m

Former passenger steamer still listed as steamer in 1982; in service on Näsijärvi until withdrawn after engine failure 1964.

Seen at Tampere half-covered by tarpaulins in 1981. Possibly used as houseboat.

TAMPERE, LAKE LÄNGELMÄVESI

PAJULAHTI

ex *Kangasala* 1927
Owner: I Kallio
Built: 1901

Former small passenger steamer built for service at Hameenlinna. From 1925 on lake Pyhäjärvi, south of Tampere; probably in service to 1964. Still in existence, perhaps as houseboat on lake Längelmävesi, east of Tampere.

KEURUSSELKÄ

ELIAS LÖNNROTT

Paddle motor vessel, replica of 1865 paddle steamer
Operator: Keuruun Matkailu
Built: 1986, Valmet, Turku; 31.3m × 5m/9m; 150 pass
Route; Keuruu–Keurusselkä Hotel (extended to Mänttä on Sundays)

Recent replica, authentic except for lack of steam engine, of Finland's last paddle steamer, scrapped in 1927. Unusual design with half-saloon on fore-deck and no upper deck. Original *Elias Lönnrott* sailed on the lake from 1891 to 1925, and was earlier on lake Pyhäjärvi, south of Tampere, 1865-1875, and lake Näsijärvi 1876-1891. Keuruu is about half way between Virrat, northernmost point of *Tarjanne's* route, and Jyväskylä. Excellent true replica of original.

Orivesi leaving Savonlinna, 1981

LAHTI, LAKE PÄIJÄNNE

JYVÄSKYLÄ

Motor vessel ex steamer, laid up
Built: 1875

Former running-mate of *Suomi*, withdrawn 1964, sold to private owner and converted to diesel. Seen at Lahti 1981, laid up and protected by guard dog. A number of other ex steamers listed below were in the same harbour, an amazing discovery made while the author was out for an evening walk.

LAHTI, LAKE PÄIJÄNNE

TARU, LEA, OLKA, VUOHIJÄRVI

All private motor yachts, of passenger steamer design; believed to be converted from passenger steamers; no recent information.

LAHTI, LAKE PÄIJÄNNE

AINO

Motor vessel, ex steam tug
Owner: Verustamo Kari & Ritva Suomalainen, Kartano
55 pass
Route: Lahti–Heinola; charters

Traditional vessel, probably converted from a steam tug in relatively recent times.

LAKE SAIMAA

ORIVESI

ex *Orivesi I* 1976, ex *Punkuharju* 1913
Motor vessel, ex steamer 1968
Owner: Verustamo Lago Lines Oy, Lahti
Built: 1906, Varkaus; 140gt; 26.5m × 6.5m; 119 pass; 12 berths
Route: Lahti–Heinola

A vessel of traditional lake Saimaa type, *Orivesi* was converted to diesel in 1968, and operated cruises from Lappeenranta to Viipuri/Varkaus along the Saimaa canal until 1986. These must be the only day excursions to Russia anywhere in the world. The canal, which connects lake Saimaa to the Baltic, was rebuilt in the sixties, and the southern half is in Russia, but is leased to Finland. There are eight locks, taking ships up to 2500 tons. The original canal, built in 1856, was restricted to 300-ton vessels, and thus the tar steamers, using the canal to take cargoes of firewood to St Petersburg and Helsinki, were built to the maximum size for the locks. *Orivesi* was built for the Savonlinna-Joensuu route, but was on Saimaa canal trips in the seventies, before a spell on the Savonlinna-Kuopio service 1977-1981. She had always had rather unsightly white plating amidships on the main deck, where the galley is situated, rather than having a walkway right around the deck like the other steamers. She was replaced on the canal cruises in 1897 by *Carelia*, former Flensburg excursion ship *Ostsee* (1969). I have no news of *Orivesi's* current service.

LAPPEENRANTA, LAKE SAIMAA

VÄINÄMÖINEN

ex *Elbe* 1971
Twin screw motor vessel, ex steamer 1960, ex gas-powered motor vessel 1947
Operator: Karelia Lines, Lappeenranta
Built: 1941, Aug Pahl, Hamburg; 444gt; 40.2m × 8.6m; 400 pass
Route: excursions from Lappeenranta

War-built vessel, for HADAG services on the Elbe at Hamburg, converted to steam after the war in order to provide more power reserve for winter sailings in ice. Converted back to diesel and modernised; sold to Lappeenranta, 1971, and in service there since, including a period 1978-81 under the ownership of Saimaan Laivamaktat.

LAPPEENRANTA

PRINCESSA ARMAADA

ex *Pikisaari 3*, ex *Uolevi*
Restaurant ship, ex tar steamer
Owner: unknown, Lappeenranta
Built: 1918

Former tar steamer, restaurant ship without engines at Lappeenranta from c1980.

IMATRA, LAKE SAIMAA

IMATRA II

ex *Luohivesi* 1984, ex *Lappeenranta* 1976, ex *Imatra II* c1969
Motor vessel, ex steamer 1983
Operator: Imatran Höyrylaiva Oy (Imatra Steamship)
Built: 1906, Varkauden Konepaja, Varkaus; 142gt; 26.8m × 6.5m; 126 pass
Route: Imatra–Lappeenranta; cruises from Imatra

Former steamer, the only one purchased at the 1982 auction by a private company, who operated her in 1982 and 1983 from Savonlinna to Mikkeli. She was dieselised after the 1982 season, and came to Imatra as consort to *Karjalankoski* in 1984 or 1985. Until the Saimaan Laivamaktat collapse in 1981 she had operated, along with *Savonlinna* and *Leppävirta*, on a Y-shaped route linking Savonlinna, Mikkeli, and Lappeenranta, with all three steamers meeting at Puumula in early afternoon. She was originally built for the Lappeenranta-Savonlinna route.

MIKKELI, LAKE SAIMAA

SAIMAA

Motor vessel, ex steamer
Operator: unknown, Mikkeli
Built: Mikkeli-Anttolanhovi
Route: excursions from Mikkeli

Veteran vessel reported to operate from Mikkeli; no further details are available. Not to be confused with the inspection steamer *Saimaa* at Savonlinna, which was built in 1893 and is still in service.

SAVONLINNA

HOPEASALMI

ex *Mikkeli*, ex *Mikkeli II*, ex *Orivesi II* 1956, ex *Mikkeli* 1956, ex *Leppävirta* 1914
Restaurant ship, steamer
Owner: Pekka Kierikka, Savonlinna
Built: 1903, Paul Wahl, Varkaus; 168gt; 26.8m × 6.5m
Machinery: compound; 138hp

Moored in the cente of Savonlinna, *Hopeasalmi* has been used as a restaurant ship since 1977. Her owner has plans to steam her again in the future, and her engine has been restored. The main deck has been carried out to the sides of the steamer, probably since she was taken out of service, giving her a slightly more modern appearance. She was built for the Leppävirta company's Kuopio-Savonlinna-Mikkeli route; her owners merged with owners of *Savonlinna* in 1951 to form the predecessor of Saimaan Laivamaktat. She changed owners 1966 and was in use on three-day tourist cruises on the southern triangle. Grounded and sank 1970 at Riistina en route from Lapeenranta to Mikkeli; then out of service for some years before purchase by present owner.

SAVONLINNA

SALAMA

Museum ship, steamer
Owner: Saimaan Purjehdusmuseoyhdistys Oy, Savonlinna
Built: 1874, Vyborg, sunk 1898; raised 1971; 31.4m × 6.7m; formerly 60 pass
Machinery: (was) 39hp; 7.5kn

This steamer, described as a steam schooner, must be the only one of its type extant anywhere in the world. She is a remarkable reminder of the transition from sail to steam, for, as originally built, she used auxiliary sails. She operated through the Saimaa canal on a regular service from Joensuu to Vyborg and St Petersburg, with occasional trips as far as Lübeck. *Salama* was refitted in 1883, when a saloon was built on her afterdeck and her passenger capacity increased from 12 to 60. In 1898 she was in a collision with the passenger steamer *Ilmari* near Puumula, and sank in 30m of water, fortunately without loss of life. In 1970 she was found when her mast was caught in the winch rope of a tug pulling a raft of logs. She was raised in 1971, by courtesy of Enso-Gutzeit, who used the lifting to test salvage gear, and taken to Savonlinna where she was restored as a museum ship, and opened to the public in 1971. Her lower deck contains an excellent exhibition of the history of shipping on lake Saimaa, and she is a must for any enthusiast visiting the area. Her engines are intact, and the hole in her side can be seen from the exhibition area, with a housing built on the outside of the hull. Her deck gear has all been rebuilt, and externally she is as she was 100 years ago. The cabins are even made up as if for overnight passengers.

SAVONLINNA, LAKE SAIMAA

SAVONLINNA

ex *Suur Saimaa* 1982, ex *Savonlinna* 1976
Museum ship, steamer
Owner: Savonlinnan Kaupunki (Town of Savonlinna)
Built: 1903, Paul Wahl, Varkaus; 169gt; 27.9m × 6.7m; formerly 180 pass, 36 berths
Machinery: compound; 200hp; 11.5kn

Former flagship of the Saimaa passenger steamer fleet, *Saonlinna* was purchased at the Saimaan Laivamaktat auction for preservation as a museum ship. She now lies near *Salama*. Most powerful of the lake steamers, she was latterly on the 'blue triangle' route linking Savonlinna. Lappeenranta and Mikkeli, having been on the Lappeenranta service from her home port most of her life.

LAKE SAIMAA

SÄYNÄMÖINEN

Motor vessel, ex steamer

Yacht-like vessel; history unknown; seen moored at remote spot on lake shore between Heinävesi and Savonlinna 1982; possibly a private yacht or houseboat.

Heino in her last year in steam, 1981

KUOPIO, LAKE SAIMAA

HEINO

ex *Anna*
Motor vessel, ex passenger steamer, ex tar steamer
Operator: Roll-Laivat, Kuopio
Built: 1914, Maaninka; 185gt; 28.1m × 6.3m; 150 pass; 52 berths
Route: Kuopio–Heinävesi–Savonlinna (12 hours)

Converted tar steamer, with standard passenger steamer design but machinery aft. Powered by tiny 50hp steam engine until after the 1981 season. Operates route with *Kuopio*, going south one day and returning the next. Formerly with Enso-Gutzeit, converted by present owner mid seventies; most attractive of the three similar vessels operated by Roll-Laivat from Kuopio.

KUOPIO, LAKE SAIMAA

UKKO

ex *Teuvo* 1970s, ex *Hosea* 1910s
Motor vessel, ex tar steamer 1970s
Operator: Roll-Laivat, Kuopio
Built: 1898; 249gt; 30.3m × 6.7m; 250 pass
Route: excursions from Kuopio, thrice daily

Another former Enso-Gutzeit tar steamer, converted directly to diesel in the late seventies with ugly tall streamlined funnel.

KUOPIO, LAKE SAIMAA

KUOPIO

Motor vessel, ex tar steamer 1982
Operator: Roll-Laivat, Kuopio
Built: 1899; 320gt; 31.2m × 6.9m; 200 pass; 70 berths
Route: Kuopio–Heinävesi–Savonlinna

Ugly former tar steamer, converted over a period of years, not fully entering service until 1983. Rebuilt for the Savonlinna service, she has been built up to give two full passenger decks.

KIANTAJARVI

KIANTA

ex *Uitto IV*
Motor vessel, ex steamer
Operator: Kianta-laivayhtymä, Ämmänsaari
Built: 1912, Lehtioniemen Konepaja, Joroinen; 80 pass; 4 berths
Route: excursions from Ännänsaari; weekend trips to Ruhtinansalmi, with overnight accommodation in log cabins

Small traditional passenger boat used on remote lake Kiantajärvi, north-east of Kajaani.

DENMARK

SILKEBORG, SILKEBORG LAKES

TERNEN (1896)
HEJREN (1909)

Ex steamers
Operator: AS Hjejlen, Silkeborg
Route: Silkeborg lakes:
Silkeborg–Himmelbjerget–Laven

Motor launches on Silkeborg lakes service along with *Hjejlen*; mainly rebuilt as waterbus-type boats.

AARHUS

ÖLAND

ex *Korsholm III*, ex *Korsholm*, ex *Öland*
Screw steamer, undergoing restoration at Stockholm for use as a conference centre at Aarhus
Owner: unknown
Built: 1931, Oskarshamns Varvet, Sweden; 422gt; 48.8m × 8.5m; formerly 34 cars, 354 pass
Machinery: triple expansion, 865hp

Built for Swedish Post Office as postal steamer and passenger ship from Kalmar to the island of Öland; larger than, but not dissimilar to, classic Swedish steamer. Sold to Umeå-Vasa Line 1958, lengthened and rebuilt for car ferry service across Gulf of Bothnia, new modern funnel fitted, converted to oil-firing. Sold to Finnish navy 1967, used as base ship until 1985. Arrived in Stockholm summer 1986, and work started on refitting her for use at Aarhus after efforts to purchase her for a museum at her old home port, Kalmar, had failed. It is planned to keep her machinery intact, and to use her as a static conference centre.

NYSTED

SCHWARZBURG

ex *DOD No VI*, ex *Schmeil*, ex *Friedrich III*
Paddle tug, museum ship
Owner: Aalholm Automobile Museum, Nysted
Built: 1896, Gebr Sachsenberg, Rosslau, River Elbe;
63.29m × 6.21/13.11m
Machinery: 400hp

Traditional two-funneled Elbe tug, in DDR fleet after 1945, and withdrawn 1970, sold to Denmark for scrapping, and bought from scrapyard for use on cruises from Aalholm Auto Museum, Nysted. Apparently she was unable to obtain a passenger certificate, and has been anchored at Nysted since then. Now the last Elbe paddle tug afloat, as *Württemberg*, the only other one in existence, is a museum on land at Magdeburg.

BORNHOLM

CHIMERA

ex *Chimaera* 1948
Wooden motor vessel, ex steam yacht
Operator: Rederi Østlandet AS, Bornholm
Built: 1912, Sandhaven, Scotland; 90gt
Route: Gudhjem–Chriatiansø

Built as steam yacht for General J G Forbes; sold in 1917 after his death in World War I for use as a pilot vessel in Bristol Channel. Sold to Bornholm owner 1947, rebuilt as passenger vessel 1955 for the service to the small island of Christiansø, off Bornholm. No recent information.

WEST GERMANY

BREMEN

FRIEDRICH

ex *Nord Bremen* 1925, ex *Sud Hamburg* 1918
Motor vessel, ex steamer, undergoing restoration
Owner: Otto W A Schreiber Reederei, Bremen
Built: 1880, Reichersteige Schiffwerft, Hamburg;
17m × 6.7m; latterly 98 pass

Very unusual two-decked steamer, with very squat appearance and upper deck saloon full size of ship; described by one writer as a 'sandwich-boat'. Operated as harbour ferry at Hamburg until 1918, having been purchased by HADAG in 1889; at that time she was a conventional small steamer with fore and aft deckhouses. Sold to Bremen owners 1918, and a new fore deckhouse was built, the aft deckhouse removed, and an enclosed upper deck added. Operated on harbour sightseeing trips at Bremen until 1963, with a diesel engine fitted in 1950; then used as workshop ship for company, with engine partially removed; preservation group founded and plans made for restoration

1987. Apparently the reason she has not been preserved before is that the owners require her or a replacement as a workshop.

LIST, NORTH SEA

GRET PALUCCA

ex *Langeoog III* 1978, ex *Binz* 1949, ex *Wilhelmsburg* 1920
Motor vessel, ex steamer 1935
Operator: D Dethlefs, List, Sylt
Built: 1901, H Brandenburg, Hamburg; 205gt;
31.9m × 6.0m; 336 pass
Route: sea excursions from List

Built for Hamburg local services; sold to Sassnitz on island of Rügen 1920; rebuilt and lengthened 1935; came to the West 1945. In service for short period for HADAG, Hamburg, then operated to West Frisian island Langeoog 1949-1978; rebuilt 1978 and on present service, from a resort at the north end of the holiday island of Sylt, since then.

DAMP 2000

ALBATROS

Museum ship, ex steamer
Owner: Rettung uber See e V Damp 2000
Built: 1912, Meyer, Papenburg; 214gt; 36.6m ×
6.3m; formerly 405 pass
Machinery: compound; 260hp

Smaller in appearance than *Alexandra*, with no upper deck, although larger on paper, *Albatros* operated out of Flensburg until 1972, then was preserved on dry land in the sand dunes of Damp 2000, a purpose-built holiday centre on the coast between Eckenförde and Kappeln. In the early fifties she sailed for a while as a cattle steamer, but her finest hour had been in 1945, when, after war service as a tender at Danzig, she carried refugees fleeing before the advancing Russian army from Danzig to Schleswig-Holstein. At that time 2½ million people fled in 115 days from East Prussia,

Albatros on the sand dunes at Damp 2000, 1986

West Prussia, and Pomerania. She is now preserved as a memorial to that operation and was taken over by the present organisation in 1983, after getting into very poor condition following use as a restaurant and disco. There is a museum on board, and the steamer is in reasonable external condition.

SCHLESWIG, RIVER SCHLEI

WAPPEN VON SCHLESWIG

ex *Brandenburger Tor* 1970, ex *Baltinn* 1961, ex *Altstadt* 1960
Motor vessel, ex steamer 1962
Operator: Schleischiffahrt A Bischoff, Schleswig
Built: 1926, Uniongiesserei, Königsberg; 84gt; 29.1m × 6.0m; 240 pass
Route: Schleswig–Kappeln–Schleimunde

Built as combined tug/passenger steamer for service at Königsberg in East Prussia. Fled to West in 1945; operated at Kiel 1954-60; to Wangerooge 1961. Later dieselised and moved to Schleswig for operation on the river Schlei since 1970.

LÜBECK

MISSISSIPPI

ex *Hessen* 1969, ex *Prinz Heinrich* 1952
Museum ship, motor vessel, ex steamer 1959
Owner: H Karsten, Lübeck
Built: 1909, Meyer, Papenburg; 266gt; 38.9m × 7.0m; formerly 390 pass

Built for service from Emden to the island of Borkum. Withdrawn 1969 and now a very unusual museum moored in centre of Lübeck; owner has sailed around the world over 40 times and steamer houses his anthropological and natural history collection, over 2000 items, although little of actual steamship interest. She has lost her funnel, and her foredeck has been covered.

Rudesheim in the Rhine gorge, 1980

HAMBURG, ALSTER LAKE

LA BARCA

ex *Alster* 1970, ex *Heinrich Dreckmann* 1947, ex
Alster 1933
Restaurant ship, ex motor launch, ex steamer
Owner: Holsteinbrauerei
Built: 1931, Oelkers, Hamburg; 22.8m × 4.4m

Last former Alster lake steam launch in
existence. Converted to diesel-electric
propulsion 1950; withdrawn 1962,
converted to restaurant ship; with present
owners since 1970.

KÖLN

RÜDESHEIM

ex *Rheinland* 1965
Paddle steamer, used as static landing stage at Köln
Owner: KD, Köln
Built: 1926, Sachsenburg, Köln-Deutz; 536t (displ);
79.1m × 8.2/14.9m; formerly 2300 pass
Machinery: compound diagonal, Sachsenburg,
Rosslau/Elbe; 750hp

In operation on the Rhine until 1982, since
when she has been reserve steamer, used in
summer as a landing stage for the
excursion motorship *Domspatz*, at Köln. She
was built as an express steamer for the
company, with deck saloons fore and aft,
and a fore saloon on the upper deck; sunk
in 1945, but rebuilt and returned to service
in 1951 with a modern profile, and an
almost full length saloon on the upper
deck. Converted to oil-firing in 1956, and
in 1979 painted in a 'nostalgia' colour
scheme, like the other paddlers, with
dummy paddle vents and a number of
other features such as special motifs on the
bow and front of the upper deck, etc. There
were plans for a new boiler to be fitted in
the early eighties, but in the event the old
one was repaired, and she was withdrawn
after the 1981 season.

MANNHEIM

MAINZ

Museum ship, paddle steamer
Owner: Gesellschaft fur Förderung des
Rheimuseums Mannheim
Built: 1929, Ruthof, Mainz; 497t (displ); 83.6m ×
8.7/16.2m; formerly 2680 pass
Machinery: compound diagonal by builder; 960hp

Withdrawn in 1980 after an engine failure,
Mainz was taken to Mannheim, lashed
alongside a tug, in late 1985, for use as a
shipping museum there. She was built for
the express-service on the Rhine, was not
badly damaged after the war, and was used
by the US occupying army as a floating
office from 1945 to 1948, returning to
service in 1949. Oil-firing was fitted in
1955, and from 1963 she was on the
normal, rather than the express, service.

DÜSSELDORF

HANSA

Restaurant ship, ex paddle steamer 1924
Owner: unknown, Düsseldorf-Volmerswerth
Built: 1885, Smit, Kinderdijk; 67.0m × 7.1/13.6m

Remarkable and little-known survivor, still
in surprisingly good condition; built for KD
as half-saloon steamer with Escher Wyss
engines; withdrawn 1924, and used as
houseboat at Köln-Riehl from around 1930
to 1940, then taken to Düsseldorf, where
she has been used as a restaurant ship ever
since. Housings have been built on the
main and upper decks, and her engines are
long since removed, but her hull is still
intact, and she must be practically the only
vessel left afloat with the backward slanting
raked bow popular in the 1870s and 1880s.

ANDERNACH

RÜDERVEREIN RHENUS

ex *Reederij op de Lek* 2, ex *Schoonhoven* 1911, ex
Culemborg 1892
floating clubhouse, ex paddle steamer
Owner: Rüderverein Rhenus, Andernach
Built: 1885, J & K Smit, Krimpen; 52.1m ×
6.5/12.7m

Former paddle steamer from the Rotterdam
to Culemborg service on the river Lek,
withdrawn 1948; used as houseboat at
Amsterdam until 1962, then at Andernach.
Much altered.

BAD KISSINGEN, RIVER SAALE

KISSINGEN

Motor vessel, ex steamer
Owner: Kur-schiffahft in Bad Kissingen
Built: unknown
Route: Franconian Saale river:

Ferry at Bad Kissingen from town to spa.
No recent information.

PRIEN, CHIEMSEE

LUDWIG FESSLER

Motor paddle vessel, ex paddle steamer 1973
Operator: Chiemsee-Schiffahrt Ludwig Fessler, Prien
Built: 1926, Hitzler, Regensburg; 53.0m × 11.6m;
675 pass
Route: Prien–Herreninsel–Fraueninsel

Half-saloon paddler, with a diesel-hydraulic
installation which replaced the original
compound engine in 1973. An interesting
vessel, sailing to the islands of
Herrenchiemsee, with one of the three
castles of King Ludwig II of Bavaria, and
Fraueninsel, with a picturesque fishing
village. *Ludwig Fessler* takes her place along
with modern motor vessels in frequent
sailings to the islands from Prien-Stock,
which is connected to Prien station by a
steam tram dating from 1887. A much
older paddle steamer, *Luitpold* (1887),
similar to *Diessen* on the Ammersee, sailed
on the lake until 1970, when she was
scrapped.

STEGEN, AMMERSEE

DIESSEN

Motor paddle vessel, ex paddle steamer 1975
Operator: Staatliche Schiffahrt Ammersee
Built: 1908, Maffei, Munich; 38.0m × 10.1m; 360
pass
Route: Stegen–Herrsching–Diessen (paddler only
sails in good weather)

Charming former steamer, of a type now
vanished elsewhere in Europe, with covered
area amidships and small upper deck, but
no deck saloons. Basic catering (bottles of
beer and soft drinks) and sale of souvenirs
is from a trestle table in this covered area.
Converted to diesel-hydraulic propulsion
1975, one of the reasons for the change
being the problem of finding trained steam
engineers. Old engines preserved privately
at Herrsching. Still a vessel of great
character, unfortunately she only sails in
fine weather, generally at short notice, and
at weekends. The vessels on the lake are
operated by the provincial organisation for
castles, gardens, and lakes, as are those on
the Starnberger See, Tegernsee, and
Königssee. The lake is surrounded by low
hills, and is a very popular sailing area.
Three post-war motor vessels also sail in
the lake, and, although their base is at
Stegen, in the north, this is little more than
a pier, and the main centre is Herrsching,
reached by the Munich S-bahn suburban
railway. Recommended

UTTING

ANDECHS

Yacht club ex paddle steamer
Owner: Bayerische Seglervereinigung e V, Utting
Built: 1908, Maffei, Munich; 38.0m × 10.1m

Sister of *Diessen*, withdrawn in 1955, in use
since 1956 as yacht club north of Utting
with engines, boiler, paddles, and funnel
removed. Former engine room now used
for drying sails. Decks still original,
thankfully with no additional housings built
on them. Placed on German equivalent of
listed building register 1980.

WEST BERLIN

SPERBER

Motor vessel, ex steamer 1962
Operator: Stern & Kreis Schiffahrt, West Berlin
Built: 1907, Klawitter, Danzig; 38.6m × 5.6m; 312
pass
Route: services from Wannsee

Modern conversion of traditional steamer,
rebuilt with maierform bow and upper deck
1949. In service as steamer until 1962;
rebuilt again, lengthened and dieselised
1967.

Diessen on the Ammersee, 1987

WEST BERLIN

DEUTSCHLAND

Motor vessel, ex steamer 1962
Operator: Reederei Bruno Winkler
Built: 1942, Winkler, Rüdersdorf; 36.8m × 7.0m;
380 pass
Route: excursions from Tegel on Tegelersee,
Heiligensee, Havel

Most interesting of the Berlin veterans; built
as replacement for an earlier motor vessel
that had been requisitioned by the
Wehrmacht and taken to the Vistula.
Steam-powered, using a second-hand tug
engine. Finally entered service in 1950; in
1952 the owners, the Winkler brothers,
along with a son and long-serving engineer,
escaped on the steamer to West Berlin, and
operations were transferred there; dieselised
1957, and funnel removed. Apart from
funnel little changed from a traditional
Berlin steamer design.

WEST BERLIN

KEHRWEIDER II

ex *Reiherstieg*
Motor vessel, ex steamer 1958
Operator: H Riedel, West Berlin
Built: 1902, H Brandenburg, Hamburg; 35.8m ×
6.4m; 400 pass
Route: Tegel–city centre

Originally in operation on local ferry route
at Hamburg. Sunk in air raid and rebuilt
when raised after war. Sold for scrap 1954,
but sold to Berlin, dieselised and enlarged
1958.

WEST BERLIN

AMOR

ex *Niederbarmin* 1945, ex *Iltis*
Motor vessel, ex steamer 1945
Operator: H Riedel, West Berlin
Built: 1907, Gebr Wiemann, Hamburg; 32.0m ×
6m; 300 pass
Route: Cottbuser Brücke–Wannsee and Pfaueninsel

Attractive former steamer, used as tug
during World War II; rebuilt and motorised
after 1945.

WEST BERLIN

BÄR VON BERLIN

Motor vessel, ex steamer 1963
Operator: Reederei Triebler
Built: unknown; rebuilt 1963; 38.0m × 5.1m; 300
pass
Route: Tegel–Pfaueninsel–Glienicker Brücke

Service runs almost the full length of the
West Berlin lake system, to the Glienicker
Brücke, which marks the border and is in
sight of Potsdam. This is the bridge over
which many dissidents have entered the
West. *Bär von Berlin* was built as the
steamer *Erna* for service from Oranienburg,
north of Berlin, and in 1961 was
completely transformed, with a diesel fitted,
and now looks like a modern vessel.

WEST BERLIN

ROLAND VON BERLIN

ex *Rudolf* 1964, ex *Deutschland* 1930s
Twin screw motor vessel, ex steamer 1964
Operator: Reederei Ursula Lodemann
Built: 1897, Stettiner Oderwerke; rebuilt 1964,
1965; 34.1m × 4.9m; 250 pass
Route: Tegel–Wannsee

Rebuilt similar to *Bär von Berlin*; originally
traditional Berlin steamer, now
unrecognisable as such.

Deutschland in West Berlin waters, 1986

Below: Kehrweider II on the Tegelersee, 1986

WEST BERLIN

HEITERKEIT

ex *Karl Wilhelm*
Motor vessel, ex steamer 1958
Operator: Reederei Horst Schmidt
Built: 1909, Gebr Maass, Neustrelitz; 27.8m ×
4.7m; 197 pass
Route: Spandau–Griebnitzsee

Formerly in service at Neuruppin and
Werbelinsee, to the north of Berlin.
Lengthened and new steam engine fitted
1930; used as tug in World War II;
dieselised 1958, rebuilt 1964.

WEST BERLIN

ALEXANDER

Motor vessel, ex steamer 1960
Operator: Reederei R Stengert
Built: 1913, Gebr Maass, Berlin
27.4m × 4.7m; 170 pass
Route: Tegel–Wannsee

Built as steamer, operated on ferry route in
city during World War II. On excursions in
West Berlin 1950 onwards; dieselised 1960,
lengthened 1979.

WEST BERLIN

VENUS

Motor vessel, ex steam tug
Operator: Reederei G Becker
Built: 1903, Stettiner Oderwerke; 21.1m × 4.3m;
141 pass
Route: unknown, possibly on canals near city centre

Former steam tug, converted to passenger
vessel 1956.

WEST BERLIN

ALTE LIEBE

ex *Godeffroy* 1969
Restaurant ship, ex motor vessel, ex steamer
Owner: L Aschmann, Lauenburg
Built: 1912, Wichorst, Hamburg; 30.8m × 7.8m;
formerly 477 pass

Former HADAG Hamburg harbour ferry,
rebuilt and motorised 1949; sold 1969 to
present owner and taken to Berlin
(presumably with upper deck removed and
later replaced). Now a restaurant ship on
the Stössensee.

Montreux before restoration of her steamer
funnel

SWITZERLAND

LAKE GENEVA

MONTREUX

Diesel-electric paddle vessel, ex steamer 1961
Operator: CGN, Geneva
Built: 1904, Sulzer, Winterthur; 322.5t (displ);
63.0m × 7.2/14.3m; 1000 pass
Route: Geneva–St Gingolph–Lausanne (2-day roster
shared with *Vevey*)

Last of a group of lake Geneva paddlers to
have their steam engines replaced by diesel-
electric machinery, *Montreux* had a tall
'steamer' funnel, white rather than the
yellow of the actual steamers, fitted in 1986
in place of her motorship funnel. This
latter funnel could always be distinguished
from similar vessels by its crest. Following
a boiler failure in 1957, she was rebuilt
from 1958 to 1961 with a new glazed
upper deck in addition to the new engines.
Her first class saloon was rebuilt then and
is now furnished in modern style. A bar
was fitted in the starboard paddle box in
1975. The diesel-electric installation is not
dissimilar to that of the former Clyde
paddler *Talisman*.

Italie and a gathering storm, 1977

VEVEY

Diesel-electric paddle vessel, ex steamer 1955
Operator: CGN, Geneva
Built: 1907, Sulzer, Winterthur; 297t (displ); 61.5m
× 7.0/14.0m; 850 pass
Route: Lausanne–St Gingolph–Geneva (alternating
daily with *Montreux*)

Slightly smaller than *Montreux*, *Vevey* and
her sister *Italie* both had similar squat
streamlined motorship funnels. She was
coal-fired until rebuilt as a diesel-electric
paddler from 1953 to 1955. Her upper deck
was rebuilt in 1975. She is one of the most
economical paddlers in Switzerland, and
often used on winter services, mainly across
the lake from Lausanne to Evian les Bains.
Her first class dining saloon is in neo-
classical style, and is little changed from
when she was built, and unlike some of the
other paddlers, the saloon has not been
reduced in size by building an office inside
near the entrance. In 1987 a new tall
steamer-type funnel was fitted, as on
Montreux.

ITALIE

Diesel-electric paddle vessel, ex steamer 1958
Operator: CGN, Geneva
Built: 1908, Sulzer, Winterthur; 296t (displ); 61.5m
× 7.0/14.0m; 900 pass
Route: St Gingolph–Lausanne–Geneva

Sister to *Vevey*, *Italie* is also used on winter
services. She was out of service from 1955
to 1958, before her diesel-electric
installation was fitted. Her dining saloon is
in Second Empire style, the style associated
with Napoleon, and can seat 100
passengers. Unlike her sister, she has a
short white funnel.

HELVÉTIE

Diesel-electric paddle vessel, ex steamer 1977
Operator: CGN, Geneva
Built: 1926, Sulzer, Winterthur; 476t (displ); 73.8m
× 8.5/15.9m; 1400 pass
Route: evening cruises from Geneva; occasional
replacement of *Rhône*

Little used since her diesels were fitted in
1977, *Helvétie* retains her tall yellow
steamer funnel. She was originally fitted
with a three-cylinder Uniflow engine which
can now be seen at the Musée du Léman at
Nyon, and was withdrawn in 1974 with

Diesel-electric paddler *Vevey*, 1977

boiler trouble. When fitting of a new boiler
could not be justified on economic
grounds, she was fitted with two second-
hand engines, built in 1954, from the
DDSG Danube tug *Goliath*, and it would
seem that they have not been too
satisfactory, in view of her little use since.
She was built as a sister ship to *Simplon*,
and her dining saloon is of similar Louis
XVI decor, but an office has been built near
the entrance, thus cutting down on the size.

LÉMAN

Twin screw motor vessel, ex paddle steamer 1942
Operator: CGN, Geneva
Built: 1857, Escher Wyss, Zürich; 185t (displ); 57.0
× 6.6m; 450 pass
Route: reserve vessel at Lausanne; little service

This remarkable veteran was built as a
flush-decked paddler for service on the
lake, and was rebuilt as a half-saloon
paddler in 1894. Her original boiler was
built by Maudslay, Sons & Field of London
for her predecessor *Léman* (1838), but she
had a further four boilers before she was
withdrawn in 1927. Rebuilding as a twin-
screw motorship started c1930, but was
stopped during the Depression from 1934

to 1939, and was not completed until 1942. She is the fastest motorship on any of the Swiss lakes, and has been in the reserve fleet since 1974. She has an unusual, though not unattractive, appearance, like a larger edition of lake Neuchâtel's *Cygne* and *Mouette*.

Note: while this book was in the process of publication the author received information that *Léman* has sadly been scrapped at Lausanne-Ouchy in September 1987.

GENEVA

VALAIS

Restaurant ship, ex paddle steamer 1962
Owner: CGN, Geneva
Built: 1913, Sulzer, Winterthur; 314t (displ); 63m × 7.2/14.3m; formerly 1100 pass

Sister of *Montreux*, withdrawn rather than dieselised in 1962 and used, with engines and boiler removed, as a booking office, landing stage, and restaurant at Geneva. In use since 1966 in this role, replacing *France* (1886) which was then scrapped.

GENEVA

GENÈVE

Static steamer, ex diesel electric paddler 1974, ex Paddler Steamer 1934
Owner: Association pour le bateau *Genève*, Geneva
Built: 1894, Sulzer, Winterthur; 334t (displ); 60.0m × 6.8/14.0m; formerly 850 pass

Pioneer diesel-electric conversion of a paddler on lake Geneva, and indeed in

Europe, *Genève* was converted as early as 1934. She was withdrawn in 1973 after about ten years of only very occasional service. Her dieselisation had seen the replacement of the classic curved bow by a raked bow and the tall funnel by a shorter one, straight rather than shaped as on the later conversions. She is now a youth club and hostel a Geneva.

THONON LES BAINS

MAJOR DAVEL

Paddle steamer, laid up
Owner: Stadt Thonon, Thonon les Bains, France
Built: 1892, Escher Wyss, Zürich; 201t (displ); 52.9m × 5.7/11.4m

Last half-saloon steamer in the CGN fleet, *Major Davel* was rebuilt and lengthened in 1911, a new boiler being fitted at that time. She operated until 1967, only three years after being converted to oil-firing. She was sold and used in the early seventies as a yacht club at Ripailles, but has lain derelict in Thonon harbour on the French shore of the lake for many years.

NEUCHÂTEL

NEUCHÂTEL

Restaurant ship, ex paddle steamer 1970
Owner: Le Vieux Vapeur, Neuchâtel
Built: 1912, Escher Wyss, Zürich; 153t (displ); 48.5m × 6.0/11.0m; formerly 550 pass

Last paddler on lake Neuchâtel, operated also via connecting canals to lake Biel and

Helvétie in her first season as a diesel, 1977

lake Morat. Half-saloon steamer, fitted with an extra saloon on top of the half-saloon by present owners, an addition not too much out of keeping with the character of the steamer. Withdrawn 1972, and engines and boiler removed. Moored in harbour at Neuchâtel.

PORTALBAN

FRIBOURG

Restaurant ship, ex paddle steamer
Owner: Hotel St Louis, Portalban
Built: 1913, Escher Wyss, Zürich; 157t (displ); 48.5m × 6.0/11.0m; formerly 550 pass

Sister of *Neuchâtel*, withdrawn 1965, at present location, a kilometre from the lake, since 1966. In poor condition due to lack of proper preservation.

LAKE THUN

SPIEZ

Motor vessel, ex steamer 1952
Operator: Bern-Lötschberg-Simplon Railway (BLS), Thun
Built: 1901, Sulzer; lengthened 1912; 53t (displ); 30.0m × 5.1m; 200 pass
Route: reserve and charter boat

Last of the former traditional Swiss screw steamers in service. Rebuilt 1912 with upper deck saloon, rebuilt 1951-52 with diesel engine and modern appearance, second new engine 1961.

Major Davel at Thonon, 1983

Below: Restaurant ship *Neuchâtel*, Neuchâtel harbour, 1987

LAKE LUCERNE

NEPTUN

ex *Obersee* 1912
Motor launch, ex steamer 1912
Operator: SGV, Lucerne
Built: 1897, Escher Wyss, Zürich; 19.5t (displ);
17.9m × 4.0m; 95 pass
Route: charters and reserve boat

Small motor launch originally on upper lake Zürich, operating out of Rapperswil until liquidation of the owners in 1910. Purchased by the DGV (predecessors of SGV), in service from 1912 at Lucerne, but with a petrol motor, replaced by a diesel in 1930, and again in 1957. Little used in recent years, but overhauled 1986; blue whales painted on cabin front could indicate that she is now being used as a party boat for charters.

LAKE LUCERNE

WALDSTÄTTER

ex *Rhein*, ex *Ben Jonson*
Motor vessel, ex paddle steamer
Operator: SGV, Lucerne
Built: 1949, DGV, on hull of steamer built 1909 by J Thornycroft, Southampton; 160.7t (displ); 51.5m × 7.9m; 550 pass
Route: Lucerne–Alpnachstad/Flüelen

Prototype for later motorships built at Lucerne, rebuilt 1960 with collapsible mast and lower wheelhouse in order to pass under the Acheregg bridge. The hull was originally part of one of a large group of paddlers built for river Thames service for the LCC. This failed after a couple of years, and the steamers were sold all over Europe, including *Ben Jonson*, which came to Lucerne. She was towed to Duisburg, then steamed up the Rhine to Basel, and was taken to Lucerne by land. She came into service in 1911, after a small deck saloon had been built, but was little used, as she did not have the covered accommodation necessary for winter services and was too small for the summer service. She did see some service as a goods steamer, but was finally withdrawn in 1939. A plan to rebuild her to a motorship in Holland had to be abandoned because of the war.

LAKE LUCERNE

BIEBO

ex *Stadt Luzern*
Bilge-water emptying vessel, ex coal-bunkering vessel, ex paddle steamer
Owner: SGV, Lucerne
Built: 1837, Escher Wyss, Zürich; 41.5t (displ); 28.8m × 5.1m

This remarkable veteran, the first steamer to operate on the lake, sailed as a passenger paddler until 1872, and then as a goods steamer until 1881. The hull was then used as an unpowered barge until 1888, when she was rebuilt as a screw steamer, and was used from 1903 to 1967 for bunkering the paddle steamers, by the end of which period the last coal-fired steamer had been withdrawn. A diesel engine had been fitted in 1924. In 1967 she was converted to

pump away the used fuel and bilge water from the lake steamers and motorships, and continues in this role to this day. A new public pedestrian walkway across the front of the SGV yard enables her to be seen readily at her normal berth.

LAKE LUCERNE

PFAHLRAMME

ex *St Gotthard*
Pile-driving vessel, ex paddle steamer
Owner: SGV, Lucerne
Built: 1843, Escher Wyss, Zürich; 40t (displ); 28.5m × 5.1m

Another astonishing survivor, the second paddle steamer to operate on the lake. She sailed as a passenger paddle steamer until 1872, then was converted to an unpowered barge for the construction of the Gotthard railway. From 1890 onwards she has been used as a pile-driving vessel, for repairing the piers on the lake, and a small steam engine was provided for the pile-driver. In 1898 she became self-propelled with a second-hand engine and boiler from the Mouettes Genevoises launch *Rhône No 3*. In 1968 she was fitted with a collapsible crane in order to pass under the Acheregg bridge, and in 1974 the steam engine was replaced by a diesel; the engine, however, was later fitted in a private launch. Like *Biebo*, she can normally be seen in the SGV shipyard. In 1987 the pile driver steam engine was replaced by a diesel.

LAKE LUCERNE

WILHELM TELL

Restaurant ship, paddle steamer
Owner: Restaurant 'Wilhelm Tell', Lucerne
Built: 1908, Sulzer, Winterthur; 320t (displ); 62.2m × 7.2/14.3m; formerly 1000 pass
Machinery: compound diagonal; 978hp

Sister ship of *Schiller*, used as restaurant since 1972. Dining saloon in Loius XVI

Waldstätter in mid-lake, 1984

style, restored to original condition. Withdrawn 1970. Well preserved and situated in the centre of Lucerne.

LAKE LUCERNE

RIGI

Museum ship, paddle steamer
Owner: Verkehrshaus der Schweiz (Swiss Transport Museum), Lucerne
Built: 1848, Ditchborn & Mare, Greenwich, London; 90t (displ); 40.2m × 8.6/4.3m; formerly 200 pass
Machinery: oscillating, Escher Wyss, Zürich, 1894

Preserved on dry land in a grassed courtyard in the middle of the Swiss Transport Musuem since 1958, *Rigi* is now difficult to see properly because of the trees that have grown up around her. She is used as a café and her engines can be turned by electricity, with a coin-in-the-slot machine. She was the smaller of two paddle steamers from this builder for a short-lived competitor to the DGV, and was lengthened in 1860 and again in 1894. New engines were fitted in 1872 and again in 1894, and a diesel engine was purchased for her in 1921, but never fitted. Rebuilt a number of times in her life, she is in her final operating condition, having been withdrawn in 1952. She is a unique veteran, taking her place beside *Salama*, *Diesbar*, and *Gisela* as relics of another age.

The Swiss transport museum also has on display portions of the paddle steamer *Pilatus* (1895-1966); on view are parts of the first class saloon and the complete engine, boiler, and paddles, which are sectioned and moving to show how a paddle steamer engine operates.

PERTISAU, ACHENSEE

ST JOSEF

Motor vessel, ex steamer 1951
Operator: Tiroler Wasserkraftwerke AG Achansee-
Schiffahrt, Pertisau
Built: 1887, Mayer, Linz; 58t; 26.4m × 4.4m; 120
pass
Route: spare vessel and charters

Original steamer on the mountain-ringed
Achensee, *St Josef* sees little use, and
normally lies at Pertisau. Rebuilt 1951 with
diesel engines and full-length upper deck.

MONDSEE

HELENE

Motor vessel, ex steamer 1951
Operator: Dr Peter Baum, Schiffahrt auf dem
Mondsee, Mondsee
Built: 1887, Dampschiff & Maschinenbauanstalt der
Österreichishen Nordwest-Dampschiffgesellchaft,
Dresden-Neustadt; 20.5t (displ); 19.5m × 2.8m; 75
pass
Route: excursions on lake from Mondsee town and
Satbauer campsite

Fascinating but little-known centenarian,
lengthened 1892; until c1985 worked

regular service to See at far end of lake,
from where until 1949 a short isolated
interurban tramway ran to Unterach on the
Attersee. Distinguished by her two masts,
unusual for such a small vessel. Although
dieselised in 1951, the raised deck to
accommodate the boiler was not brought
down to main deck level until 1970. It is
reported that the original steam engine was
kept in situ as ballast at the conversion in
1951, but it is not clear if it is still there.
Has been in the ownership of the Baum
family all her life.

WOLFGANGSEE

KAISER FRANZ JOSEF I

Motor paddle vessel, ex paddle steamer 1954
Operator: Österreichische Bundesbahn, St Wolfgang
Built: 1873, Mayer, Linz; 46.4t (displ); 33.0m ×
4.3/8.5m; 200 pass
Route: St Gilgen–St Wolfgang (express service)

Europe's only remaining flush-decked
paddler, *Kaiser Franz Josef I* puts up a fair
turn of speed on her service. As the two
towns are not connected by road, except
around the far end of the lake, there is a
considerable traffic from St Gilgen, and the
Kaiser runs a non-stop shuttle service
throughout the day. She is a paddler of
character, although one would imagine the
bare below-deck saloons, lit only by tiny

Kaiser Franz Josef I at St Wolfgang, 1979

portholes, must get claustrophobic in rainy
weather. A steam rack railway runs up the
Schafberg mountain from St Wolfgang,
which has two jetties, one in the centre of
the town, the other at the railway station.
She was the original steamer on the lake,
and was owned until 1957 by
Salzkammergut Lokalbahn, whose narrow
guage railway from Salzburg to Bad Ischl,
passing alongside the lake, was closed in
that year.

WOLFGANGSEE

ELISABETH

ex *Kaiserin Elisabeth*, ex *Pannonia* 1888
Motor vessel, ex steamer 1924
Operator: ÖBB, St Wolfgang
Built: 1873, Pest-Fiumer Hajogyar RT, Budapest;
24.0m × 3.5m; 100 pass
Route: St Gilgen–St Wolfgang

In use until 1886 as a Danube ferry at
Budapest, and, by a remarkable
coincidence, of the same vintage as *Kaiser
Franz Josef I*. Brought over pass from
Mondsee, pulled by 36 horses. Lengthened
1914; dieselised 1924; new engine 1973,
when the funnel was replaced by an extra-
large wheelhouse, and the windows of the

Dance restaurant *Johann Strauss*, Vienna, 1987

fore and aft saloons were enlarged. Now has dark green hull, and a certain amount of imagination is necessary to picture her as such a veteran. Used to provide a strengthened service on the western half of the lake to the modern motorships *Salzkammergut* and *Austria*, which run the full length of the lake from Strobl to St Gilgen.

GRUNDLSEE

RUDOLF

ex *Rudolf Erlbacher* 1946, ex *Fürstin Kinsky* 1938
Motor vessel, ex steamer 1954
Operator: Schiffahrtunternehmen P u G Zimmerman, Grundlsee
Built: 1903, Schiffswerft Linz; 19.3m × 3.5m; 80 pass
Route: Grundlsee–Gösl (fine weather only)

Little-known veteran, on small lake east of Bad Aussee. Renamed after notable Nazi following Anschluss in 1938 (interestingly, large hoards of Nazi gold were found sunk in the nearby small lake after the war). Used for three-lakes trip, with rowing boat on Toplitzsee, and by foot to the tiny Kammersee. Dieselised 1954; new engine 1964; rebuilt 1965 with modern funnel and new saloons. Note that no services operate at all in wet weather.

VIENNA

JOHANN STRAUSS

Restaurant ship, ex paddle steamer
Owner: Walzerkonzert-Café 'DDS Johann Strauss', Vienna
Built: hull 1853, Schiffswerft Budapest; superstructure 1913, Linz; recontructed 1950, Linz; 70.0m; 7.9/15.8m

Well-restored as a café on the Danube Canal in the heart of Vienna, *Johann Strauss* was in operation until 1972, when she was withdrawn after a paddle shaft fractured, having latterly been on the Wachau service. She was laid up 1972-1974, used as a restaurant at Regensburg 1974-1985, and has been at Vienna since then. Her engines and boiler have been removed. She is used as a dance-café, with exhibition dances of the traditional Viennese waltzes composed by her namesake, and reportedly is attracting 1500 visitors a day. She was constructed in 1950, using the hull of the paddle steamer *Grien* (ex *Carl Ludwig* 1938) of 1853, and the engine and parts of the superstructure of *Johann Strauss* (ex *Erzherzog Franz Ferdinand*) of 1913, which had been bombed and sunk at Linz in 1945. She retains her character, and is a favourite venue for weddings, etc. Well worth visiting.

THE NETHERLANDS

AMSTERDAM

KAPTEIN KOK

ex *Kurpfalz* 1977, ex *Reederij op de Lek 6* 1948
Motor paddle vessel; ex restaurant ship, ex paddle steamer
Operator: W Key, Hilversum
Built: J & K Smit, Kinderdijk, 1911; rebuilt 1977; 59.0m × 7.0/13.65m; 400 pass
Route: charters from Amsterdam

Built for service on the river Lek from Rotterdam to Culemborg, and in operation there until 1948. Then steamed up the Rhine to Ludwigshafen where she was used as a restaurant. Rescued in 1977 by present owner, musician Wijnand Key, and towed back to Holland for a complete rebuild, with new saloon in traditional style and diesel-hydraulic machinery. This is so compact that no full-width paddle shaft is required, and the engine is below main deck level. The paddle can be seen revolving through large picture windows. Restored to service 1977, used for a year or two on public sailings from Amsterdam to Rotterdam, and to IJmuiden, but has been purely on charters since then. Her saloon was extended around 1979, and she normally lies at Amsterdam. Named after her last captain when on the Lek, who took her to Ludwigshafen; he visited her immediately after she returned, but died a few weeks later. A new upper deck saloon, similar to one she had carried during her

Kaptein Kok at Amsterdam, 1986

years on the Lek, was added in 1984, and her name on the paddle boxes changed from *Raderboot Kapt Kok* to *Radersalonboot Kapt Kok*. In her days on the Lek she had been the last to be built of a fleet of six paddle steamers, providing about half a dozen sailings daily from Schoonhoven and a few from Culemborg to Rotterdam. After withdrawal of the service in early 1948, she operated charter trips in the 1948 and 1949 summers before being sold to Ludwigshafen.

AMSTERDAM

HYDROGRAAF

Motor vessel, ex survey steamer
Operator: De Vaerende Museum, Amsterdam
Built: 1910, Fijenoord, Rotterdam; 260t (displ);
40.5m × 6.7m
Route: excursions and charters from Amsterdam

Built as coastal survey vessel, operated until c1961; history since then unclear, but she seems to have been dieselised at some time. Seen at Amsterdam 1986, apparently recently restored; restoration very good quality, to original condition, except engine. Appears to operate charters and locally advertised public trips. Owners refuse to answer letters, so regrettably no further

information available. Owners also operate *Elisabeth Smit*, apparently an old sailing ship, but actually rebuilt from Royal Navy minesweeper *MMS 54*, built at Buckie in 1941, and used by the Dutch Sea Scouts until converted in 1981.

HOORN, IJSSELMEER

STAD ENKHUIZEN

ex *Pax IV* 1976, ex *Scherpenhof I* 1975, ex *J H D Koppe* 1972, ex *IJsselstroom* 1964, ex *IJssel* 1943
Motor vessel, ex steamer 1956
Operator: C H de Jonge, Hoorn
Built: 1931, Verschure, Amsterdam; 200gt; 49.8m × 7.3m;
Route: Hoorn-Volendam;
Hoorn-Enkhuizen-Medemblik

Built for owner's Amsterdam-Lemmer passenger/cargo service across IJsselmeer; dieselised 1956; used on Enkhuizen to Stavoren route 1959-1972; also on Amsterdam harbour cruises 1964-66; used for excursions on the IJssel 1972-1975; on present service in conjuction with preserved railway since 1976. Tickets are available from Hoorn to Medemblik with travel in one direction by ship, and the other by train. Originally of unusual type, fairly common at one time in Holland, with long foredeck with hold, and all passenger accommodation in after part of ship.

Rebuilt 1964 with full length passenger saloons on main and upper decks.

LEMMER, IJSSELMEER

JAN NIEVEEN

ex *Wolga* 1977, ex *IJsselhaven* 1960, ex *Jan Nieveen* 1975
Motor vessel, ex steamer 1952
Operator: Maatschappij tot Exploitatie MS *Jan Nieveen*, Lemmer
Built: 1928, Arnhems Scheepsbouw Maatschappij; 45.4m × 6.4m
Route: Lemmer-Enkhuizen; Lemmer-Medemblik; occasionally Lemmer–Amsterdam

Built, like *Stad Enkhuizen*, for the Amsterdam to Lemmer night service, with similar design. Operated this route until service withdrawn 1958, having been dieselised in 1952. Operated excursions to Zuiderzee works 1928, when enclosing dam was being built. Lemmer was a transshipment point for cargo from the barges from Groningen and other points to the larger steamers for Amsterdam. Rebuilt as excursion boat 1960, with passenger cabin where hold had previously been; operated from Rotterdam to Delta works; then in 1975 and 1976 on the Biesboch. Returned to Lemmer and restored to something approaching original condition, but still with new passenger cabin and extended upper deck aft; operated on excursions from Lemmer since 1978.

ELBURG, IJSSELMEER

JACQELINE H

ex *Georg Friedrich Handel*, ex *Fritz Reuter*, ex *Baurat Bolten*
Twin screw motor vessel, ex steamer 1960
Operator: Rederij Randmeer, Harderwijk
Built: 1906, K Fock, Itzehoe; 110gt; 3.1m × 6.2m; 400 pass
Route: Elburg–Urk

Built as steamer for Hamburg-Blankenese route; converted to diesel and rebuilt with modern appearance 1960 (possibly converted to single screw then); sold to present owners mid-seventies. Owners also have a vessel named *Caroline*, which may well be the former HADAG ferry *Neuenfelde I* of 1927, which was sold to this company in 1968.

ROTTERDAM

DE NEDERLANDER

ex *C Bosman*
ex steamer
Built: 1915, J & K Smit, Kinderdijk
67.1m × 9.9m

Built as sister of present *Flandria 20* for Enkhuizen-Stavoren passenger rail-connection ferry service; withdrawn 1956; engine and boiler removed. In static use as training ship in Haringvliet until 1981; laid up at Rotterdam.

ZEELAND

ZIJPE

ex *Willemsdorp*
Twin screw (double-ended) motor vessel, ex steamer, car ferry
Operator: N V Streekvervoer Zuid West Nederland, Zeirikzee
Built: 1930, De Biesboch, Dordrecht; 195gt; 40.5m × 11.0m; 150 pass, 28 cars
Route: Zijpe–Anna Jacobspolder

Originally tall-funnelled open deck steam car ferry; built as sister of *Dordrecht*, now *Melittaland* (see Malta); rebuilt and dieselised as late as 1972; service planned to be replaced by bridge as final part of delta plan c1987.

NIJMEGEN

K S C C SCHIPPERSZENTRUM

ex *Jos Franken* 1986, ex *Hugo Basedow* 1962
Floating office, ex paddle steamer
Built: 1925, WUMAG, Dresden-Übigau; 58.1m × 13.2m

Built as rather ugly paddle steamer for service on the Elbe at Lauenburg; operated until service withdrawn 1962. Sold to Holland; used as floating supermarket at Rotterdam until c1986, then moved to Nijmegen; very much overbuilt, little trace of original. There are a number of relics of *Hugo Basedow* at the Elbe shipping museum in Lauenburg.

RIVER RHINE

BASILEA

ex *Bern* 1956
Twin screw motor vessel, ex steam paddle tug 1956
Operator: Van Holst Scheepvaart BV, Rotterdam
Built: 1923, J & K Smit, Kinderdijk; 77.0m × 9.0m; 94 pass
Route: Düsseldorf–Rüdesheim

Former typical Rhine paddle tug, built for Swiss owners; rebuilt as cargo/passenger ship 1956, later as cruise vessel.

RIVER RHINE

ROTTERDAM

ex *Kronprinzessin Cecilie* 1960
Twin screw motor vessel, ex steam paddle tug
Operator: F Broere Reizen, Rotterdam
Built: 1914, Sachsenburg, Rosslau; 65.5m × 8.1m; 135 berths

Built as two-funnelled Elbe paddle tug; sold to Holland 1960, converted to cruise vessel. No recent information.

BELGIUM

ANTWERP

FLANDRIA 20

ex *R van Hasselt* 1966
Twin screw motor vessel, ex steamer 1966
Operator: Interprovinciale Stoombootdiensten Flandria, Antwerp
Built: 1915, Smit, Kinderdijk; 732gt; 69.5m × 9.9m; 800 pass
Route: Antwerp–Vlissingen; excursions from Antwerp to Ostend, Zeirikzee, Veere, Middelburg, Rotterdam (no single journeys possible on these latter excursions)

Built for rail connection ferry route from Enkhuizen to Stavoren across the Zuider Zee (now the IJsselmeer); laid up 1950, but reactivated 1956-1959 on this route, and then on excursions for a while. Sold to Flandria 1964; rebuilt and dieselised; in

Rebuilt veteran *Flandria 20* at Antwerp

present service from 1966; new engines 1975. Modern appearance, cruiser stern only clue to age of vessel. Shares Antwerp-based excursions with four other vessels in fleet.

DINANT, RIVER MEUSE

TOURISTE I *(200 pass)*
TOURISTE IV *(300 pass)*
LE MOUCHE *(350 pass)*
MEUSE-ARDENNES *(200 pass)*

Motor vessels, ex steamers
Operator: Croisières Mosanes 'Bateaux-Mouches', Dinant
Route: river Meuse from Dinant downstream to Namur and upstream to Agimont

Unfortunately, I have no record of the history of these vessels, or even dates of building. *Touriste I* and others able to be identified positively from photographs are of unusual design, with saloons on both lower and upper decks, and would appear to be modern rebuilds of old passenger screw steamers. There are other smaller vessels at Dinant, but these would appear to be waterbuses.

FRANCE

PARIS

NOMADIC

ex *Ingenieur Minard*, ex *Nomadic* 1934
Restaurant ship, ex twin screw steamer
Owner: unknown, Paris
Built: 1911, Harland & Wolff, Belfast; 1273gt; 67.3m × 11.3m; formerly 500 passengers

Built for the White Star Line, for use as a tender to *Olympic* and *Titanic* at Cherbourg, *Nomadic* is the last surviving ship of that once great line. She passed into French ownership in 1934, (although she had always been French flagged, being actually owned by a subsidiary of White Star), and was renamed, operating under steam until 1968 at the French port. She tendered the Cunarders *Queen Mary* and *Queen Elizabeth* right to the end of their service, *Queen*

Elizabeth 2, however, called at Le Havre instead of Cherbourg. Sold for demolition in 1968, she was later purchased for use at Paris, and is little altered from her days as a tender, except for the cutting down of the funnel and masts, and the extension of some accommodation over the fore-deck. It is not certain if the engines are still in situ.

PARIS

(STEAM LAUNCH)

Route: Bois de Boulogne, Paris; Lac Inferieure

Steam launch reported in Gault Millau restaurant guide as serving 'Chalet des Isles' restaurant, which is on an island in the middle of the Bois de Boulogne in Paris. It is known that steam launches were used there around the turn of the century, and the guide mentioned indicates specifically that the boat is steam-powered. No further information is available, however.

PARIS

PRINCESS ELIZABETH

Restaurant ship, ex paddle steamer
Owner: Association de Défense des Arts Typographiques, Paris
Built: 1927, Day Summers Ltd, Southampton; 388gt; 59.4m × 7.4m; 338 pass
Engines removed

Built for the Southampton, Isle of Wight and South of England Royal Mail Steam Packet Co Ltd, commonly known as Red Funnel Steamers, *Princess Elizabeth* ran on excursions from Bournemouth and Southampton until 1958. She, like many other paddlers, took part in the Dunkirk evacuation in 1940. She operated at Torquay (1960-1), Bournemouth (1962), and Weymouth (1963-5) for new owners, and was sold for scrap in 1967. Purchased after her engines and boiler had been removed, she has had a number of owners since, and was at London from 1970, spending the greater part of that time as a restaurant ship upstream from London Bridge. Sold to French owners December 1987 and towed to Rouen prior to berthing on the river Seine in Paris as a museum and cultural centre. She has been used as a memorial to the Dunkirk evacuations, and carried a list on board of the 'little boats' used there.

PARIS

L'HIRONDELLE

Motor vessel, replica of 1889 steamer
Operator: Bateaux-Monches, Paris
Route: charters on Seine at Paris

Replica or possibly rebuild of a true veteran, based on original 'Mouche' steam launch, referred to briefly in Bateaux-Monches literature; I have been unable to trace either photograph or technical data. Note that an ugly modern *L'Hirondelle* also exists in the Bateaux-Monches fleet.

SPAIN

CANARY ISLANDS

LA PALMA

Yacht club, ex steamer
Built: 1912, Harkness, Middlesborough; rebuilt 1950; 894gt; 67.0m × 9.1m; formerly 190 pass
Machinery: triple expansion

Last of a trio of veteran steamers, which operated all their lives principally on services between the various Canary Islands, but also sailing to Mauritania and Spanish Sahara, and in later years to the Spanish enclaves in northern Morocco of Ceuta and Melilla. They were of a type which had long vanished elsewhere in Europe, Norway's *Kysten I* being the nearest equivalent survivor. *Viera Y Clavijo* was sold in the mid-seventies to a Dutch scrap merchant who was so impressed by her that he operated her as a museum at Zierikzee for a few years before she went for scrap around 1980; *Leon Y Castillo* was scrapped in 1982; while *La Palma* was removed from Lloyd's Register c1985 with a note that she had been converted to a yacht club. I have no information as to where this was, but it is presumably on Tenerife or Las Palmas. Further information would be welcomed.

PORTUGAL

LISBON

CASTELO

ex *Lichtwark*1977
Motor vessel, ex steamer 1958
Operator: Transtejo, Lisbon
Built: 1928, H C Stülcken, Hamburg; 144gt; 23.6m × 7.1m; 453 pass
Route: Lisbon-Cacilhas and Montijo

Former HADAG Hamburg harbour passenger ferry; sank 1946 while carrying marines with the loss of 101 of the 110 on board; raised and returned to service; rebuilt and converted to motorship similar to post-war HADAG vessels 1958; sold to Portugal 1977.

ITALY

LAKE MAGGIORE

TORINO

Motor vessel, ex steamer 1950
Operator: NLM, Arona
Built: 1913, Bacigalupo Sampierdarena, Genoa; rebuilt 1950, 1965-1969; 203t (displ); 443m × 5.8m; 500 pass
Route: variety of lake services on Italian half of lake

Completely rebuilt 1950 from tall-funnelled screw steamer which was bombed, burnt and sunk in 1944; rebuilt again 1959; now almost indistinguishable from modern motorships on lake.

ARONA

LOMBARDIA

Restaurant ship, ex paddle steamer
Owner: unknown, Arona
Built: 1908, N Odero, Sestri Ponente; 52.0m × 6.5m

Former paddler, withdrawn in 1958, used as restaurant ship at Baveno until 1969, since then at Arona. Engines and boiler removed, altered internally and roofed over with rows of lights above this. Not at all well restored; Similar in original design to *Italia* on lake Garda, with funnel aft of the paddle boxes.

LAKE COMO

MILANO

Screw motor vessel, ex paddle steamer 1925
Operator: NLC, Como
Built: 1904, N Odero, Sestri Ponente; 182t (displ); 43.2m × 5.9m; 496 pass
Route: Como-Bellagio-upper lake

Still of paddle steamer design, with overhanging sponsons and deckhouses on these, *Milano* was originally built as a paddle steamer. She has a half-saloon aft, originally richly ornamented but now with plain decor. In 1926 she was rebuilt as a screw motor vessel, but keeping her sponsons and general paddler design. A tall funnel remained until replacement with the present one after 1945. She is an extremely interesting survivor of the transition from steam to diesel, a number of other similar conversions on the Italian lakes having either been rebuilt later with a more modern appearance, or been scrapped.

LAKE COMO

BARADELLO

Motor vessel, ex steamer 1959
Operator: NLC, Como
Built: 1908, Escher Wyss, Zürich; 98t (displ); 34.7m × 5.5m; 400 pass
Route: spare vessel

Originally built as a screw steamer, with half-saloon aft and paddle-steamer style sponson housings. Bombed and sunk 1945 by Allied air raid, then rebuilt with a

Italia leaving Limone, 1979

modern aft saloon, but still with steam propulsion. Entered service in 1950, and was converted to diesel between 1956 and 1959, emerging looking similar to lake Garda's *Baldo* with an open foredeck, the remainder of the main deck enclosed with flat glass sides, and an open upper deck.

LAKE COMO

BISBINO

Motor vessel, ex steamer 1956, laid up
Owner: NLC, Como
Built: 1907, Escher Wyss, Zürich; 98t (displ); 34.7m × 5.5m; 400 pass

Although built as a sister of *Baradello*, she remained in her original condition until rebuilt and dieselised from 1955-6. She retains her small half-saloon, but the midships section was extensively rebuilt at that time. In 1982 she was withdrawn from service, but as far as is known she is still in existence, laid up at the company's yard at Como-Tavernola.

LAKE COMO

PLINIO

Restaurant ship, ex paddle steamer
Owner: Centro Nautico Alto Lario, Colico
Built: 1903, Escher Wyss, Zürich; 51.0m × 6.4m

Well-preserved paddler, used as yacht club and bar-restaurant moored inside breakwater at Colico, at the north of lake Como. Engines and boiler removed, but

paddles still intact, and appearance little changed from her time in service. Half saloon steamer, withdrawn mid-sixties, moored at Colico from 1970. One of Europe's better paddle steamers preserved as restaurant ships.

LAKE ISEO

ISEO

Motor vessel, ex steamer
Operator: Navigazione Lago d'Iseo
Built: 1910, Cant Bacigalupo, Sampierderna; 28.8m × 4.2m; 220 pass
Route: Iseo–Tavernola–Lovere

Small single deck motor launch, probably sole veteran on this lake, which lies north of Brescia. Built for a railway connection service from Pisogne to Lovere, dieselised 1929; damaged by air raid 1944 with 41 casualties; returned to service after World War II; operates with four smaller post-war motor boats and the new motor vessel *Citta di Brescia* (1986).

LAKE GARDA

ZANARDELLI

ex *Giuseppe Zanardelli*
Diesel-electric paddle vessel, ex steamer 1982
Operator: Navigaziona Lago Garda, Peschiera
Built: 1903, Escher Wyss, Zürich; 253t (displ); 48.6m × 6.2/11.6m; 500 pass
Route: mainly charters on lake

A more conventional-looking paddler then *Italia*, *Zanardelli* is of a fairly standard Swiss type. She was fitted with a glassed-in upper deck saloon and a more upright funnel in 1964, and was withdrawn after running aground in 1976. Her engines were then replaced by diesels, and she did not re-enter service until 1983. She offered similar cruises to those of *Italia* in that year, but in 1987 appeared to be at Peschiera, used solely for charters.

LAKE GARDA

ITALIA

Diesel-electric paddle vessel, ex steamer 1975
Built: 1909, N Odero, Sestri Ponente; 304t (displ); 52.5m × 6.5m; 600 pass
Operator: NLG, Peschiera
Route: afternoon excursions from various places on lake

An unusual paddler with a tall straight funnel, which was at one time even taller, *Italia* has been on the special cruise roster, with a different starting point each day of the week, since re-entering service in 1977 after modernisation and dieselisation. She

Plino at Colico, 1987

has a totally glassed-in upper deck saloon aft, used as a dance-saloon, and an ugly modern wheelhouse; these alterations were made in 1970. The effect of this upper deck alteration has been to enclose half the funnel, thus giving an odd effect. She was bombed and sunk off Sirmione in January 1945 while in use as a German hospital ship, and did not come back into service until 1952

LAKE GARDA
BALDO

Screw motor vessel, ex paddle steamer
Operator: NLG, Peschiera
Built: 1900, N Odero, Sestri Ponente; 149t (displ); 42.8m × 5.2m; 480 pass
Route: services on lake Garda

The seemingly similar modern-looking motorships on lake Garda have considerably different histories. *Baldo* was built as a paddle steamer, and rebuilt in 1925 to a screw motorship, but keeping her sponsons and steamer profile, and aft half-saloon, looking something similar to *Milano* on lake Como. Then, in 1959, she was rebuilt again into a modern two-decked motorship. Sister *Mocenigo* was treated similarly, but scrapped in 1985.

LAKE GARDA
(PILEDRIVER)

ex *Garda*
Owner: NLG, Peschiera
Built: 1888

Built as screw tug; converted to passenger steamer 1890; and to motorship (like *Baldo*) and lengthened in 1925; probably used as piledriver since 1940s at least. Identified by former name on hull.

VENICE
32

ex *Burano*, ex *32* 1939
Motor vessel, ex steamer 1939
Built: SAVINEM, 1908; new engine 1979; 81gt; 24.8m × 4.5m; 234 pass
Route: lagoon services

Traditional 'vaporetto' waterbus, rebuilt 1939 for service to Murano and Torcello, rebuilt again with raised wheelhouse as prototype for new vessels *33* to *36*, built 1974 to 1981

VENICE
39

ex *Capitano Bragadin*, ex *No 39*
Motor vessel, ex steamer 1929
Built: 1916, SAVINEM; 84gt; 24.6m × 4.5m; 250 pass

41

ex *Murano*, ex *41* 1939
Motor vessel, ex steamer 1939
Built: 1917, SAVINEM; 91gt; 24.6m × 4.5m; 250 pass

Both rebuilt, like number *32*, in 1939.

VENICE
51, 54, 59, 60

ex *Teodoro Maggiolago*; ex *Arturo Salvato*; ex *Giglio Boscari*, ex *Luigi Boscari*; ex *Tita Fumei*
All vaporetto motor launches, ex steamers c1949
Built: 1935, Cantiere Navale ed Officine Meccaniche; 25gt; 20.9m × 4.2m; 221 pass; 224 pass; 234 pass; 215 pass

45, 48, 49, 53

ex *Franco Gozzi*; ex *Luigi Passoni*; former name unknown; ex *Arrone Cazzogon*
All vaporetto motor launches, ex steamers c1949
Built: 1935, Cantiere Navale ed Officine Meccaniche; 53gt; 20.9m × 4.2m; 234 pass; 234 pass; 234 pass; 236 pass

42, 46, 47, 58, 61

ex *Annibale Foscari*; ex *Ugo Pepe*; ex *Severino Francesco*; ex *Leonio Contro*; ex *Ferruaio Poloni*
All vaporetto diesel-electric launches, ex steamers c1949
Built: 1935, Cantiere Navale ed Officine Meccaniche; 53gt; 20.9m × 4.2m; all 234 pass

In these three batches, the difference between the tonnages of the first group and those of the remainder is probably accounted for by the fact that the first have an open foredeck, while the second and third have an enclosed foredeck; the vessels of the third group are listed in the ACTV list as diesel-electric, although the entire list may in fact be diesel-electric. All were built as oil-fired steamers named after fascist martyrs, renamed after the war, and, as noted, re-engined in about 1949. Apart from numbers they are indistinguishable from recent buildings, which go from *84* to *99*, and from *1* to *13*. All Venice vessels are operated by Azienda del Consorzio Trasporti Veneziano (ACTV), Venice.

There is a also a small non-standard batch, *66*, *68* and *69*, built by Breda in 1955, which have a funnel. Vaporetto have cream upperworks, and are used on routes along the Grand Canal, and from the station to the Lido, whereas some of the other routes run along canals which are too small for the vaporetti. These vessels are known as 'motoscafi'.

Of these smaller motoscafi, which have white upperworks, *122* was built in 1942, and the remainder (*126* to *214*) from 1950 onwards.

TRIESTE
NAVE RISTORANTE TRAGHETTO

ex *Mojolner* 1972, ex *Mjølner* 1970
Restaurant ship (probably never opened); ex screw steamer
Owner: B Mauri, Trieste
Built: 1930, Svendborg, Denmark; 360gt; 45.0m × 8.3m
Machinery: quadruple expansion, Christiansen & Meyer; 460hp

Former Danish steamer, used between Korsør and Lohals; sold to Italy 1970; seen lying laid up at mole at Trieste 1983. No recent information.

BAY OF NAPLES
PELORITANO

ex *Fehmarn*
Motor vessel, ex double-ended steam ferry 1951
Operator: N Assenso, Formia
Built: 1927 Nobiskrug, Rendsburg; 397gt; 62.0m × 8.2m; approx 250 pass; unknown no of cars
Route: Puzzuoli–Ischia

Converted former German train ferry; used on Straits of Messina service 1966-1974; rebuilt and lengthened Naples 1974-6, and at that time she was converted from a double-ended ferry to a stern loader and more passenger accommodation was fitted. Occasionally used on Formia-Ponza service c1981 in addition to present service; originally operated as train ferry on route across Fehmarnsund, but bridge built 1963 when route became major international route by Puttgarden-Rødby ferry to Denmark; dieselised and lengthened 1951.

ISCHIA
CITTA DI ISCHIA

ex *Langeland* 1961
Landing stage for hydrofoils, ex motor car ferry, ex steamer
Owner: Libera Nazigazione Lauro, Ischia
Built: 1926, Helsingør; 483gt; 48.5m × 9.3m

Another former Danish ferry, built for Svendborg-Rudkøbing train ferry route to Langeland; sold to Naples 1961. Extensively rebuilt from original condition with two tall funnels to a modern single-funnel vessel 1967; possibly dieselised then, or after she arrived in Italy. Operated at Naples until c1982, then used as a hydrofoil terminal at Ischia, having been mainly on the Puzzuoli-Ischia route before withdrawal.

SALERNO
BUCANIERO

ex *Ischia* 1972, ex *Partenope* 1949, ex *St Elian* 1927, ex *Hörnum* 1922, ex *M140* 1919
Restaurant ship, ex twin screw steamer
Owner: C Lauri, Salerno
Built: 1919; Tecklenborg, Geestemunde; 553gt; 56.0m × 7.4m; formerly 500 pass
Machinery: triple expansion; 1800hp; 16kn

Remarkable survivor, built as World War I German minesweeper; rebuilt 1919 for HADAG's East Prussian and Helgoland services; sold to Liverpool and North Wales SS Co 1922, used as *St Elian* on excursions from Llandudno until sold to SPAN in 1927; then on Bay of Naples routes until withdrawn 1972, having been renamed following post-war reconstruction and conversion to oil-firing in 1949; used since then as restaurant ship at Salerno; with upper deck built over. It is not known if the engines remain in situ.

VILLA SAN GIOVANNI

LERICI

ex *Unione Operaia*
Motor vessel, ex steamer
Operator: La Calabria, Villa San Giovanni
Built: 1906; 141gt; 34.7m
Route: excursions on Calabrian coast

Built as small traditional two-decked steamer for service in Gulf of La Spezia; rebuilt with modern superstructure. Operated by local authority from 1956 until replaced by modern vessels and withdrawn from local route 1982, sold and placed on excursion service; sold to present owners 1987.

MALTA

MALTA

MELITALAND

ex *Dordrecht* 1973
Motor vessel, car ferry, ex steamer 1956
Operator: Gozo Channel Co, Malta
Built: 1933, Meyer, Zaltbommel, Holland; 1434gt; 70.5m × 10.4m; 600 pass; 80 cars
Route: Cirkewwa–Gozo

Built for use in Holland across the Hollandsch Diep at Moerdijk as sister of present *Zijpe*; operated for PSD, Vlissingen, on Kruiningen-Perkpolder route 1936-1972. Lengthened 1955; dieselised 1956; sold to Malta 1973, but did not actually arrive there until mid-1974, after an engine failure in the Bay of Biscay; rebuilt for Gozo route; with present owners since 1980.

GREECE AND CYPRUS

PIRAEUS

ARIS

ex *Pindos* 1987, ex *Pindos II* 1965, ex *Sylvana* 1949, ex *Maid of Honour* 1923
Screw steamer, present status unknown
Owner: Commercial Bank of Greece
Built: 1907, Ailsa Shipbuilding Co Ltd, Troon; 421gt; 53.3m × 7.5m
Machinery: triple expansion

Remarkable veteran, believed long since scrapped, but noted as renamed in 1987, so she must presumably still be afloat, although ownership by a Greek bank usually indicates that the owner has gone bankrupt and the bank has repossessed the ships. Built as a typical pre-1914 steam yacht with clipper bow and very fine lines. Used in World War I as auxiliary patrol vessel, and World War II as minelayer, and later as minesweeper base ship. Sold to Greece 1949, converted to passenger/cargo steamer; owner in late sixties was John Tripos, but no more recent information; possibly converted to cargo vessel.

PIRAEUS

MESSARIA

ex *Blekinge* 1945, ex *Landskrona* 1941, ex *Polhem* 1930
Cargo motorship, ex passenger steamer
Owner: I Dimakis, Piraeus
Built: 1889, Södra Varvet, Stockholm; 35.9m × 7.4m

Built for Swedish Gotland Company's passenger/cargo service; sold 1930 for Landskrona-Copenhagen service; sold and operated on Swedish coastal routes from Stockholm 1941-1945; then sold to Greece and converted to cargo motorship; believed to be still afloat.

PIRAEUS

APOLLONIA

ex *Sidi el Abbes* 1963
Twin screw turbine steamer, laid up
Owner: Hellenic Mediterranean Lines
Built: 1949, Swan Hunter & Wigham Richardson, Newcastle; 5324gt; 122.7m × 16.3m; 476 pass; 50 cars

Former French passenger steamer, built for SGTM routes from Marseilles, bought by HML 1963, and converted to side-load cars. Used until late seventies on Hellenic Mediterranean lines route from Venice to Piraeus, Cyprus, and Haifa; laid up at Chalkis since then; unlikely to sail again. No recent information (last noted 1985).

LIMASSOL

SOL PHRYNE

ex *Aeolis* 1977, ex *Taisetsu Maru* 1967
Twin screw motor vessel, ex steam train ferry
Operator: Sol Maritime Services, Limassol, Cyprus
Built: 1948, Mitsubishi; 6151gt; 121.3m × 15.9m; 630 pass
Route: Piraeus–Limassol–Haifa

Former Japanese Railways turbine-powered train ferry, originally built with four funnels (two sets of twins) and used on the ferry from Hakodate on the main island of Hokkaido to Aomori on the northern island of Honshu. Sister ship *Toya Maru* capsized in a typhoon in September 1955 with the loss of 1172 lives, a catastrophe little-known in the West, and magnified by the loss of four further train ferries in the same typhoon. *Taisetsu Maru* was converted to a diesel car ferry after sale to Greece; initially operated by ill-fated Efthymiadas Lines, and from the mid-seventies by her present owners, she was a remarkably stable fixture in the much-changing world of Greek ferries.

Note: she was seized in November 1987 in lieu of her owner's debts, and in February 1988 was purchased by a Palestinian group. She was renamed *The Return* and intended for symbolic use carrying deported Palestinians back to Israel. Shortly before she was due to sail she was sunk by a bomb, claimed by the Palestinians to have been planted by Israeli agents.

ISTANBUL

HEYBELİADA

Twin screw steamer, laid up
Built: 1928, Ateliers & Chantiers de Provence, Port Bouc, France; 699gt; 61.2m × 9.1m; 1389 pass
Machinery: two triple expansion by builder's Marseilles yard; 700hp; 11kn
Route: If; spare on other routes

Although built some sixteen years later, an identical sister of *Burgaz*, also converted to oil-firing c1961; used as relief on a number of routes, including Princes islands, in recent years. She was withdrawn from service in December 1987 when a survey found her unsafe.

ISTANBUL

SARAYBURNU

ex *Sarayburnu/Bosporus No 65*
Twin screw steamer, laid up
Owner: Zarbo Denizcilik
Built: 1910, Fairfield, Glasgow; 434gt; 46.8 × 7.9m; formerly c900 pass
Machinery: two triple expansion by builders; 455hp; coal-fired; 10kn

In service until 1985; I sailed on her in 1984, and she seemed in good condition and was in intensive use. Reportedly withdrawn because of boiler problems. A beautiful veteran steamer, and one which should really be brought back to the Clyde as part of a maritime museum; reported sold in 1986 to Zarbo Denizcilik for conversion to a restaurant cruise vessel.

ISTANBUL

ALTINKUM

ex *Altinkum/Bosporus No 74*
Twin screw steamer, laid up
Owner: Ufuk Denizcilik
Built: 1929, Fairfield, Glasgow; 415gt; 47.0m × 7.9m; formerly 887 pass
Machinery: two triple expansion by builders; 455hp; coal-fired

Built to same design as earlier steamers, although much later; on Bosporus commuter runs 1984; withdrawn 1985, reportedly sold for conversion to tourist service or to be rebuilt as coaster. Seen at Gelibolu scrapyard late 1987, but still intact at that stage, so could either be scrapped, or having upper works removed as first stage of conversion to coaster.

ISTANBUL

GÖZTEPE

ex *Göztepe/Bosporus No 69*, ex *Hüseyin Haki/Bosporus No 69* 1933
Twin screw steamer, undergoing conversion
Owner: Ufuk Denizcilik
Built: 1911, Ateliers & Chantiers de France, Dunkirk; 567gt; 47.4m × 7.6m; formerly 788 pass
Machinery: two triple expansion by builders; 547hp; coal-fired; 9kn

Transferred to AKAY company for Princes Isles service 1933, and renamed; withdrawn

Heybeliada off Şirkeci, 1984

Below: Sarayburnu in her last season, 1984

1983; sold 1986 for conversion to diesel tourist ship. Seen at Gelibolu with *Altinkum* late 1987 where work was to be done.

ISTANBUL

KOCATAŞ

ex *Kocataş/Bosporus No 75*
Screw steamer, laid up
Built: 1938, Hasköy, Istanbul; 157gt; 33.0m × 6.6m
Machinery: triple expansion, allegedly built by
McTaggart Scott, Leith, 1913; 330hp

Last of a group of four small single screw steamers built between the wars; used latterly as rush hour relief on the Golden Horn service; withdrawn late 1984; still on sale list as far as is known. Engines are rather a mystery, as McTaggart Scott made reversing gear; if they were second-hand presumably the builder's plate from McTaggart Scott was the only one that survived the presumed changeover from another steamer when *Kocataş* was built.

ISTANBUL

MUDANYA

Screw steamer, car ferry, in static use
Built: 1940, Swan Hunter & Wigham Richardson,
Newcastle; 691gt; 54.9m × 12.3m;
Machinery: triple expansion by builders; 750hp

Withdrawn a number of years ago, and used was a floating office with accommodation built over the car deck, *Mudanya* is a survivor of a class of twelve landing craft type steam car ferries built in Britain in the early 1940s for the Turkish navy. For some reason they were not requisitioned, and all sailed out to Turkey in convoy, during the height of the submarine war between 1940 and 1942. Eight came from Swan Hunter, and the remainder from Ferguson Bros of Port Glasgow. Only one failed to make it to Turkey, *Murefte* being sunk in the Mediterranean in September 1941 by gunfire from an Italian submarine. Two survive with the Turkish navy, *TCG Tuzla* (Y1168), ex *Sarkov*, and *TCG Kilya* (Y1166), which are based at Bükükdere, on the upper Bosporus. *Mudanya* was one of three transferred to civil use after the war, probably being used on the Dardanelles car ferry service.

ISTANBUL

HAYDARPAŞA

Twin screw steamer, laid up
Built: 1948, J & K Smit, Kinderdijk, Holland; 561gt;
54.4m × 10.5m; formerly 1041 pass
Machinery: triple expansion, Verschure,
Amsterdam; 680hp; coal-fired

One of a Dutch sextet of steam ferries, withdrawn c1984 and laid up on Golden Horn; reportedly still for sale late 1987.

ZONGULDAK

BÜYÜKADA

Twin screw steamer
Built: 1948, J & K Smit, Kinderdijk, Holland; 561gt;
54.4m × 8.4m; formerly 1041 pass
Machinery: triple expansion, L Smit, Kinderdijk;
680hp, coal-fired

Withdrawn c1986; reportedly sold to town of Zonguldak, a coal port on the Black Sea, for use as a restaurant, and taken there in 1986-7.

ISTANBUL

RUMELI HISARI

Twin screw steamer, laid up
Built: 1948, Werft Gusto, Schiedam; 561gt; 54.4m
× 8.4m; formerly 1041 pass
Machinery: triple expansion, De Klop, Schiedrecht;
680hp; coal-fired

Withdrawn late 1986, having been on the rush hour Besiktaş-to-Üsküdar shuttle in that year with occasional stand-in on the Bosporus commuter runs; reportedly for sale 1987.

ISTANBUL

ANADOLU HISARI

Twin screw steamer
Built: 1948, Werft Gusto, Schiedam; 561gt; 54.4m
× 10.9m; formerly 1041 pass
Machinery: triple expansion, L Smit, Kinderdijk;
680hp; coal-fired

Withdrawn late 1986, having been on the rush hour Besiktaş-to-Üsküdar shuttle in that year with occasional relief duties on Bosporus commuter services; reportedly for sale 1987.

ISTANBUL

A KAVAGI

Twin screw steamer, laid up
Built: 1961, Fairfield, Glasgow; 781gt; 69.9m ×
13.6m; 1952 pass
Machinery: two compound in tandem on each
shaft, Christiansen & Meyer, Hamburg; 1600hp

Ninth member of Fairfield class, badly damaged by fire 1985, fortunately shortly after a full load of passengers had disembarked, and without casualties. Originally planned to be rebuilt, retaining steam machinery, but later put up for sale.

ISTANBUL

ŞIHAP

ex *Şihap/Bosporus No 52*
Screw steamer, status unknown
Built: 1905, Fairfield, Glasgow; 116gt; 30.6m ×
5.9m
Machinery: compound, by builders; 190hp

Smaller steamer withdrawn mid-seventies, still listed in Lloyd's Register, although probably scrapped.

ISTANBUL

CAMIALTI I
CAMIALTI II

Screw steamers, status unknown
Built: 1961, Haliç, Istanbul; 162gt; 32.7m × 6.6m
Machinery: compound, Arnhemsche Scheeps
Maatschappij, Arnhem, 1934; 150hp; 8kn

Rather ugly small launches used on Golden Horn service; withdrawn c1983; not seen since then and may have been scrapped, or tucked away somewhere awaiting conversion to diesel. Engines presumably originally came from earlier steamers, probably *Bebek/Bosporus No 55* and *Göksu/Bosporus No 56* (1905), which had been re-engined in the thirties and scrapped around 1960.

ISTANBUL

PARADISE

ex *Sariyer* 1986
Motor vessel, ex steamer
Operator: unknown, Istanbul
Built: 1938, Hasköy, Istanbul; 150gt; 33.0m × 6.6m

Former sister of *Kocataş*, withdrawn 1983; converted 1984-1986 for use as restaurant cruise motorship, with rebuilt superstructure and new modern twin funnels.

ISTANBUL

SHERAZAD

ex *Rumelihisari/Bosporus No 73* 1986
Dummy paddler, motorship, ex steamer
Operator: Hilton Hotel, Istanbul
Built: 1927, Schichau, Elbing, Germany; 140gt

Former single screw steamer, sister of *Üsküdar*, which sank in 1958 during a storm in the Gulf of Izmit with the loss of over 200 lives, and slightly smaller version of *Kocataş*. Sherazad was withdrawn c1983, and re-entered service after a hideous conversion in 1986. She now looks like the Sultan's toy paddle steamer, with narrow dummy side wheels, a funnel with a crown on the top, and a fancy curly design on the rails. She is powered by a Caterpillar diesel engine driving a single screw. A bar and dance floor has been installed on the upper deck, and she is operated on very expensive cruises on the Bosporus, including a meal and wine, for around £25.

ISTANBUL

ERENKÖY

ex *Erenköy/Bosporus No 70*, ex *Ziya/Bosporus No 70* 1933
Twin screw motor vessel, ex steamer 1984
Owner: Gümüs Kepi
Built: 1911, Ateliers & Chantiers de France,
Dunkirk; 567gt; 47.4m × 7.6m; formerly 788 pass

Transferred to AKAY company for Princess Isles service 1933, and renamed; withdrawn c1983; sold and used as restaurant cruise ship on similar service to *Boğaziçi*. Seen laid up off Kabatas May 1986, but was not there later that summer; believed converted to diesel by new owners, but this is unconfirmed.

ISTANBUL

RAHMI KAPTAN

ex *Demirhisar* 1983, ex *Cihat* 1938, ex *Aydın* 1933,
ex *Ihsanie* 1926, ex *Fauvette* 1924, ex *Chryssalis*
1917, ex *Honfleur* 1911
Motor cargo vessel, ex steamer 1936
Owner: M K Basak
Built: 1873, Aitkem & Mansel, Glasgow; 489gt;
53.8m × 7.3m

Amazing survivor, built for the London &
South Western Railway routes from
Southampton to the Channel Islands, and
also a route from Jersey to Granville. Re-
engined 1883; sold to Greek owners 1911;
taken over by French Government 1917;
and owned by a succession of Turkish
owners since 1924. Diesel fitted 1936;
second diesel fitted 1956; machinery moved
aft and new aft superstructure built early
seventies. Still recognisable by antique hull
lines. One of a number of little known
veteran coasters in Turkish waters.

ISTANBUL

KAPTAN SUKRU

ex *Sahilbent/Bosporus No 27*
Motor cargo vessel, ex paddle steamer
Built: 1872, Maudslay, Sons & Field, London; 455gt

Built as an early 'roro' paddle ferry for
Şirketi Hayriye for carrying horses and
carriages across the Bosporus, converted
1927 when the passenger deck was
removed to make her more suitable for use
as a car ferry; withdrawn 1954, converted
to diesel coaster (screw propelled).

ISTANBUL

TAMANLAR

ex *Hizir Kaptan* 1977, ex *Sütlüce/Bosporus No 63*
1974
Twin screw motor cargo vessel, ex steamer 1975
Built: 1909, Ateliers & Chantiers de France,
Dunkirk; 397gt; 50.0 × 8.0m

One of a trio of slightly smaller steamers
then *Küçüksu*, which came from the same
builders. The other two, *Sultaniye/Bosporus
No 61* and *Hünkar İskelesi/Bosporus No 62*,
were lost in World War I. Withdrawn 1974
and converted to motorised sand carrier.

ISTANBUL

OSMAN NURI AYANOLĞLU

ex *Şevki Kaptan* 1981, ex *Kurtuluş 2* 1980, ex
Petma 1976, ex *Eregli* 1973, ex *Ben Voirlich* 1936
Motor tanker ex passenger/cargo steamer, ex
steam trawler
Owner: Osman Nuri Ayanoğlu, Istanbul
Built: 1900, Hall Russell, Aberdeen; 176gt; 32.3m ×
6.4m

I nteresting veteran, built as steam trawler
for North British Steam Fishing, Aberdeen;
sold to Turkish owners and used as
passenger/cargo steamer 1924-1934;
converted to diesel coaster 1936, and again
to tanker 1969.

EAST GERMANY
(German Democratic Republic)

DRESDEN, RIVER ELBE

SCHMILKA

ex *Sachsen* 1936, ex *Meissen* 1928, ex
Höhenzollern 1919
Paddle steamer, laid up
Owner: Weisse Flotte Dresden
Built: 1897, Werft Blasewitz, Dresden; 56.1m ×
5.0/10.2m
Machinery: compound oscillating, Kette, Dresden-
Übigau; 145hp; coal-briquette fired

Out of service since 1977 with boiler
problems, *Schmilka* was planned to be re-
boilered with a second-hand dredger boiler,
but it would appear that this has not
worked out. She now lies in Neustadt
harbour, away from the other steamers. As
the present sailings are well covered by the
operating steamers, it would seem unlikely
that she will return to service. She was the
second steamer in the fleet to have been
built as an upper-deck steamer, and was
originally designated a 'first-class' steamer.
She was seized by Czechoslovakia in 1945,
but returned to Dresden in 1947, a
reminder that some six paddlers, built
between 1899 and 1915, were taken to the
USSR in 1945 and never heard of again.
This is clearly a contributing factor to the
survival of so many nineteenth-century
steamers here.

KLOSCHWITZ

KRIPPEN

ex *Tetschen* 1946
Restaurant ship, ex paddle steamer
Built: 1892, Werft Blasewitz, Dresden; 54.6m ×
4.8/9.9m; formerly 628 pass
Machinery: simple oscillating by builders; 110hp

Similar steamer to *Diesbar*, in service until
1979, then used as reserve steamer until
1983, when she was towed to Kloschwitz

Rahmi Kaptan, former *Honfleur* (Selim San)

on the river Saale, near Halle. She lay here
until spring 1987 before finally being
placed on dry land for use as a restaurant
ship. Her engines were designated a
technological monument a few years ago,
so I would imagine they will be retained in
situ. They are similar to *Diesbar*'s in that
they are still simple expansion rather than
compound. She was the first steamer in the
fleet to be fitted with electric lighting when
built, and was unchanged throughout her
life, except for the addition of a wheelhouse
when steam steering was fitted in 1928,
and the fitting of a canopy over the after
deck in 1967.

SEEBURG

SEEPERLE

ex *Königstein* 1973, ex *Lobositz* 1949, ex *Köningen
Maria* 1937, ex *Lobositz* 1936, ex *Graf Moltke*
1919
Restaurant ship, ex paddle steamer
Built: 1892, Werft Blasewitz, Dresden; 54.7m ×
4.7/9.8m; formerly 621 pass

Situated on land on the bank of the Süssen
See at Seeburg, near Eisleben, since 1973,
Königstein was in operation until 1971. She
was seized by Czechoslovakia in 1945, but
returned in 1947. In 1936, for the
centenary of the company, she was
renamed and rebuilt for one season as a
mock up of the original paddle steamer
Köningen Maria of 1836. After withdrawal
her engine and boiler were removed and
she was cut in two, being taken to her
present site by road, where a large after
deck saloon was added; other alterations
make her rather a monstrosity.

Pelikan at Berlin Treptow, 1986

EAST BERLIN

HEINRICH ZILLE

ex *Panke* 1958, ex *Baurat Hobrecht* 1948
Twin screw motor vessel, ex steamer 1958
Operator: Weisse Flotte Berlin
Built: 1896, Stettiner Oderwerke; lengthened 1958;
38.1m × 6.2m; 292 pass

Former steamer of Type III, built for the
Stern company, major operators in the city;
typical rebuilt Berlin ex steamer with
enclosed upper deck and open foredeck.

EAST BERLIN

ADOLF VON MENZEL

Twin screw motor vessel, ex steamer 1958
Operator: Weisse Flotte Berlin
Built: 1904, Stettiner Oderwerke; 29.9m × 5.7m;
279 pass

Former type I steamer, built for the Stern
company; dieselised 1958; one of few
Berlin veterans to have kept the same name
all her career; bombed 1945, and did not
return to service until 1954; rather ugly
appearance.

EAST BERLIN

FRIEDENSWACHT

ex *Neptun* 1960, ex *Fürst O v Bismarck* 1951
Twin screw motor vessel, ex steamer 1960
Built: 1904, Stettiner Oderwerke. lengthened 1960;
36.6m × 5.6m; 329 pass

Former Type I steamer, sunk by the SS at
the end of the war, but repaired and

returned to service by 1947; lengthened
and motorised 1960 at Aken on river Elbe.

EAST BERLIN

ARCONA

ex *Cäcilie* 1928, ex *Hoffnung* 1917
Twin screw motor vessel, ex steamer 1970
Operator: Weisse Flotte Berlin
Built: 1905, Gebr Maass, Neustrelitz; 25.4m ×
4.8m; 250 pass

One of the more interesting survivors, and
last of East Berlin's steamers to be
dieselised, *Arcona* is an attractive vessel,
and was one of the last to be taken over by
the Weisse Flotte, having been family
owned prior to 1974, and chartered to the
Weisse Flotte. She has been designated a
'Tradition Ship' and will be destined for
preservation if ever withdrawn from service.
Originally she was used as a tug and
icebreaker as well as a passenger steamer.
In the World War I she served as a
hospital ship in France and Belgium, and
operated at Brandenburg for a while
between the wars. Used in the latter
months of the World War II as part of the
essential transport system in the bombed
city. Operated by the Weisse Flotte until
withdrawn in 1967, she was dieselised in
1970 and returned to service, probably now
mainly on charters. Unlike the larger
vessels, her lower saloon only has portholes
and not full size windows.

EAST BERLIN

PELIKAN

ex *Mariendorf* 1969
Motor vessel, ex steamer 1958
Operator: Weisse Flotte Berlin
Built: 1906, Stettiner Oderwerke; 32.6m × 6.0m;
40 pass
Route: luxury charters

Type II steamer built for Teltower
Kreisschiffahrt, which later merged with the
Stern company to form Stern & Kreis
Schiffahrt, now the premier West Berlin
operators. In DSU service from 1945,
rebuilt to motorship 1958, rebuilt a second
time in 1973 for only 40 passengers for
nostalgia charters for congresses, etc. Main
saloon laid out with small tables and
armchairs for dinner cruises rather than the
usual bench seating.

EAST BERLIN

HAVELLAND

ex *Oberspree*
Motor vessel, ex steamer 1940s, ex motor vessel
1940s
Built: 1925, Berlin; 25.4m × 4.7m; 99 pass
Route: Friedrichshagen–Woltersdorf–Alt Buchorst;
charters

Built as motor vessel, but steam engine
fitted during the war because of diesel fuel
shortages; new diesel fitted late forties, and
current engine fitted 1958. Half saloon
vessel, similar to standard Thames type.

EAST BERLIN

SPREE

ex *Wintermärchen II* 1957, ex *Europa*, ex *Leopold-Wilhelm*
Motor vessel, ex steamer 1962
Built: 1890, H Schmidt, Küstrin, rebuilt 1962-4, Aken/Elbe; 67.2m × 8.2m; 86 pass (berthed)
Route: cruises from East Berlin to Frankfurt/Oder, Sczeczin, Dresden and Prague

Built as a standard passenger steamer; renamed *Wintermärchen II* for winter service; taken over by Weisse Flotte 1957; rebuilt from 1960 to 1964 at Aken for cruise work, being almost doubled in length; little remaining of old steamer. May have been withdrawn in early eighties.

POTSDAM, RIVER HAVEL

CAPUTH

ex *Anna II* 1962
Twin screw motor vessel, ex steamer
Operator: Weisse Flotte Potsdam
Built: 1887; 31.1m × 5.2m; 285 pass
Route: excursions from Potsdam; Potsdam–Brandenburg

Used immediately post-war, before the railway line was reconstructed, for a passenger/cargo service from Berlin to Fürstenburg on the river Oder. Fitted with steam engine from *Professor Rudolf Virchow* in 1962; dieselised and rebuilt 1966.

POTSDAM, RIVER HAVEL

SEEBAD TEMPLIN

ex *Professor Rudolf Virchow* 1960
Twin screw motor vessel, ex steamer
Operator: Weisse Flotte Potsdam
Built: 1904, Stettiner Oderwerke; 35.0m × 5.6m; 371 pass
Route: excursions from Potsdam; Potsdam–Brandenburg

Built as Type I steamer for Stern company; to DSU 1948; rebuilt, lengthened, dieselised at Aken 1960.

POTSDAM

CONCORDIA

Twin screw motor vessel, ex steamer 1927, laid up
Built: 1886, Stettiner Oderwerke; 24.9m × 4.9m; 198 pass

In operation for Stern company from 1889; motorised 1927; in Soviet sector in 1945 and used at Potsdam since 1946, being one of first vessels to operate in the Eastern zone; withdrawn 1978. No recent information.

PREMNITZ, RIVER HAVEL

DORA

ex *Gilda* 1945, ex *Nixe* 1920s, ex *Biene* 1902
Built: 1875, Reihersteigwerft, Hamburg; 21.4m × 4.9m

Houseboat at Premnitz, lower Havel; built as tug, rebuilt 1902 for passenger steamer on Alster Lake at Hamburg, sold for scrapping at Warnemünde 1923, but later operated at Zehdenick, in the Uckermark

region; moved to Berlin 1945. One source claims that she was in fact a rebuild of the passenger launch *Aline* (1859) and not a new building in 1875. This latter was converted to a tug in 1862, and in 1870, at the outbreak of the Franco-Prussian war, sailed for Kiel for use as a Naval Auxiliary, but was sunk in the Elbe near Mühlenburg by an English cargo steamer, with the loss of life of three of the crew. She was raised, but was then reportedly only fit for scrapping.

BRANDENBURG, RIVER HAVEL

MAXIM GORKI

ex *Venus* 1965, ex *Graf H Moltke* 1948
Twin screw motor vessel, ex steamer 1965
Operator: Weisse Flotte Brandenburg
Built: 1904, Stettiner Oderwerke; 32.6m × 6.0m; 200 pass
Route: excursions from Brandenburg; Brandenburg–Potsdam

Built for Stern company as Type I steamer; taken over by DSU 1948 and renamed, in service at Brandenburg; rebuilt, lengthened and dieselised 1965.

KYRITZ, RIVER HAVEL

SEEBÄR

ex *Seid Beriet* 1965, ex *Hertha* 1950
Motor vessel, ex steamer 1956
Built: 1886, Stettiner Oderwerke; rebuilt 1965; 22.8m × 4.6m; 263 pas
Route: excursions from Kyritz

Built as sister of *Concordia*; first steamer to enter service after 1945; taken over by DSU 1948. Rebuilt to motorship 1958; in service at Berlin until 1965; major rebuild 1960s for present service.

ODERBERG

RIESA

ex *Habsburg* 1919
Museum ship, ex paddle steamer
Owner: Oderberger Schiffahrtsmuseum, Oderberg
Built: 1897, Werft Blasewitz; 56.1m × 5.0/10.2m; formerly 740 pass
Machinery: compound oscillating, Kette, Dresden-Übigau; 145hp

Now berthed on dry land at Oderberg, on a subsidiary stream of the river Oder, near the Polish border east of Berlin, and in use there as a museum ship since 1979. She is an identical sister of *Pirna, Junger Pionier* and *Schmilka*, and was in use until 1976, having received two second-hand ex-tug boilers, in 1963 and 1972 respectively, but being withdrawn after failure of the latter one. She was used as a floating office in 1943-4 at Dessau by the Junkers factory, but returned to Dresden and was blown up and sunk by the Hitler Youth at the close of the war. She re-entered service in 1947, with a new fore-part. She was towed to Oderberg with paddle-boxes removed in order to pass through the canals en route, and was pulled up on the river bank there, the paddle boxes remounted, and the steamer opened as a museum in 1979.

STRALSUND, BALTIC SEA

DEUTSCHE-SOWEJETISCHE FREUNDSCHAFT

ex *Sowjetischefreundschaft* 1954, ex *Direktor Ehmke* 1947, ex *Sedan* 1921
Twin screw motor vessel, ex steamer
Operator: Weisse Flotte Stralsund
Built: 1895, Stettiner Oderwerke, Stettin; 42.8m × 6.1m; 402 pass
Route: Stralsund–Hiddensee Island

Built as a coastal-type screw steamer, similar to *Albatros*, for service from Stettin on the river Oder; owned after 1896 by a company at nearby Greifenhage; has been at Stralsund since 1945; apparently used on all the year-round service to the holiday island of Hiddensee, west of Rügen. Rebuilt with modern fore-saloon with wheelhouse and aft saloon, and also dieselised, but the hull and the midship section would appear to be not too different from her original condition.

ROSTOCK, BALTIC SEA

UNDINE

ex *Kronprinz* 1945, ex *Kronprinz Wilhelm*
Motor vessel, ex steamer 1953
Built: 1910, Neptun Werft, Rostock; 158gt; 3.4m × 6.8m; 405 pass
Route: harbour excursions from Rostock

Built for excursion service from Rostock to Warnemünde and resorts along the Baltic coast; bombed 1943, repaired and re-entered service; later modernised, upper deck saloon fitted, and dieselised.

WITTOW, BALTIC SEA

WITTOW
BERGEN

Bergen formerly *Jasper von Malzahn*
Motor vessels, car ferries, former train ferries, ex steamers 1916
Built: 1896; 24m × 5.65m
Route: Wittower ferry, north of Rügen Island

Former train ferries for the narrow gauge (750mm) Rügener Kleinbahn, connecting the main island with the peninsula known as Wittow Island. This section of railway was closed in the late sixties, although another section, from Puttbus to Göhren, survives, and is still fully steam. The ferries continue on this route for vehicles. The ferries are believed to have been dieselised as early as 1916.

UCKERMÜNDE, BALTIC SEA

UCKERMÜNDE

ex *Walter* 1963, ex *Grossherzogin Alexandra* 1930
Motor vessel, ex steamer 1955
Operator: Stadt Uckermünde
Built: 1905, AG Neptun, Stettin; 48gt; 130 pass
Route: excursions from Uckermünde

Originally operated at Ribnitz on Saaler Bodden (a *bodden* being the large lagoon-lake found on the Baltic coast of Germany and Poland); built as small coastal passenger/cargo steamer; rebuilt 1955-60. In service with Weisse Flotte until 1963, then at present location.

JADWISIN

GEN SWIERCZEWSKI

ex *Stanislaw* 1948, ex *Titanic* 1919
Paddle steamer, laid up
Built: River Shipyard, Plock, 1914-1919; 56.1m ×
5.9/10.6m; formerly 465 pass; 100 berths

Amazingly named *Titanic* while on the
stocks; laid down 1914 but not completed
until 1919 because of World War I; in used
on Vistula; sunk 1944; rebuilt after war in
1948, and again rebuilt in 1957 and 1963;
withdrawn c1976. It would appear from
photgraphs that the large deckhouses were
only added at this latter rebuilding. Latterly
operated on an overnight service from
Warsaw to Gdansk; according to owners
she was not run in recent years because of
low water levels; laid up since withdrawal
at Zegrzyn lake, Jadwisin.

WARSAW

RAKLAWICE

ex *Naurycy*
Paddle steamer, derelict on dry land
Built: 1881, Schichau, Elbing; 50.8m × 5.0/9.7m;
formerly 345 pass

In service at Warsaw until 1974, then used
as Club FSO at Warsaw-Praga until 1986;
now derelict, in poor condition.

TORON

KILINSKI

ex *Dniestr* 1948, ex *Krakus* 1939, ex *Sobieski* 1921,
ex *Krakus* 1919
Hotel ship (on land), ex paddle steamer
Built: 1899, Schichau, Elbing; 51.1m × 4.5/7.9m;
formerly 250 pass

In service at Plock on river Vistula; taken
over by Polish River Navigation Co 1927;
sunk 1944 by Germans along with other
paddlers; returned to service 1948;
withdrawn 1963. Used as hotel ship at
Wloclawek up to 1975; moved onto land,
used as clubhouse 1975-1982, and as
private hotel since 1985.

WARSAW

FELIKS DZIERZYNSKI

ex *Halka* 1952, ex *Polska* 1933
Paddle steamer, laid up
Owner: Zegluska Warszawska, Warsaw
Built: 1914-1925 Rivers Shipbuilding, Warsaw; 61.6m
× 5.8/9.8m; formerly 340 pass

Construction started 1914, but stopped
during World War I, and steamer was not
completed until 1925. Used at Warsaw on
river Vistula; sunk 1944 during German
occupation; returned to service 1951;
withdrawn 1972; still in existence, but
derelict.

PLOCK

ANIELA

ex *Traugutt* 1978, ex *Nur* 1950, ex *Gontec* 1939
Paddle steamer laid up
Owner: unknown, Plock
Built: 1926, Schichau, Elbing; 57.1m × 5.4/10.0m;
formerly 700 pass
Machinery: compound diagonal; 120hp

Built for Vistula service; renamed while
country under German occupation; sunk
1944; reconstructed 1945-49. In service

Raclawice in dilapidated condition, 1984
(Waldemar Danielewicz)

until c1975, then used as workers' hostel at
Plock until early eighties; now derelict, but
may possibly be rebuilt.

WARSAW

BALTYK

ex *Alina* 1985, ex *Baltyk* 1975, ex *Prinz Eugen* 1945,
ex *Baltyk* 1939
Paddle steamer, laid up
Built: 1929 Danziger Werft, Danzig (now Gdansk);
63.0m × 6.5/11.6m; formerly 540 pass
Machinery: compound diagonal; 200hp

Operated on Vistula prior to 1939; an
accommodation ship at Danzig during
World War II, and again on Vistula until
1975, then used as a hostel for river
maintenance staff until 1981. Now reserve
steamer (for motor vessels presently
operating at Warsaw, or perhaps for a newer
hostel) in Bialobrzegi harbour near Warsaw.
Typical of the Polish paddlers, with rather
ugly chunky deck saloon aft.

SZCZECIN, RIVER ODER

GRYFIA

ex *Prom Kolejowy 2* 1953, ex *Swinemünde 2* 1947,
ex *Tyras* 1940s
Steamer, car ferry, ex train ferry
Owner: Szczecin Ship Repair Works
Built: 1887, Stettiner Vulcan, Bredow; 146gt; 33.3m
× 4.8m
Machinery: compound, 100hp

Built as a train ferry for harbour use in
Stettin (now Szczecin) and used to provide
rail access to various factories in the
harbour rather than as part of a through rail
route. Moved to Swinemünde and converted
to a vehicle ferry during World War II;
returned to Szczecin 1947, in service until
1983, now a technical monument.

HUNGARY

WARSAW

DIANA

ex *Preussen* 1949
Restaurant ship, ex screw steamer, now derelict
Built: 1911, J C Tecklenborg, Wesermunde; 48.9m
× 9.2m

Built as Weser ferry, sold to owner in
Elbing, East Prussia 1936; sunk in Gdansk
1945; rebuilt 1949 for local routes at
Gdansk. Withdrawn 1962 and used as
restaurant at Rynia, near Warsaw for some
time; now derelict. Possibly originally sister
to *Jarl*, see Sweden.

MIELNO

SMIALY

ex *Hluboka* 1945, ex *Beethoven* 1926, ex *Gresham*
c1912
Clubhouse, ex paddle steamer
Built: 1905, J Thornycroft, Southampton; 32.3m ×
3.2/5.5m
Machinery: compound diagonal, Scott, Greenock;
350hp

Last survivor, and first to be completed in
May 1905, of group of 30 paddle steamers
built for London County Council for
commuter service on the Thames, a service
which only operated until 1907, by which
time it was found to be uneconomic.
Gresham was one of a number of the
steamers sold to City Steamboat Co for
continued service, and later was sold to
owners at Memel, East Prussia, c1911, (at
one stage possibly she went to Köln for
Köln-Mulheim local service). In service on
rivers Oder and Vistula as passenger
steamer and tug, then sold in 1926 for use
on the river Vltava at Prague as a tug.
Requisitioned by the Wehrmacht in 1942,
as owner was Jewish, and taken to river
Vistula; sunk 1944; rebuilt 1947 and again
1955; used as inspection steamer for river
administration at Plock until 1958, then at
Tczew until withdrawn in 1968. In use at
Mielno as clubhouse on land; still in
existence as late as 1984. Surely a
candidate for a return to a maritime
museum in Great Britain and preservation?

Wreck of *Feliks Dzierzynski* (Waldemar
Danielewicz)

CZECHOSLOVAKIA

PRAGUE, RIVER VLTAVA

ODRA

ex *M8* 1981, ex *Odra* 1963, ex *P9*, ex *D9*, ex
Roztoky 1940, ex *Žernoeky* 1937, ex *P 9* 1934, ex
Reichenburg 1922
Motor vessel, ex steamer 1957
Built: 1909, Dresden Übigau; 26.5m × 6.5m

Former tug, in use 1934-1940 as passenger
steamer at Prague; used as tug after 1940;
now owned by young pioneers, operated for
excursions.

USTI, RIVER LABE (ELBE)

MARIE

Motor launch, ex steamer
Built: 1908, Dresden Übigau; 13.2m × 3.2m; 55
pass
Route: ferry across Elbe at Üsti

Dieselised 1950, rebuilt 1985.

SKALKA DAM LAKE

OHŘE

ex *Augusta*
Motor launch, ex steamer
Built: 1897, Dresden-Neustadt; 9.5m × 2.3m; 30
pass
Route: Skalka Dam lake, near Cheb

Former river ferry, dieselised 1955.

BRATISLAVA

DĚVÍN

ex *Tabau*, ex *Megyer*, ex *Dunaj*
Paddle steamer, awaiting restoration
Built: 1911, Pressburg; 33.5m × 3.0/7.7m; formerly
200 pass
Machinery: compound diagonal; 110hp

Formerly a ferry on the Danube at
Bratislava, withdrawn 1966; possibly used
as a restaurant for a while; now derelict,
awaiting preservation. Similar to the Elbe
paddle ferry *Bad Schandau I*, whose engines
are preserved at Lauenburg.

HUNGARY

BUDAPEST

KOSSUTH

ex *Leányfalu* 1953, ex *Rigo* 1936, ex *Ferencz
Ferdinand Foherczeg* 1919
Museum ship, paddle steamer
Owner: Topco-op/Hungarian Transport Museum,
Budapest
Built: 1914, Ganz-Danubius, Budapest; 62.4m ×
8.0/16.5m; formerly 1350 pass
Machinery: compound diagonal; 580hp

Withdrawn from service in 1978, *Kossuth*
had previously been employed on the
popular promenade excursions on the
Danube at Budapest. She is typical of the
smaller Danube paddlers also operated by
the DDSG. Her boiler was replaced in 1953
by one from the German paddle tug
Regensburg, which had been bombed and
sunk in Hungarian waters during World
War II. Opened as a museum and
restaurant steamer in centre of Budapest
1986, with an exhibition of shipping
history in the lower saloons, the engine
room restored and in original condition,
and a restaurant and bars in the upper
deck saloons in an unusual but enterprising
co-operation between a national museum
and a restaurant. Built as part of a
modernisation programme of the Hungarian
Danube fleet by state company MFTR (now
MAHART).

BUDAPEST

PETÖFI

ex *Szent László* 1960
Paddle steamer, laid up
Owner: MAHART, Budapest
Built: 1920/26 MFTR, Komarom; 60.0m ×
8.0/15.5m; 1450 pass
Machinery: compound diagonal; 580hp; new boiler
1960

Hungary's last operating day paddle
steamer, *Petöfi* ran on the Budapest
promenade trips until 1984. She was
expected in service again in 1985, but new
management took over in early 1985, and
she was deemed to be uneconomic and
withdrawn. In that year she was used as a
workers' restaurant in city centre, but I am
uncertain if she has has continued since
then. She operated on the day excursions
to the Danube bend until *Kossuth* was
withdrawn in 1979, and her name was
changed following a major refit in 1960,
when she received a new oil-fired boiler
and her fore saloon was remodelled. Laid
down as one of the five passenger steamers
planned in a 1914 modernisation plan, but
not completed until 1926.

BUDAPEST

VISEGRÁD

ex *Imre*
Hotel/restaurant ship, ex paddle steamer
Built: 1896; formerly 850 pass; 350hp

Former paddler moored, with engines and
paddle wheels removed, at Margaret Island

184

Petöfi as a workers' canteen, Budapest, 1984   *Below: Budapest* at Budapest, 1985 (Waterways World)

at Budapest, and used as hotel/restaurant ship for a good number of years.

BUDAPEST

BUDAPEST

Paddle steamer, laid up
Owner: SZOT (Hungarian Council of Trade Unions)
Built: 1960, Schiffswerft Budapest; 71.4m × 9.25/15.4m; 350 pass (250 berths)
Machinery: compound diagonal; 550hp; 18km/h

Last of the 63 type 737 paddle steamers to be built (see USSR); *Budapest* was also probably the last commercial paddle steamer to be built anywhere in the world, as any more recent examples have been replicas or fake-antique steamers. Used for long-distance cruises on the river for the Hungarian Trade Union movement, and fitted with cabins on both main and upper decks, with a sun deck above the upper deck. Withdrawn 1986 after boiler failure and economic problems.

SZEGED

FELSZABADULAS

ex *Szent Imre* 1948, ex *Sas* 1926, ex *IV Karoly* 1919
Hotel/restaurant ship, ex paddle steamer
Built: 1917, Ganz-Danubius, Budapest; 75.0m × 7.7/15.3m; formerly 800 pass/175 berths
Machinery: triple expansion diagonal; 800hp

Large two-funnelled paddle steamer, withdrawn 1974. Converted 1965 with cabin accommodation for long distance cruises downstream to Iron Gates. Used as canteen vessel for shipping company; sold to Szeged town 1979; towed there via Yugoslavia, Szeged being on the river Tisza which flows into the Danube in that country. At one stage an English preservation group were interested in purchasing her. Built as part of previously mentioned modernistion programme, as larger edition of *Kossuth*.

LAKE BALATON

KELÉN

Motor vessel, ex steamer 1961
Operator: MAHART, Siófok
Built: 1891, Schoenichen & Hartmann, Budapest; 35.2m × 4.9m; 160 pass

Very attractive clipper-bowed former steamer; probably only used nowadays as reserve ship, based at Siófok; deck saloon added at fairly recent date, as old photographs show her with a simple shelter amidships; has operated on Lake Balaton since building. It is planned to restore her to 1891 condition with her crew also dressed in 1890s costume for tourist excursions. The steam engines of both *Kelén* and *Hekla* are preserved in the Budapest Transport Museum. Later steamer *Jokai* (1913) was also dieselised c1964, and was transferred in 1980 to the river Körös in eastern Hungary. It is unclear if she is still in service.

LAKE BALATON

ERCSI, ZEBEGÉNY, SZENTENDRE

ex *LI*, ex *Tbiliszi*, ex *LI*; ex *LIV*; ex *LV*
Motor vessels, ex steamers 1963/1963/1966
Operator: MAHART, Siofok
Built: 1921; 37.3m × 6.3m; 400 pass

Built as part of a group of six identical screw steamers for local commuter services at Budapest; original design rather striking with large straight funnel and saloons on two decks. Completely rebuilt in slightly different styles, with *Ercsi* with a full width upper deck saloon, and *Zebegény* and *Szentendre* with narrower upper deck saloons; dieselised; moved to lake Balaton 1967-68.

BALATONBOGLÁR

BALATON

ex *FK319* 1981, ex *Irma*, ex *Mohacs* 1901, ex *Alexandra* 1896, ex *Balaton* 1879
Motor vessel, ex steamer, undergoing restoration
Built: 1872

Operated as a passenger steamer until 1876 on lake Balaton, then on Danube, coming under the ownership of Prince Albrecht from 1879 until 1896; used from 1913 as a sand carrier, and returned to Balaton in 1954 for use in a water management project. Withdrawn 1978, and undergoing restoration since 1981 at Balatonboglár. Oldest existing lake Balaton vessel.

Balaton under restoration, Balatonboglár, 1987 (Prof J Parratt)

BALATONFÜRED

HELKA

Museum ship, ex motor vessel, ex steamer
Owner: Hungarian Transport Museum
Built: 1891, Schoenichen & Hartmann, Budapest; 35.2m × 4.9m; 160 pass

Sister of *Kelén*, preserved on land since c1980 at Balatonfüred as a museum by Hungarian Transport Museum, possibly also used as restaurant.

BULGARIA

RUSE

ISKER

Houseboat, ex screw steamer
Built: 1924, Monfalcone, Italy
Machinery: 300hp

Former passenger ferry on Danube between Ruse and Giurgiu, seen near railway museum at Ruse 1985, apparently in use as houseboat. Originally had a sister named *Vit*.

River ferry *Isker* at Ruse, 1984

Below: Restaurant *Libertatea* at Galatz, 1984

RUMANIA

RIVER DANUBE

ANGHEL SALIGINI

ex *Continental* 1922, ex *Schruns* 1921, ex *Habsburg* 1919
Paddle steamer, laid up, derelict
Built: 1884, Schifswerft Linz; 50.3m × 5.6/11.9m; 300 pass
Machinery: compound diagonal, Escher Wyss, Zürich; 400hp

Built as a flush-decked paddler with small deck-house amidships for Austrian Railways routes on Bodensee; rebuilt 1895 with fore-saloon; withdrawn 1919. Sold to Rumanian owners, moved to Linz by land and rebuilt with aft saloon and upper deck; operated in Rumania on Danube delta and river services until late seventies; then used as restaurant; damaged by fire and seen lying on river bank 1985, possibly later scrapped.

GALATI

LIBERTATEA

ex *Luceaferal*, ex *Nahlin* 1937
Restaurant ship, ex twin screw turbine steamer, ex steam yacht
Built: 1930, John Brown, Clydebank; 1392gt; 90.2m × 11.0m
Machinery: two geared turbines; 4000hp

This rather tatty restaurant ship moored on the Danube at Galati was actually built as a magnificent steam yacht, one of the last large steam yachts to be built in Britain, designed by the famous yacht designer G L Watson, built by John Brown, and originally owned by Lady Yule. In 1936, King Edward VIII chartered her for a Mediterranean cruise with Wallis Simpson, and the resulting furore in Britain led to the abdication. Apparently, Helen Lepescu, mistress of King Carol of Rumania, was so enthralled by the 'romantic' nature of this episode that she persuaded him to buy the yacht. This he did in 1937, but she apparently made only one cruise as the Rumanian royal yacht, and then, after Rumania became a republic, *Libertatea* was used as a passenger steamer for NAVROM until withdrawn, probably in the late sixties, since when she has been a café-restaurant. Surely this must be a possibility for repatriation to the Clyde as centrepiece of a maritime museum, telling the story of the river that once produced so many ships, or as a luxury hotel in the style of Stockholm's *Mälardrottningen*, formerly Woolworth heiress Barbara Hutton's yacht, now a first class hotel and restaurant in the centre of the city.

USSR

VOLZHSH

SPARTAK

Paddle steamer
Route: Volzhsh–Leningrad

Former Tsarist paddler, still in service until recent years, probably typical of many such.

SHUSHENSKOE

S V NIKOLAY

Preserved paddle steamer
Built: c1892

Steamer which carried Lenin into Siberian exile in 1897, reportedly restored 1977 and placed in village of Shushenskoe, Siberia. The whole village has been preserved as a memorial to Lenin, who lived in exile here from 1897 to 1900 and also as an example of a Siberian taiga village of the turn of the century. No further details of steamer available.

LAKE BAIKAL

ANGARA

Screw steamer, undergoing restoration
Built: 1899, Armstrong Whitworth, Newcastle; 60.9m × 10.7m; 150 pass
Machinery: triple expansion; 1215hp

Two-funnelled passenger steamer, built to partner train ferry *Baikal* on lake Baikal service; entered service 1900. Like *Baikal*, she was shipped in parts, but the journey was easier, only taking two months, because by that time the railway had been opened. Seen laid up, and partially sunk, at Irkutsk, but I have no information as to whether this was carried out. *Baikal*, was a triple screw train ferry with two screws forward and one aft, also built by Armstrong Whitworth at Newcastle in 1895. She measured 4200 tons displacement, and was used as a train ferry before the railway was built across the lake. Transported to the lake in sections, 7200 parts were shipped by barges pulled by men and by horses along the 1100 miles of the Angara river from the then railhead at Krasnoyarsk. After three years transporting these parts, she was completed and entered service 1899, and was normally used for freight and for transporting carriages and wagons across the lake, while *Angara* normally took the passengers. Both steamers used as icebreakers and for general passenger/cargo service on lake Baikal after completion of railway around the southern shore in 1904. It is thought that *Baikal* was destroyed during the Revolution, although no positive news of her scrapping has materialised.

As far as is known, there are now no veteran coastal passenger ships in the Soviet Union. The turbo-electric *Baltika* (1939/7494), long on the Leningrad-London route, was scrapped in early 1987, and veteran Black Sea cruise liner *Admiral Nakhimov*, ex *Berlin* (1925/17053) was tragically sunk in 1986. Another remarkable

veteran scrapped recently was *Morskaja II*, ex *Jakutia* ex *Imperator Veliky* (1913/5878), which went to Korean breakers in 1987 after a long period as an accommodation ship. She had originally been built by John Brown of Clydebank, but spent a long period out of use after sinking in World War I, and was in service in the Far East after World War II. It is reported that the Russians have started to withdraw all older ships since the *Admiral Nakhimov* disaster, in view of the bad publicity, although the enquiry into the disaster pointed to human error as the casue of the collision with the coaster.

A number of Elbe and other German paddle steamers, and German and Polish coastal steamers, were removed to Russia after 1945; generally there has been no further information on any of them. It is possible that there may still be veteran passenger vessels, for example, serving the islands on the Estonian coast; the Soviet Union, not being a consumer society, would not require the car ferries that have revolutionised coastal shipping in Western countries, yet it is also a society dedicated to standardisation, and so older vessels may well have been replaced by hydrofoils and standard classes of 1940s motorships.

VLADIVOSTOCK

KRILYON

ex *Preussen* 1945
Built: 1909, Vulcan, Stettin; 2972gt; 113.8m × 15.5m; 800 pass

Former train ferry on Sassnitz-Trelleborg run; seized by Russians after World War II; rebuilt as passenger steamer for Far East service; withdrawn 1970, used as hostel ship for workers building new harbour at Vostochny, near Vladivostok. No recent information.

BLACK SEA

ABKHAZIA

ex *Lensoviet* 1962, ex *Marienburg* 1954
Twin screw turbo-electric steamer
Built: 1939, Stettin, not completed until 1955 by Mathias These, Wismar 6807gt; 131.6m × 18.3m; 549 pass

Originally designed for express service from Germany to East Prussia, used on Russian Black Sea service when finally completed.

APPENDIX
FURTHER INFORMATION

History

There are a large number of books available on the history of steamers and motor vessels in various languages, for different areas of operation. The best British importer of such books is Mainmast Books, Saxmundham, Suffolk, IP17 1HZ, who publish regular lists including mini-reviews. They also operate a second-hand and antiquarian book service. They are a very efficient and friendly firm to deal with.

Motor Books, St Martins Court, London, and Albion Scott, who advertise regularly in the shipping enthusiast magazines, are also useful for European books.

Two German booksellers, WEDE Fachbuchhandlung, Grosse Bleichen 36 in Hanse Viertel, D2000 Hamburg 36, and Christian Schmidt, Sauerbruchstrasse 10, D8000 München 70, publish regular maritime catalogues, and are happy to ship orders to the UK.

Societies

The Paddle Steamer Preservation Society publishes an excellent magazine *Paddle Wheels*, four times a year. This is available to members, and membership details are available from the Membership Secretary; Rev Clem Robb, Sorn Rd, Catrine, Mauchline, Ayrshire, KA5 6NA. Current rates (1987) are £9 per year. The society also has regular meetings in winter in London, Glasgow, the North of England, the Bristol Channel area, and Wessex.

The Coastal Cruising Association publishes a comprehensive monthly news magazine *Cruising Monthly* covering all British coastal operations. Membership Secretary is Ian Somerville, 'Birkenhill', 90 Old Greenock Rd, Bishopton, Renfrewshire. The CCA has monthly meetings in winter in London and Glasgow, and occasional meetings in the North-West of England.

The Clyde River Steamer Club has regular monthly meetings in Glasgow, and publishes an annual review of Scottish shipping operations and an annual illustrated magazine with historical articles about Clyde steamers. Membership details are available from the Membership Secretary, 21 Keith Avenue, Giffnock, Glasgow G46 6LG, and the current subscription is £7.

The West Highland Steamer Club has a monthly meeting in Glasgow in winter, and publishes twice-yearly a detailed review of Caledonian McBrayne's operations in the West Highlands. Subscription details are available from the Membership Secretary, Wardiebank House, 21 Boswell Rd, Edinburgh, EH5 3RR.

Geoffrey Hamer, 77 St Marys Grove London, W4 3LW, publishes a monthly *Trip Out* newsletter on passenger vessels operating in England and Wales. Subscription rates vary, depending on whether a *Trip Out* guidebook is included or not.

Swiss and other European steamers are covered by the excellent magazine *Dampferzeitung*, 2 Hirtenhofenring, CH 6005 Luzern, Switzerland. The annual subscription is 27SFr for five well-illustrated issues.

Stiftelsen Skärgårdsbåten, Nybrogatan 76, 114 41 Stockholm, Sweden, the Stockholm enthusiast group, also publishes a first-class magazine. *Skärgårdsbåten* appears four times a year. Subscription is 85SKr.

Sällskapet Ångbåten, Box 2072, 403 12 Göteborg, Sweden (owners of *Bohuslän*) also publish a magazine *Ångbåten*; this is normally about thrice yearly and subscription is 50SKr per year.

Loggen is the magazine of the Swedish Society for Tugs and Passenger Ships; it appears six times annually and some articles are in English and some in Swedish. Subscription is 100SKr per year. Contact address is Einar Madsen, Box 9007, 250 09 Helsingborg, Sweden.

Antonio Scrimali, Via Magellano 17/B, 10044 Pianezza (To), Italy, publishes a monthly newsletter *Latest News from the Mediterranean*. This often carries information not published elsewhere, and is illustrated by photocopies of photographs, a large selection of which are also available from him.

Finally, *Steamboat Bill*, the quarterly magazine of the Steamship Historical Society of America, has occassional European articles, and regular European news. The magazine has been published since 1940, and production is first class, with excellent reproduction of photographs. Subscription is $20 plus $4 for overseas postage; SSSHA, 345 Blackstone Blvd, H C Hall Bldg, Providence, RI, USA 02906.

Current timetables, etc

Essential for any enthusiast are the *Trip Out* guides published by Geoffrey Hamer, 77 St Marys Grove, London, W4 3LW. *Trip Out* appears every other year, and includes brief details of every passenger ship and boat operating in the British Isles, along with the operator's address and telephone number. *Trip Out in Northern Europe* and *Trip Out in Southern Europe* cover all passenger vessels over 100 tons on coastal waters in Europe, also with operators' addresses and telephone numbers. The Northern Europe edition last appeared in 1985, and the Southern Europe in 1987, and annual amendment lists are issued.

In many cases timetables can be obtained from tourist information offices, local, regional, and national. The offices of the various national tourist offices in London can be very helpful in some cases, such as Finland and Switzerland, and worse than useless in others, such as some of the Eastern Bloc countires, and Holland, who refuse to publicise any individual operator, and indeed any individual tourist attraction, to avoid any semblance of favouritism or advertising.

The national rail timetables of Norway, Finland, West Germany, Switzerland, Austria, and Hungary contain full information on local shipping services, while other countries have a limited amount of such information.

Cook's European timetable, published monthly, has timetables for the Rhine and a number of the Swiss and Italian lakes, as well as ferry services in the Baltic and Mediterranean.

The *ABC Passenger Shipping Guide* has many services in it, and is published monthly. It also includes operators' names and addresses.

In general these timetables include point-to-point services rather than non-landing excursions.

Cook's timetable can be obtained from any branch of Thomas Cook; the ABC Guide from the publishers, ABC Travel Guides, World Timetable Centre, Dunstable, Beds LU5 4HB; and the Swiss timetable is available from the Swiss National Tourist Office, Swiss Centre, 1 New Coventry St, London.

All European Rail timetables, including the above, are available from BAS Overseas Publications Ltd, 48-50 Sheen Lane, London SW14 8LP, who from time to time have sale lists of out-of-date timetables at bargain prices. They publish an annual price list of timetables, and are a very efficient firm.

Details of German and certain other European inland water passenger vessels are in two guides:

Schiffstouristik: Adressen & Routen der Weissen Flotten by Weickert Touristik Verlag GMBH, D 6251 Waldbrunn 1, Steinbacher Str 14, West Germany, is really aimed at coach tour operators and travel agents; it has full details of addresses and routes, but no times, and little more detail than names of ships. It is, however, very comprehensive for inland Europe, filling the gap between the two *Trip Out* guides.

Deutsche Binnen & Kusten Personenschiffahrt Kursbuch, Jægerverlag, Darmstadt, is a new (1986) annual pocket-book sized timetable of German inland and coastal ship and boat services. It is a nicely presented production, published in April each year, with actual timetables, some interesting advertisements, and a number of photographs.

INDEX OF VESSEL NAMES